WHAT HAPPENED IN THE GARDEN

WHAT HAPPENED IN THE GARDEN

The Reality and Ramifications of the Creation and Fall of Man

John MacArthur and The Master's College Faculty

ABNER CHOU
EDITOR

Kregel Academic

What Happened in the Garden: The Reality and Ramifications of the Creation and Fall of Man
© 2016 The Master's College

Published by Kregel Publications, a division of Kregel, Inc., 2450 Oak Industrial Dr. NE, Grand Rapids, MI 49505-6020.

The Hebrew font (NewJerusalemU) and the Greek font (GraecaU) are available from www.linguistsoftware.com/lgku.htm, +1-425-775-1130.

ISBN 978-0-8254-4209-4

Printed in the United States of America
16 17 18 19 20 / 5 4 3 2 1

To God our Creator, whose deeds we proclaim

*In memory of the founders of Los Angeles Baptist Theological Seminary
and Los Angeles Baptist College, now The Master's College,
who established us on a course to uphold the authority, accuracy,
historicity, and inerrancy of all of Scripture, from beginning to end*

*To our students to whom we have entrusted this cause;
may you always uphold the authority of God's Word.*

*In loving memory of Taylor Jones
faithful brother, scholar, and friend*

Contents

Contributors

Ernie Baker, D.Min., Westminster Theological Seminary
Professor of Biblical Counseling

Abner Chou, Th.D., The Master's Seminary
Professor of Bible

George A. Crawford, J.D., UCLA School of Law
Adjunct Instructor

Joseph W. Francis, Ph.D., Wayne State University
Chairperson, Departments of Biological and Physical Sciences, and Mathematics
Professor of Biology

Alexander Granados, Ph.D., Biola University
President, Southeastern Bible College

Grant Horner, Ph.D. (A.B.D.), Claremont Graduate University
Associate Professor of English

Taylor B. Jones, Ph.D., The University of Texas at Austin
Late Professor of Chemistry

John MacArthur, Litt.D., D.D., Talbot Theological Seminary
President
Professor of Bible

R. W. Mackey, II, Ed.D., Pepperdine University
Professor of Business Administration

Jo Suzuki, Ph.D. (A.B.D.), University of Texas at Arlington
Associate Professor of English

Paul R. Thorsell, Th.D., Dallas Theological Seminary
Former Professor of Theology

William Varner, Ed.D., Temple University
Professor of Biblical Studies

Todd Charles Wood, Ph.D., University of Virginia
President, Core Academy of Science

PREFACE AND ACKNOWLEDGMENTS

In a lot of ways, this book is a labor of love. The original idea for it came from Dr. Steven Boyd, who desired to serve God and the church by writing a response to recent skepticism against the historicity of Genesis 2–3. Dr. Boyd had the vision to bring us all together to write a more thorough examination of this issue from our various disciplines. Dr. Boyd's efforts, however, were hindered by series of medical complications concerning his eyes. As a result, I took on the editorship of this work. Nevertheless, the credit should go to him. Thus, as we acknowledge a variety of individuals in this preface, Dr. Boyd is at the top of the list, for this book really is his brainchild. We are thankful to the Lord for his determination in upholding the cause of this book even in the face of great trial.

Putting together a book like this requires a gargantuan effort. For editors, such anthologies are a nightmare because working with so many people, deadlines, writing styles, and subject matter is quite overwhelming. While editing will always have its challenges, the faculty who contributed to this book deserve great accolades, as they made the process as smooth as it could be. Some have joked that faculty are anarchists who share a common parking lot. The contributors for this work proved otherwise. They showed incredible unity and humility in finishing the job well and on time. I want to honor their sacrifice and efforts (and I am aware of this, for at times we were exchanging emails in the wee hours of the morning!).

However, the effort goes beyond the contributors. Their families (particularly their wives) should be acknowledged for the strong support they gave. The sacrifice of time, their encouragement in difficulty, and their efforts to drive this entire process along are not seen within the book, but in actuality the book itself is the visible evidence of their work. So, even though we are already thankful to the Lord for them, this occasion only increases the reasons for our appreciation and love.

In addition, we would like to express our sincere and heartfelt appreciation to the president and administration of The Master's College for their unswerving commitment to the Scripture and for supporting this project. We are also thankful for the students who have been patient with an even more "absent-minded professor" in their classes. We hope that this book demonstrates that we practice what we preach about the careful study of research and the art of communicating.

Special thanks goes to Megan Low, administrative assistant in the Bible Department, who read many of the chapters with a sharp eye. Also, I must acknowledge my research assistant, Chris Williams, who did a heroic job at going through every chapter for readability as well as style. His diligence, eye for detail, and tenacity to get the job done not only continually astounds me but also makes me tremendously thankful that the Lord provided him for this time.

We would be remiss if we did not mention our aspiration that this book honor the Creator, the divine Author of Genesis 1–3. Our prayer is that this book inspires you to think more deeply about a portion of Scripture that has been recently under fire. May we not only defend it but also further seek to live in submission to the One whose Word is truth.

INTRODUCTION

Abner Chou

Evangelicals are no strangers to the issue of creation and evolution. Traditionally, that discussion involved issues within Genesis 1–2 (e.g., the length of days or a gap in the opening part of the creation story). However, recently, the debate has spread to the issues of Adam, Eve, and the Fall (Gen 2–3). If we accept evolution, our conceptualization of Adam also needs to be changed. Adam and Eve could not be the parents of all humanity if evolution were true.

At this point, we might wonder if this really matters. What will change if we reinterpret the opening chapters of the Bible? Perhaps, for some of us, we might believe that this will have little impact on our lives. We can contain the repercussions of a new reading of Genesis 2–3 to our understanding of those chapters of Scripture and our comprehension of science. Outside of that, nothing else will change.

However, reinterpreting the first chapters of Scripture does not stop at the end of Genesis 3. The story of Genesis 2–3 is the foundation for the rest of the story in Scripture. Change one part of that and we will shift our entire theology. Even more, theology is not just ideas in an ivory tower but the way we understand reality around us (cf. Prov 8:22–36). It intersects every point of life. And so a modification of this passage will have a "snowball effect"—it will rework how we understand the Bible and alter how we understand all of life. What would change when you reinterpret the opening chapters of Genesis? In a word: everything.

This reality originally compelled the faculty from various disciplines to come together and address this matter. Our understanding of Genesis 2–3 is not something confined just to the Bible and science departments; it is something acutely felt in all disciplines. This collection of essays investigates this topic from a variety of angles to help us see the reality and ramifications of Genesis 2–3.

The first several chapters deal with the Fall's reality. Should we read Genesis 3 as history? We begin with Abner Chou's chapter on hermeneutics and Genesis 2–3. Although some scholars contend that the opening chapters of Genesis never intended to communicate actual events, the evidence shows otherwise. Reading the text as history corresponds with the Scripture's concern for history as well as with the way Scripture interprets itself. Hence, to read Genesis 2–3 otherwise is to break out of the pattern and logic within the Bible. The correct interpretation of Genesis 2–3 is to read it as an accurate record of the past.

Such an interpretation of Genesis 2–3 might be reasonable were it not for recent scientific objections. Hence, the next two chapters, both coauthored by Joseph W. Francis and Todd Charles Wood, tackle these scientific issues. How similar are humans and chimpanzees? Does genetics demand that a historical Adam and Eve not exist? Francis and Wood discuss the evidence and remind us that the evolutionary framework *is not the only viable way to interpret the evidence*. There are ways to account for these observations in a creationist model. In fact, the end of Genesis 4 provides a model for harmonizing current scientific observations with what the opening chapters of Genesis teach. Accordingly, science does not (and should not) overthrow what we have observed about the text.

Grant Horner rounds out this section with reflections on the literary nature of Genesis 3. From a literary point of view, Genesis 3 does not read like a pure allegory. In biblical literature, theological sophistication does not undermine historicity. Genesis partakes in a larger plotline of Scripture which one reads consistently as historical. If one rejects Genesis 3 as historical, then belief in the historicity of the gospel is questionable. In the end, the problem is not with the text but rather with the reader. Genesis 3 itself then becomes the explanation of why people want to misread the text. If Genesis 3 was historical, we would expect that fallen, unrepentant man would distort that which convicts his soul. Thus, even the controversy surrounding the issues of the book points to the reality of Genesis 3.

Having discussed the reality of the text, we move to dealing with the theological ramifications of the Fall. Genesis 2–3 illustrate that the issue of the Fall is not a trivial matter. Indeed, changing the interpretation of these chapters will cause a major shift in our theology. Paul R. Thorsell discusses a foundational doctrine in the Christian faith: the doctrine of original sin. Contrary to those who would believe that this view came as a result of Augustine, Thorsell points out that the doctrine not only was in Paul but also ultimately in Genesis 3 itself. Likewise, William Varner reminds us that the Messiah is promised in Genesis 3. Contrary to some skeptics, the first promise of the gospel is in Genesis 3:15. Because of this, if we take away the "history" of the text, the reality of Messiah is also threatened.

However, the historicity of Adam and the Fall is not merely a matter of theology. Genesis 1–3 impacts various areas of life. Certain chapters deal with "what you would expect," assuming the Fall was historical. These implications are suggestive and provide indirect evidence of its historicity. R.W. Mackey, II writes about the nature of the Fall in the world of enterprise. We can observe the particular dynamics of the Fall in the distortion of communication, presence of scarcity, and need for management and accountability. Similarly, Taylor B. Jones presents a scientific study highlighting how thermodynamics changed in the Fall. The details of Genesis 3 accord with what we observe about the nature of entropy in our world.

The idea of "what you would expect" continues to the area of law. George A. Crawford demonstrates that the ideas of natural law, its distortion and need of codified law, as well as the judicial process all look back to fundamental tensions in Genesis 1–3. On one hand, man is created in God's image and should be just. On the other hand, the need for such regulation and our warped view of justice are accounted for by the Fall. The legal system is what you would expect if Genesis 1–3 is true.

Our reading of Genesis 3 also shapes a variety of issues we deal with in the modern day. Ernie Baker shows that psychology is one of those areas. If we want to help people change, it is essential to remember Genesis 3 and that the root of all problems is ultimately the influence of sin on our entire person. Sin has impacted our bodies and souls; we sin and are sinned against. The historicity of Genesis 3 grounds our worldview so that we really can help people be more like Christ.

Gender relations is another matter which is heavily predicated upon Genesis 1–3. Jo Suzuki demonstrates that only a careful reading of Genesis 1–3 allows us to correctly wade through this sensitive issue in our culture. These chapters are the grounds of having a truly biblical understanding of the roles of men and women. Alexander Granados explains that the historicity of Genesis 3 is a major issue in education. Although our culture has argued that we cannot mix faith and intellectual pursuits, Granados reminds us that Christians should desire to understand their Creator in every area. However, that can only be done if we submit every thought to the lordship of Christ. Hence, keeping Adam real matters, if we want to have a truly Christian education.

John MacArthur sums up the various discussions in this book with a passionate plea. The removal of Adam's historicity erodes the reality of sin, undermines the authority of Scripture, and will shift our entire paradigm of the nature of the world. Genesis 3 provides the answer not only to why the world is the way it is, but also provides the solution to this problem: the Second Adam, who is as real as the first.

Before continuing into the body of our discussion, I should preface this with one final comment. The issues within and stemming from Genesis 3 are complex and technical by nature. There is a delicate balance of trying to be accessible yet showing that our conclusions are well-grounded. Thus, we have endeavored to be as clear as possible for the lay reader, and put more technical detail in the footnotes. Even then, certain chapters are by nature more technical. However, all of that is essential to show that we have done our homework and are not shying away from the difficulties. We have tried to be clear yet accurate and thorough.[1] For some readers, such data will be slightly more difficult (but I encourage you to take the challenge). For others, it will be necessary. This work is to be a reference for both. Through it, we learn how to honestly tackle the challenges of our day. It further models to our own students how we desire them to serve God through scholarship. With that in mind, let us dig in to contemplate the reality and ramifications of what happened in the Garden.

---

1. One example of this is the spelling of Neandertal. While the more common spelling is Neanderthal, many paleontologists spell it Neandertal, which is the spelling adopted in this book.

PART 1:

REALITY OF GENESIS 2–3

CHAPTER 1

"Did God Really Say...?"— Hermeneutics and History in Genesis 3

Abner Chou

The supposed conflict between Genesis 3, its historicity, and science presumes certain realities. For one, it assumes certain conclusions on the level of science which my colleagues cover in chapters 2–3 of this book. It equally assumes a certain interpretation of Genesis 3. Traditionally we view Genesis 1–3 as *historical*, describing particular events that happened in the past. Hence, we might read Genesis 3 as follows: At the beginning of human history, when there was only one man and one woman (Gen 2:22–23), a serpent tempted the woman and Adam to eat the forbidden fruit (Gen 3:1–8). Adam succumbed, plunging creation into the consequences of sin (vv. 14–24). Although the text seems to say this at first glance, the advent of modern science causes such a scenario to be questioned on a variety of fronts.

However, what happens if the interpretation I gave is wrong? What happens if we misconstrued God's intent and He never claimed what we stated? Perhaps this entire debate is misguided because we have drawn the wrong conclusions.

Before shrugging off these ideas, we need to understand that these issues are important. Do we really want to misrepresent what God has said?[1] The Lord

---

1. This assumes a hermeneutic of authorial intent. I will not spend time to defend that view in

has demanded careful handling of His Word (cf. 2 Tim 2:15).[2] False teachers are those who twist the Scripture to their own destruction (2 Pet 3:16) and we do not want to fall anywhere near that camp. Thus, we should never handle these accusations lightly. They should spur us on to take another serious look at the text and to make sure "thus says the Lord."

Accordingly, this raises the question much like the one the serpent posed to Eve, "Did God really say...?" (Gen 3:1). Admittedly, this is a double entendre. On one hand, the question of this entire book asks whether God really said these words to Adam. Was any of that historical? On the other hand, particularly for this chapter, we also want to know what God really intended in these opening chapters of the Bible. Have we just assumed that our reading of Scripture is correct? How do we know if it is true?

This brings us to the subject matter of hermeneutics or the study of how the Bible works and how we read it.[3] My goal in this chapter is for us to tackle certain hermeneutical issues that surround Genesis 1–3. Through this, we can have more confidence that the way we have read Genesis 1–3 is accurate. Even more, I hope that we will be able to better read the Bible as a whole as we understand how history and theology work together in the Scriptures.

THE HERMENEUTICAL ISSUES

What are the hermeneutical issues that surround Genesis 1–3? Why could we be mistaken in our reading of that text as history? Objections against interpreting Genesis 1–3 revolve around two major arguments. One concerns the nature and claims of Genesis 1–3 itself. The other discusses how hermeneutics works in general. The following will help us understand these issues better.

Exegetical Issues Surrounding Genesis 1–3

The first objection focuses upon the textual features of Genesis 1–3. Scholars contend that the author of Genesis never intended for the text to portray actual events. Instead, the writer used stories to communicate certain

---

this chapter but refer the reader to other robust works that do so on the theological and philosophical levels. See Hirsch, *Validity in Interpretation*; Vanhoozer, *Is There a Meaning*; Stein, "The Benefits of an Author-Oriented Approach to Hermeneutics"; Stein, *A Basic Guide to Interpreting the Bible*.

2. Knight, *Pastoral Epistles*, 412.
3. Thomas, "The Principle of Single Meaning"; Zuck, *Basic Bible Interpretation*, 9–26.

theological truths about man, the world, and the purpose of Israel.[4] The story was not designed to show *how* people were made but rather the *purpose and nature* of their existence. Instead of *formation* the passage concerns *function*.[5] Thus, people who read it as historical narrative miss what the text actually claims. Just as we do not believe a parable necessarily happened in history, we should not think that Genesis 1–3 occurred in the past.[6] To do otherwise grossly misinterprets the text. In essence, these scholars argue that we have read the text asking the wrong set of questions.

What is the evidence for this? To begin with, one might compare Genesis 1–3 with other ancient near eastern (ANE) myths. Scholars observe that ANE stories do not concentrate upon material origins. For example, in some ANE stories, pagan gods create lesser gods (or humans) who represent different vocations.[7] This would communicate to the ancient audience the different tasks in the world and how they were to operate. Such "creation stories" are really trying to explain the way the world works. This is function over formation.

Even more, the Genesis account seems to parallel these stories in a variety of ways. For example, *Enuma Elish*, a Babylonian myth, records the presence of a firmament with waters above and below like in Genesis 1:6. The same story discusses a goddess named "Tiamat" which sounds a lot like the word for "depths" in Genesis 1:2 (תְהוֹם, tĕhôm). On top of this, we observe that both Genesis 1–3 and ANE stories deal with agriculture by irrigation (*Enuma Elish*; cf. Genesis 2:5) as well as describe plants that confer immortality (*Gilgamesh Epic*; cf. Genesis 2:9), serpents (*Gilgamesh Epic*; cf. Genesis 3:1), and how man angers the gods (*Atrahasis*; *Eridu Genesis*; cf. Genesis 3:8–11).[8]

Since we are covering the issue of Adam, we can specifically note parallels between ANE myths and the formation of man in Genesis 2:7. In *Atrahasis*, humans are made out of clay, flesh, and blood to serve the gods.[9] In *Enki and Nimah*, Enki, the god of subterranean waters, makes man from some excess clay.[10] The

---

4. Walton, "A Historical Adam: Archetypal Creation View," 89–90.
5. Walton, *The Lost World of Genesis One*, 21–35.
6. Walton, "A Historical Adam: Archetypal Creation View," 117.
7. Ibid., 98–102.
8. Enns, *The Evolution of Adam*, 39–56.
9. Lamoureux, "No Historical Adam: Evolutionary Creation View," 58. See also *Atrahasis*, line 210 in Hallo and Younger, *Context of Scripture*, 450.
10. Lamoureux, "No Historical Adam: Evolutionary Creation View," 58. See also *Enki and Nimah*, lines 30–35 in Hallo and Younger, *Context of Scripture*, 517.

Gilgamesh Epic also makes reference to how man was made out of clay.[11] Does this not sound somewhat similar to Genesis 2:7?

These parallels are substantial. If ANE stories are meant to explain the order of the world (as opposed to its origins) and if the biblical record sounds like these tales, then why would the original audience ever have thought that Genesis 1–3 concerned the origins of the world? Based upon this, scholars argue that reading Genesis 1–3 as history would be foreign to the audience.[12] They would never have read the text with that in mind and neither should we.

Evidence for a more parabolic reading is not only based upon external evidence (ANE background) but also upon internal factors. For instance, the organization of days seems to indicate that the text's emphasis is on the functionality of creation. Days 1–3 provide differing locales, which days 4–6 respectively fill. By the stars filling the heavens (Gen 1:16), the fish occupying the sea (Gen 1:20–21), and man and animals living on the land (Gen 1:24–26), we observe that God shows how creation is to operate. Thus, scholars suggest that Moses intends to communicate function over formation.[13]

In addition, Walton argues that words like "create" (ברא, *br'*), "make" (עשׂה, *'śh*), and "form" (יצר, *yṣr*) all pertain to the notion of shaping something for a purpose as opposed to material creation.[14] Of particular interest is the term "create" (ברא, *br'*) since the word in its English translation would seem to indicate how God made the world materially. However, Walton points out that God creates immaterial entities (like a "pure heart," Ps 51:10, or a "new thing," Jer 31:22), which may imply that the Hebrew idea may not fundamentally be "to create" as we think of it. The word may not refer to making something but rather giving something purpose. Again, the stress would be on function over formation.

Advocates of reading Genesis 1–3 ahistorically would also point out that the text has rich theology.[15] To them, Eden appears to be like a cosmic temple and, indeed, the tabernacle and temple seem to draw from the imagery of Eden.[16] In

11. Lamoureux, "No Historical Adam: Evolutionary Creation View," 58. See also *Gilgamesh Epic* in Pritchard, *Ancient Near Eastern Texts Relating to the Old Testament*, 72–97.
12. Walton, "A Historical Adam: Archetypal Creation View," 102.
13. Walton, *The Lost World of Genesis One*, 53–70.
14. Ibid., 36–45.
15. Walton, "A Historical Adam: Archetypal Creation View," 102–104; Lamoureux, "No Historical Adam: Evolutionary Creation View," 63–65.
16. Walton, *The Lost World of Genesis One*, 77–85; Beale, *Temple and the Church's Mission*, 29–80. Beale does not discuss the historicity of Genesis 1–3 but rather the theological emphasis of Eden in the account.

fact, Postell observes some fascinating parallels between God's work in Eden and Moses' labor on the tabernacle.[17] In addition, Adam seems prototypical of great kings like Solomon. Both of them share knowledge over trees, cattle, flying creatures, creeping things, and fish (1 Kgs 4:33), which mirrors the language of Genesis 1:26–28. Thus, the story of Adam appears to be about the theology of a true king. Some also suggest that Adam's and Eve's expulsion from the Garden may parallel Israel's expulsion from their own land.[18] Scholars, observing such great theology, conclude that this is the main point of Genesis 1–3 and say that concentrating on the historicity of Genesis 1–3 misses the point.

Overall, scholars point to the historical backgrounds of Genesis 1–3 as well as internal evidence to suggest that historicity is not the text's focus. The original readers would never have read it that way. We should not read these chapters to learn how mankind was *formed* but rather how humanity *functions* in this world. For certain scholars, that is the way to read the text per the author's intent.

Hermeneutical Issue of History and Theology

The second camp of scholars does not disagree with what has been said above. Nevertheless, they not only see exegetical issues surrounding Genesis 1–3 but they also take issue with traditional hermeneutical methodology. This pertains to how we deal with history and theology. Traditional hermeneutics gives equal weight to both of these things. It cares about the history that a text supposedly described and to the theology it communicates. However, these scholars would say that such an interpretative methodology is flawed based upon how God wrote the Bible. They assert that God accommodated His message to the ancient readers so that they would understand His truth. Thus, He communicated His ideas in the stories, cultural practices, language, and even the (flawed) worldview of the writer and his audience.

Based upon this, scholars argue that stories, like in Genesis 1–3, were merely an accommodation to the audience. They were just a vehicle that communicated truth but were never meant to be taken as the truth. Thus, our hermeneutical practice must separate the "incident" or "story" from the eternal message.[19]

---

17. Postell, *Adam as Israel*, 111. The comparisons include how God completed the work for Eden (Gen 2:2) and Moses completed the work of the tabernacle (Exod 40:33b). Also, God sees everything He made (Gen 1:31a) and Moses saw all the work they had done (Exod 39:43a).
18. Ibid., 147; Enns, *The Evolution of Adam*, 67.
19. Lamoureux, "No Historical Adam: Evolutionary Creation View," 63.

This is not only the case in Genesis 1–3 but is also to be applied across the Scriptures.[20]

According to these theologians, this new methodology is not as drastic of a shift as one might think. They would contend we already do this quite frequently. For example, do we believe that the heavens are a solid dome? I think most of us would answer negatively. However, the Bible uses the word "firmament" (רָקִיעַ, *rāqîaʿ*), which may denote that idea.[21] Similarly, do we believe in a three-tiered universe of heavens above, the earth, and the underworld? The biblical texts seem to assert that very paradigm (Phil 2:10). We could also cite instances where the Bible describes how the sun rises and falls (2 Sam 23:4; Ps 104:22) and the earth does not move (Ps 93:1). One scholar cited Jesus' parable of the mustard seed as an illustration since our Lord claims that the mustard seed is smallest of the seeds (Matt 13:32) when it actually is not. Should we accept His claim about the size of mustard seeds or see the truth He is trying to illustrate?[22] Thus, it appears that those who take Genesis as history are inconsistent. On one hand, we argue that Genesis 1–3 is history and must be accepted as the account of our origin. On the other hand, we reject other texts' claims about the nature of the universe. To these scholars, this is evidence that we ought to separate theology from the accommodation that God made to His original readers.

My intent in discussing these theories is not to scare or overwhelm the reader. I also am not claiming that I adhere to these ideas. Rather, my point is that the hermeneutical objections against historicity are real and substantial. They pertain not only to Genesis 1–3 itself but also to broader questions of how God wrote the Bible and how we ought to read it. It is with this background that we can better see how to evaluate our own understanding of hermeneutics and sharpen our reading of Genesis 1–3.

INDIVISIBILITY OF HISTORY AND THEOLOGY

Thesis: History as Grounds of Theology

In approaching these issues, I will first deal with whether or not we need to adjust our overarching hermeneutic. Should we separate the event described in the text from its message? Does the Bible divorce history from its

---

20. See also, Rogers, *The Authority and Interpretation of the Bible*; Sparks, *God's Word in Human Words*.
21. Lamoureux, "No Historical Adam: Evolutionary Creation View," 52–53.
22. Ibid., 60.

theology? As discussed, these types of questions presume that the Bible works a certain way. Namely, God views the stories of Scripture as merely a vehicle that illustrates or communicates the truth. The following discussion seeks to address whether that is the case. How do the biblical writers define the relationship between history and theology?

Within this, our first step is to gain a working definition of how history and theology interact. To do this, I suggest we look at several examples where the inspired authors present their rationale of how history and theology operate. From there, we can see if this initial idea plays out through the rest of Scripture.

Undoubtedly, Paul's view of the resurrection is the clearest example of how Scripture associates history and theology. He argues that if the resurrection never occurred, then our faith is in vain, our preaching is false, we have no hope, and thus are to be most pitied (1 Cor 15:19). Notice that the apostle's logic is not that the theology of the resurrection can still be true even if the historicity of the resurrection is false. Rather, in Paul's mind, if the history fails, so does our faith. I would suggest that such a concept is at the core of how the Bible relates history and theology.

Although Paul's discussion of the resurrection may be the clearest, it is not the only text in which the Bible demonstrates such logic. Peter's view of the Flood similarly follows Paul's logic about the resurrection. In his second epistle, Peter confronts false teachers who are indifferent to God's eschatological judgment (2 Pet 3:3). They base their indifference upon the fact that the earth has continued on as it was since the beginning (2 Pet 3:4). Peter argues that a precedent for judgment actually exists: the global judgment of the Flood (2 Pet 3:6). In context, Peter's point cannot be that the Flood is merely a metaphor for how God hates sin. That would not disprove the false teachers' supposition. Rather, the apostle contends that the world has not continued as it was since the beginning. God *actually judged* the whole earth and that historical reality supports that He can do it again.[23] In sum, Peter reasons that the historicity of God's past acts is the grounds for His promises about the future, a logic parallel to Paul's.

God seems to have the same paradigm in discussing the Exodus. In Deuteronomy, the Lord warned His people that if they disobeyed, they would be exiled (Deut 4:27). Nevertheless, God promised to deliver them in the end because of His great compassion (Deut 4:31–32). What assurance did Israel have of such future redemption? God compares Himself with the other "gods" and states that

---

23. Davids, *The Letters of 2 Peter and Jude*, 270; Schreiner, *1, 2 Peter, Jude*, 37:376.

no one else has delivered a people with signs and wonders (Deut 4:34; cf. Exod 7:14–12:51). God alone accomplished this in the Exodus and thus Israel should trust Him. His amazing work in the past guarantees that He can do a repeat performance in the future.[24] Such logic seems to mirror Peter's and Paul's. Even more, God portrays that the Exodus event actually *makes* the theological point of God's uniqueness. If God did not do this work, then He would not be distinct from the other gods and would lose the basis of His claims.

In addition, the apostles tightly intertwine history and theology. Christ's life and death provide an example of godly suffering and humility for us to follow (Phil 2:5–11; 1 Pet 2:21). God demonstrated His love in that while we were yet sinners, Christ died for us (Rom 5:8). Christ died on behalf of the ungodly so that we would become the righteousness of God (2 Cor 5:21). His death demonstrates that God is both just and justifier (Rom 3:25–26). His resurrection conquers death and gives us hope for a new creation (Rom 6:5–8; 2 Cor 5:17).

In these passages, the historicity of Christ and His work is essential. We can ask the following question about the texts just cited. If Christ never came, did God actually love us in the way Paul describes? If Christ never died, then did God forgive sin? If Christ never atoned, is God still just and justifier? If Christ never rose and conquered death, why would we rise from the dead? These passages seem to argue that when we take away the history, we also take away the reality of the theology. Paul's presentation of the gospel is case in point. He does not claim that we are saved because God is kind and gracious. Rather, he argues that Christ's death for our sins and His resurrection on the third day is the gospel that saves (1 Cor 15:2–4). Theology is worked out in history itself.

These examples give us a different picture of how the Bible works from what was suggested in the previous section. Instead of seeing history as merely some accommodation to communicate theology, the prophets and apostles based their reasons for certain theological points upon God's past acts. More precisely, they see that history grounds theology in reality. Peter's point is that God's judgment is not some theoretical idea but rather is *real*. Not only did the Flood demonstrate that He *could* act in wrath but that He, in fact, *did*. Likewise, God is not only unique because He says He is but because He has shown it in events like the Exodus. God's love is not some ethereal concept but is tangibly ours because of Christ's incarnation. Forgiveness of sin is not just potential but actual because of Christ's death. Our own resurrection is not hypothetical but guaranteed based

---

24. Merrill, *Deuteronomy*, 4:131; Craigie, *The Book of Deuteronomy*, 143.

upon the precedent of Christ's own resurrection. These correlations allow us to define the relationship between history and theology one step further. *The biblical writers do not see history as merely a means of communicating theology; rather, they see history as the means of actualizing theology.* History is the vehicle by which theological truth comes into our world and impacts our lives. Far from separating history from theology, the Bible seems to tie them inextricably together.

As stated above, this notion that history grounds theology is preliminary. The preceding examples do not prove that this is the way Scripture as a whole operates, but helps us to begin to define the relationship. The question becomes whether or not this paradigm operates throughout the entirety of the Bible. That is where we now must turn.

The Logic of Scripture

The amount the scriptural authors write about history hints that they thought of it as a vital mechanism for theology. We can see this in the major narratives of the Bible found in Genesis, Exodus, Joshua, Judges–Nehemiah, the Gospels, and Acts. We can also witness this in the way biblical writers repeatedly summarize the storyline of Scripture (Deut 1–3; Josh 24:1–28; Neh 9; Pss 78; 104–6; Dan 9:1–19). In looking at these texts, we can observe that the logic mentioned above is repeated over and over again. As such, history as the actualization of theology is not an isolated idea but the logic of the Bible; it is the way the Bible works.

Before delving into the details of this, I would like to provide three more sweeping observations of these texts that support what we have considered thus far. First, throughout these texts, the biblical writers discuss history for the sake of worship. The Levites in Nehemiah call upon the people to bless the Lord (Neh 9:5) for the works He has accomplished (Neh 9:6–15). The psalmist calls upon his audience not only to give thanks to the Lord for His deeds, but also to make them known amongst the people (Pss 104:1; 105:1).[25] God's activity, particularly Creation, distinguishes Him from idols and demands awe and trust (Jer 10:5–12). Thus, the people of God are commanded to worship God *for what He has done.* Such a sentiment does not relegate these stories as a vehicle to communicate some ethereal idea. Rather, this rationale arguably indicates that the biblical writers viewed these stories as fact (otherwise what would they

25. This raises a significant question of whether God would be demanding that His people propagate untruths about Himself.

be worshipping God for?) and made biblical history the grounds for our worship. They wrote with the logic that history is foundational for our theology

Second, we can notice that the writers of Scripture frequently recount the narratives of Scripture to show how the storyline connects theology with their readers. Moses discusses the past to show how the Lord's work for Abraham continues with Israel (Deut 1–3). Accordingly, they needed to obey and conquer the promised land (Deut 4:1). In Nehemiah, the people understand how they have sinned and God was faithful to provide them another chance. Hence, they desire to re-establish a covenant with the Lord (Neh 9:38 [Heb 10:1]). In the New Testament, Stephen and Paul recount history in order to show how that climaxed in Christ and how all are accountable to believe in Jesus (Acts 7:1–53; 13:13–42). The author of Hebrews, in the famous "hall of fame of faith," provides a historical recounting of those who trusted God so that believers in the church age would continue to persevere and rely upon the Lord (Heb 11).[26] In all of these examples, the inspired authors situate their audience in the story of the Bible. That was the way the authors helped their readers theologically understand their circumstances and what they presently needed to do. History was the bridge between the theology of the past and its relevance in the present. Again, the writers see that history is what binds theology to reality.

Third, at certain points, the biblical writers highlight how certain events fulfill prophecy or work out particular promises. Israel's conquest of the land demonstrates how God's promises to the patriarchs did not fail (Josh 23:14). Israel's exile (2 Kgs 17:5–23) carries out what God warned them against in the days of Moses (Deut 28:36). Jesus' birth (Matt 2:1; cf. Mic 5:2 [Heb 5:1]), life (Matt 8:17; Isa 53:4), death (Mark 10:45; Isa 53:5–11), and resurrection (Acts 2:31; Ps 16:10) fulfill Old Testament predictions. This, too, demonstrates the nature of how the writers thought about and used history. They viewed it as the means by which the promises and intentions of God worked their way into reality. God's acts in history make His past guarantees (whether predictions or promises) actual. These notions of prophecy and promise reinforce that history actualizes theology.

These more prevalent features of scriptural narratives support what we have suggested above. From here, we can proceed to examine the way the authors discussed history in its breadth and detail. In doing so, we can see that what has been discussed is how the Scripture consistently sets up its own storyline. This shows that the paradigm of "history grounds theology" is the way the Bible works.

---

26. O'Brien, *The Letter to the Hebrews*, 395–96.

This begins with creation. The Levites in Nehemiah's day include God's work of creation (Neh 9:6) as part of the storyline and do not differentiate it from the life of the patriarchs, the Exodus, or the exile (Neh 9:7–37). Similarly, the psalms not only recount the life of Abraham (Ps 105) and Israel's wilderness wanderings (Ps 106), but also God's wisdom in creation (Ps 104). Although we will address the way that the Scripture reads Genesis 3 in a later section, suffice it to say that the Scripture does not treat Creation separately or differently than other historical narratives. It is viewed the same way.

As such, Creation parallels other historical events that operate as the actualization of theology. When the psalmist reflects upon the lives of the patriarchs, he claims that God confirmed His promises by His acts for them (Ps 105:8). God's dealings demonstrate the certainty of His promises thereby (Ps 105:8–10).[27] The Exodus is also the working out of God's promises in the Abrahamic covenant (Ps 105:23–45). His acts of deliverance work to fulfill those guarantees (Ps 105:42). The conquest as well marks God's fidelity to His promises. Not one good word of the Lord failed (Josh 23:14–15). From the patriarchs to the conquest, history brings what God promised to reality. That is how the biblical authors portrayed these stories and how later writers understood it.

As Israel settles in the land, they disobey and God punishes them. Such punishment extends from the time of the Judges (Judg 2:10–15) all the way to the exile (2 Kgs 25:1–21). This fulfills God's warning that He would curse disobedience (Deut 28:15–68). In fact, the specific judgments of drought (1 Kgs 17:1; cf. Lev 26:19), famine (Ruth 1:1–6; cf. Deut 28:23–24), siege (2 Kgs 6:24–25; cf. Deut 28:52), or eating one's children (2 Kgs 6:28–29; cf. Deut 28:56–57) all attest that history worked out what God had warned. As later writers reflect upon this era, they do not see them as a parable illustrating God's wrath but, rather, state that they experience the outcomes of that wrath as they live in exile, slaves of another country (Lam 1:1 and Neh 9:36). The reality of past history and theology becomes their own reality. This again highlights that the historicity of the Bible's story and theology all go hand in hand.

However, Israel's history is not purely one of judgment. Rather, after the time of the judges, God also fulfills His promises to bless. The Lord raises up kings, like David and Solomon, whose kingdoms facilitate God's blessing to the nations (cf. 1 Kgs 10:9). This fundamentally demonstrates how God fulfills His promises to raise up a king (cf. Gen 17:16). It also works out what God prom-

---

27.   Allen, *Psalms 101–150 (Revised)*, 58.

ised in the Abrahamic (Gen 12:1–4) and Davidic (2 Sam 7:9–14) covenants. The paradigm again is one where history brings God's promises to reality.

The New Testament views Old Testament history and theology through the same lens. The apostles recount that the situation of the New Testament directly stems from what happened in the Old. Israel's sins have led to the exile, which is the backdrop of the Gospels (Luke 1:71; 3:4–6) and for believers in the church age (1 Pet 1:1–2). The Old Testament anticipations of how God would work (Isa 40:1–3) are answered in the New (Mark 1:1–4). This illustrates that one way the Old connects with the New is via history. As mentioned above, history not only weds theology and reality but also connects realities past with realities present.

Moreover, the New Testament fulfills Old Testament expectations by showing how God brought His prophecies and promises to fruition in the life of Jesus. Christ's birth fulfills prophecies (Mic 5:2 [Heb v. 1]; cf. Matt 2:1–6). His baptism and temptation complete certain Old Testament concepts (Matt 4:1–11; cf. Deut 6:16; 8:3; 10:20). The location of His ministry fulfills prophecy (Matt 4:13; cf. Isa 9:1 [Heb 8:23]). His miracles demonstrate that He is the Messiah (Matt 8:17) and fulfill what the prophets said (cf. Isa 53:4). As discussed above, His crucifixion and resurrection defeat death (Heb 2:14) and allow believers to have eternal life (1 Cor 15:22). The New Testament writers show that God's purposes are not mythical, but actual, by the work He did in Christ. History actualizes theology.

In addition, the Great Commission (Matt 28:18–20) is itself theology breaking into reality via history. God prophesied that the nations, even the ends of the earth, would see the salvation of the Lord in the Messiah (Isa 49:6). For this reason, Jesus commands His disciples to be His witnesses even to the ends of the earth (Acts 1:8). The work of the twelve and of Paul makes this command a reality. Acts then shows how God enacts salvation to the ends of the earth. In fact, as we partake in that same command, do we not actualize theology into reality? Do we not make real what God had intended to display in Christ? God's focus upon history demonstrates His concern with reality—a reality we need to live out.

The storyline continues from the church age to consummation. I suppose one could argue that this is not "history" in the sense that it is not of the past. Nevertheless, we can make two important observations about eschatology. First, the prophets and apostles anticipated actual events in the future. Christ's return is not a metaphor, but something to be expected (1 Pet 1:13), seen (Matt 24:30), and experienced at a given time, albeit unknown (Matt 24:36). This confidence in the reality of future events reflects on how they thought about the reality of earlier events. Second, His coming changes the world. Death is conquered and tears are wiped away (Rev 21:4). Again "future history" actualizes theology. With that, the ending of the story matches the biblical writers' paradigm throughout the entire storyline.

From this discussion, we can make two major observations. First, the biblical writers were consistent in their approach to history. They viewed it as the grounds for and the actualization of theology. In our survey above, the biblical writers do not view the past as merely an illustration of God's character. Instead, they see it as the cause for why certain realities exist. History binds not only theology with reality but also past truths with present. Theology is not merely real because God declares it so but also because He has demonstrated it in history. Succinctly put, theology is not merely what is but also what happens. In fact, one could even argue that God's promises by nature are guarantees to shape history. Making Abraham a great nation (Gen 12:2a), blessing the world (Gen 12:3), cursing for disobedience (Deut 28:15–68), and sending His Son to save (Isa 42:1–9) are arguably all things that cannot come to pass without history. That too shows the Bible's focus on the fact that history is a vital mechanism for theology.

Second, such a perspective is not only consistent but also comprehensive. This survey shows that the scriptural writers viewed the stories of the Bible *from creation to consummation* in such a light. For our discussion, the inclusion of creation in this paradigm is important. It shows that it is no exception to the pattern we have seen above. Even more, it demonstrates that this is the way stories operate in Scripture as a whole. Put differently, *the logic of Paul about the resurrection is the logic of Scripture about all of its history.*

Having stated all of this, we can return to the larger issue of our discussion. Should we change our hermeneutical method to separate the incident of Scripture from its message? The argument for this was based upon how the Scripture works; how God wrote it. However, instead of finding evidence that the stories in Scripture are merely an accommodation to the audience, we see that history is essential in undergirding the reality of its theology. Take away the history and one also takes away the theology. The way the Bible operates actually makes it imperative to care *both* about history and theology because they are interconnected. That should be our hermeneutical conviction.

Perhaps a counterargument might be that the biblical writers were wrong in this thinking. I would challenge this based upon my own conviction of how God operates in inspiration (2 Pet 1:20–21). Nevertheless, even if that was true, we would need to admit that the hermeneutical shift is warranted, not by evidence in the Scripture itself, but rather, by external factors. If we are committed to interpret Scripture the way it actually works—the way God working through the authors seems to make it work—then seeing the necessity of history as the grounds for theology is imperative. This should be our hermeneutic.

Addressing the Issue of Language

One matter still remains in this hermeneutical discussion. Scholars suggested that we already split incident from theology in other texts. Examples included the idea of a solid dome (Gen 1:6), a three-tiered universe (Phil 2:10), the sun rising and setting (Matt 5:45), and the mustard seed (Mark 4:31). Does the above discussion demand that we accept a solid dome of the sky or a three-tiered universe?

In response, for these objections to work, scholars must assume that such language is a reflection of what an author believes as opposed to using cultural terms or idioms. However, is that even the case with us? Do our words reflect everything we believe? After all, we talk about the sun rising and setting yet know that the earth revolves around the sun. We talk about "going up north" even if north might not be higher in elevation. In light of this, it is not unreasonable to accept that biblical writers used language phenomenologically and rhetorically. They used language to describe what they saw (from their perspective) as well as used figures of speech to make a point.

This is especially reasonable when the biblical writers do not always describe a "three-tiered universe" (cf. Gen 1:1; Deut 32:1). Their variation of wording arguably demonstrates that this was not their belief, but rather, their use of language to describe. Similarly, the Hebrew word "firmament" or "expanse" probably does not even talk about a solid dome (רָקִיעַ).[28] Even more, biblical writers view the sky and rainfall quite differently than a "solid dome" (cf. Job 26:7–8; Ps 147:8). Hence, when the writers of Scripture talk about the "firmament," they were not intending to communicate a certain idea about the sky. Rather, they were simply referring to it. Finally, commentators agree that Jesus, in context, was speaking hyperbolically about the mustard seed to prove a point about the growth of the kingdom.[29] It was never His intent to make a scientific claim.

Hence, these objections do not require a hermeneutical shift. In fact, dis-

---

28. Walton, "No Historical Adam: Response from the Archetypal View," 67–68; Barrick, "No Historical Adam: Response from the Young-Earth View," 82.

29. Edwards, *The Gospel According to Mark*, 144; France, *The Gospel of Mark*, 215.

cerning through this issue is based upon a consistent hermeneutic of heeding the author's intent. With that, the biblical writers' uniform rationale that history actualizes theology resurfaces. We should heed their intent about history and theology as well. This should cause us to see the necessity of going back to Genesis 3 and addressing the actuality of those events as they bring the theology of man, sin, and salvation to reality.

GENESIS 1–3 AS HISTORICAL

With the mention of authorial intent, some might object to my analysis with the assertion that Moses never intended Genesis 1–3 to be read with history in mind. To them, my emphasis on the hermeneutical logic of history and theology is misplaced because that only applies when the author claims his writing represents history (which Moses supposedly never did). That brings us to the second objection against reading Genesis 1–3 as history: the objection that the features within Genesis 1–3 do not pose it as historical. We observed two major arguments for why Genesis 3 never intended to portray history. First, Genesis 3 has striking parallels with ANE myths. Just as ANE myths concentrated upon function over formation, so Genesis 3 does as well. Second, Genesis 3 has different structural and thematic features that make it an account more about theology rather than history. In addressing these issues, we can determine if Genesis 1–3 claims that it is historical in nature and thereby abides by the logic we stated above.

Myth or Mythbusting?

Scholars point to the substantial parallels between ANE myths and Genesis 1–3. At the same time, how alike are the similarities? Is the overlap as considerable as it seems? I have listed six often-cited correspondences between Genesis 1–3 and ANE literature. We can go through them to determine how parallel they really are.

1.   Scholars observe the presence of a firmament in *Enuma Elish* and in Egyptian cosmologies. This matches what is described in Genesis 1:6. However, *Enuma Elish* might not have even existed in the time of Moses.[30] Scholars acknowledge that it is late, perhaps existing no earlier than Nebuchadnez-

---

30.   This presumes Mosaic authorship. See discussion in Grisanti, "The Pentateuch," 162–69.

zar I (ca. 1100 BC).[31] Even if one accepts that Genesis interacted with an ancient tradition(s) behind *Enuma Elish*, there are still problems. In *Enuma Elish*, the context of the firmament is how the god Marduk rips Tiamat in half forming the upper heavens and earth. Marduk additionally creates a "lower heaven."[32] The formation (violence versus speaking) and material (goddess's body versus water) of the firmament are completely different between ANE literature and Genesis 1–3. The stories are not that similar.

2. Scholars also cite *Enuma Elish* to compare the goddess Tiamat with the Hebrew word "deep" (תְּהוֹם, *tĕhôm*). This too may demonstrate how Genesis paralleled the ANE account. In addition to the chronological problems with associating *Enuma Elish* with Genesis, we can make a simple observation. Tiamat is a goddess and in Genesis 1, the "deep" is not divine or living in any sense. It is just water (הַמָּיִם, *hammāyim*, 1:2). Again, though there may be some kind of overlap, there are categorical differences. This is not strict borrowing. Furthermore, the story of *Enuma Elish* seems to parallel another myth, the Baal Cycle. Just as Marduk fights Tiamat, Baal fights Yam (the sea).[33] However, the Baal Cycle concerns not creation but seasons.[34] *Enuma Elish* may have some hint of that as well. If this is the case, then that further reinforces that the suggested similarities function contextually in entirely different ways (creation versus the seasons).

3. Scholars also observe that light came before the light bearers in certain ANE myths. However, if the focus is upon seasons (see above point), then the reason the ANE myths discuss this is entirely different from what Genesis portrays.[35]

4. Scholars point out that both ANE myths and Genesis 1–3 depict agriculture by irrigation. That should not be too surprising since irrigation is often involved in agriculture. Furthermore, in Genesis 2 the "irrigation" involved is divinely ordained (Gen 2:5–6) but in ANE myths (like *Eridu Genesis*), the irrigation is manmade. Even in something more "common," differences exist.

---

31. Lambert, "Enuma Elish," 527.
32. Ibid., see *Enuma Elish* 4:135–40.
33. Gronbaek, "Baal's Battle with Yam—A Canaanite Creation Fight," 35.
34. Ibid.
35. Ibid., 29–35.

5. Scholars point out that ANE myths describe how man angers the gods just like in Genesis 3:11. However, the reasons are different. In *Atrahasis* and *Eridu Genesis*, the gods become angry over the great noise made by an overpopulated earth.[36] In Genesis, the problem is clearly not overpopulation (since it seems to portray just two human individuals) but disobedience.

6. Scholars mentioned that the *Gilgamesh Epic* contains mention of a serpent and a plant that confers immortality. This sounds quite similar to Genesis 3. However, Gilgamesh's plant is on the bottom of the ocean. He desires to eat it to thwart his death but the serpent ends up eating it instead. Genesis does not view the tree of life as a solution to death since death seems not to be present until after disobedience (cf. Gen 2:17; 3:19). The snake does not eat from that tree either.[37] To be sure, similarities of the stories exist but there are some substantial differences.[38]

My point in discussing the above is to show that while parallels exist, such similarities are used in different contexts for different purposes. Thus, we cannot simply argue that because the ANE myths operate in a particular way, so Genesis operates the same way. Genesis may be interacting with the ANE myths but doing something entirely different with those cultural ideas. Though similarities exist, we need not over exaggerate them. Rather, we need to define the precise relationship between what occurred in Genesis 1–3 and the ANE.

A further examination of the differences between Genesis 1–3 and the ANE stories can help us solidify that relationship. For example, ANE myths commonly portray "creation" as a battle. We have observed above that Marduk rips open Tiamat to form heaven and earth. Baal fights Yam, which results in the seasons. However, Genesis contains none of this. God is supreme and creates by His Word without contest. We can also observe a major contrast between the Genesis account and Egyptian cosmologies. The latter portray creation as a sexual activity.[39] That also does not occur in the biblical account.

Other theological differences also exist. ANE myths portray man as insignificant whereas the Bible describes man as important (Gen 1:26–28; 2:5–7). ANE myths portray the world as an imperfect place whereas the Bible de-

---

36. Hallo and Younger, *Context of Scripture*, 451, 514.
37. Pritchard, *Ancient Near Eastern Texts Relating to the Old Testament*, 72–97.
38. One might even suggest that these stories are perversions of what actually happened.
39. Hallo and Younger, *Context of Scripture*, 6. See *Book of Nut* for some descriptions of this.

scribes it as very good (Gen 1:31). ANE myths do not deal with the issues of disobedience and sin, while that is the focus in the narrative of Genesis 3 (v. 11). All of these differences (and more[40]) have led scholars to suggest that the creation narrative was a way for Moses to argue against the false ideas of the surrounding nations.[41] Thus, initially we may conclude that the relationship between Genesis 1–3 and ANE myths is a polemical one.

However, other differences between these two accounts help us to sharpen that definition. For instance, a noticeable distinction between the two is the lack of consistent poetic parallelism in Genesis 1–3. ANE myths like *Enuma Elish*, Sumerian myths, and even the *Gilgamesh Epic* are poetic in nature rather than narrative. In addition to the lack of parallelism, Genesis 1–3 contains a verb form (*wayyiqtol*) which is a standard marker of narrative.[42] The prevalence of the verb form is found in other historical narratives including Genesis 12–50, Exodus, 1 and 2 Samuel, and 1 and 2 Kings.[43] Granted, genre itself does not attest to whether something is historical or not. After all, poetry itself can communicate historical events (cf. Pss 78; 104–6). However, narrative genre in the Old Testament (and even in ANE literature) does not communicate myth.[44] My point here is that if Moses was combating certain ANE ideas, he did so in a way totally different than the stories of his contemporaries. His claims are put in a genre form (narrative) associated with history rather than mythical poetry. This suggests that he used history to combat myth.

Moreover, the biblical record demythologizes elements of ANE myths. For instance, ANE myths talk about the sky, ocean, depths of the sea, and even death as divine. Their stories are pantheistic in nature. However, Genesis 1 portrays all of those entities as merely physical objects created by God. This is completely unique to ANE literature. As Waterman states, "We may ven-

---

40. Interestingly enough, ANE myths have a form of evolution. Egyptian cosmologies show how the world develops like an egg. Translators even use the term "evolve" to describe this process. Civilizations in *Eridu Genesis* and *Atrahasis* imply the ongoing development of civilization. However, the Bible does not describe a long process but rather instantaneous creation. It does not depict a civilization reaching its peak but rather that creation was at its peak and then fell.

41. Enns, *The Evolution of Adam*, 50; Barrick, "A Historical Adam: Young-Earth Creation View," 225.

42. Boyd, "The Genre of Genesis 1:1–2:3: What Means This Text?"

43. Ibid.

44. One arguable exception might be Judges 9:8–15 where Jotham tells a "parable" using a narrative genre. However, even that is historical in nature since his speech is actually a historical event. Thus, the author of Judges still makes a claim of history. Jotham, at a certain time and place, spoke that parable. Thus, the narrative genre still is closely tied with history.

ture to say that Genesis, chapter 1, with its almost completely depersonalized nature forces is by contrast a triumphant work of creative art."[45] From this, it appears that Moses' agenda is to describe things as they really are as opposed to playing into the mentality within ANE myths.

Finally, scholars note that while certain ANE myths deal more with seasons and cycles, the Bible is distinctively creational in nature. Gronbaek analyzes the Baal myths and contrasts them with Genesis in this way: "Naturally creation is not equally prominent in all of the contexts in which the concept appears. It seems to be unique in Genesis 1, which relates a once-and-for-all event at the beginning of history."[46]

What do the differences show? They not only indicate the polemical nature of Genesis 1–3 but also hint at the precise logic involved. The differences of genre, content, and purpose argue that Moses was not merely countering a myth with a myth, but with history. He countered with what really happened. That is why he uses historical narrative as a genre, demythologizes the ANE myths, and discusses the beginning event of all history. His focus was not on trying to give a nice story that counteracted the story of the ANE. He was giving something totally different: the history of what God did. Arguably, that best accounts for these marked distinctions and the precise way he polemicizes against the myths of the time. The contrasts help us to see Moses' claim of historicity.

As discussed, one of the arguments that Genesis 1–3 never portrayed history was due to its parallels with ANE literature. Upon further examination, we find that the opposite is true. Moses was not giving more myths. Rather, he was a myth-buster. The differences show a deliberate emphasis upon reality rather than mythical storytelling or ideas. To the original audience, such stark contrasts would most likely alert them to the fact that Genesis 1–3 was completely different than the myths they had heard. It was history and not parable or myth.

History and Theology

In addition to external factors (ANE myths, see above), scholars also suggested that internal factors point out that Genesis 1–3 concerns a theological message rather than the origins of man. The underlying assumption seems to be that history and theology are somewhat exclusive of each other. This may also stem from the conception that Genesis 1–3 is more "mythical," like the ANE

---

45. Waterman, "Cosmogonic Affinities in Genesis 1:2," 181.
46. Gronbaek, "Baal's Battle with Yam—A Canaanite Creation Fight," 38.

stories. We dealt with that latter point above and found that these similarities do not substantiate reading Genesis 1–3 ahistorically. Even more, we have discovered that a separation between history and theology is not the paradigm in which the biblical writers operated. They viewed history as the grounds and the actualization of theology. Thus, having a theological message does not preclude history. Rather, all of the history in the Scripture is theological in nature. Instead of seeing this as an either/or, it is better to see this as a both/and.

Accordingly, rather than seeing that the formation of man was merely an expression of his value, we could see that the reality of man's value is in how God actually made Adam.[47] Rather than seeing this as a parable about man's role to serve God, we could see that Adam did serve God. This sets the paradigm for why God's people serve Him not only in real historical events of the past but also in an anticipated future eternal state (Rev 22:3). Rather than seeing words such as "create" (ברא) as purely functional in nature, why not see them as both creative (as lexicographers agree) as well as providing function?[48] While some of the theological points above should be qualified, we could apply this rationale to essentially each one of them.[49] Again, the internal evidence brought up does not indicate that we should read the narrative ahistorically. Theology does not diminish the need for history; in actuality, per the Bible's logic, it demands it. The polemic of Israel's theology against ANE ideas is rooted in how the truth of history trumps the fanciful myths of their time.

THE WAY THEY READ IT

A final argument that Genesis 3 is historical in nature concerns how the biblical authors read it. As noted above, their logic is consistently that history actualizes theology. My argument here is that they applied that rationale to Genesis 3. This not only supports that a historical reading of the text was intended but also that it is necessary. Changing one part of history alters the

---

47. Matthews, *Genesis 1–11:26*, 195–97.
48. *HALOT*, 1:153–54. See also, Schmidt, "1:255," ברא.
49. Qualification would include that Eden is to be equated with the temple. The temple might be recapitulating Eden but to read the tabernacle back onto Eden might be anachronistic. Similarly, Israel's expulsion from the land may have echoes of what happened to Adam in the Garden but it should not be read back onto the narrative of Genesis 1–3. Genesis 1–3 sets up for these realities later on in the storyline but what is later does not cause us to re-read what came earlier. Genesis 1–3 is the foundation (literary and theological) for later revelation.

rest of the storyline of Scripture. We can initially observe this in the following discussion. This is particularly important since scholars sometimes charge that the Bible (particularly the Old Testament) cares little about Adam.[50]

The Reading of Moses and Paul

Certain allusions made by Moses and Paul indicate that they read Genesis 1–3 as a portrayal of history. For Moses, it is interesting that he consistently treats Adam as an individual.[51] For example, following Genesis 3, Adam has children (Gen 4:1, 25) and is mentioned in a genealogy (Gen 5:1–5). If he was not a historical individual, then are his children actual? Is his genealogical line fictional? If so, then why are Noah, Abraham, Isaac, Jacob, David, Joseph, and Jesus not fictional (Luke 3:23–38)? If their ancestry was false, why are they not a creative literary figure like their "forefather" was? Already, we may observe that by changing one part of the story, we can end up changing all of it. More to the point, Moses seems to consistently treat Adam as a historical individual.

We can also discuss Paul. We might be tempted to jump to Romans 5 and 1 Corinthians 15, where Paul discusses Jesus as the second Adam. However, we will save that for the next subsection. I want to draw our attention to Paul's message on Mars Hill (Acts 17:16–34). Paul claims that God made every nation on the earth from one man (Acts 17:26). Commentators overwhelmingly see this as a reference to Adam.[52] For Paul's logic to work, certain realities need to be true. Paul views Adam not as an archetype but as "one man." That presumes Adam's historicity in Genesis 1–3. Paul views this individual as the source of all the nations. This reflects that Genesis 1–3 is not merely providing a record of functionality but of formation. It records not only theological truth but also the origins of all the nations. That is history. Such history becomes part of Paul's argument that God is creator (Acts 17:24–26), man is in his image (vv. 27–29), and must repent (v. 30). Even more, it is the basis for why God has appointed another man to judge in the end (v. 31). For Paul, Adam's historicity becomes the grounds of reality and the grounds for the second Adam.

---

50. Enns, *The Evolution of Adam*, 84–85.
51. See Walton, "A Historical Adam: Archetypal Creation View," 89; Collins, *Did Adam and Eve Really Exist?*, 55–57; Barr, "One Man, or All Humanity?," 9.
52. Peterson, *The Acts of the Apostles*, 497; Polhill, *Acts*, 374; Bruce, *The Book of the Acts*, 337; Bock, *Acts*, 566. Some may counter that this is Noah and not Adam. However, the reference to creation in context makes Adam a more likely referent.

Everyman's Story or One Man's Story?

We can now expand upon that latter thought. Some have suggested that Genesis 2–3 is an archetypal story or the story of "everyman."[53] However, the focus of Moses and later biblical writers is not on how Genesis 2–3 is the story of every human being, but the story of one man in relation to humanity. Moses depicts Noah as a recapitulation of Adam. For example, God commands both to be fruitful and multiply as well as fill the earth (Gen 9:1; cf. Gen 1:26–28). Abraham follows in this vein as well. God mediates His blessing through Abraham to the rest of the world (Gen 12:3; cf. Gen 1:28). David and Solomon follow in suit. Both of them are associated with fulfillment of the covenants (2 Sam 8:1–14; 1 Kgs 4:20–34) and the reversal of the curse (1 Kgs 4:20–34). As mentioned above, Solomon exercises wisdom over trees, cattle, flying creatures, creeping things, and fish (1 Kgs 4:33).[54] He thereby parallels Adam who was to have dominion over these same creatures (Gen 1:26–28). David also parallels himself with Adam. In Psalm 8, David discusses his role as a king in terms of Adam. He characterizes himself as a son of man (Ps 8:4) in both his lowliness (8:4b) and his role as one who has dominion over creation (8:5–9; cf. Gen 1:26–28). David thereby understands his own position as one who takes up what God commissioned in Genesis 1:26–28.[55]

David and Solomon also anticipate one who will exercise ultimate dominion (cf. Ps 72:8). The wording of such rule is interesting. The term "to have dominion" (רדה) is not often used in the Old Testament. The first time it is used is in Genesis 1:26–28, with how man was to have dominion over all creation. The psalmist predicts a king who will have that dominion to the ends of the earth (Ps 72:8). Later, Daniel beholds this individual. In Daniel 7, the prophet sees a vision of various beasts coming out of the sea. The one who has dominion over all of these beasts (representing nations) is one like a son of man (Dan 7:14). We can make two observations about this vision. First, it seems to echo creation with its mention of the sea (Dan 7:2; cf. Gen 1:10), various creatures (Dan 7:2–8; cf. Gen 1:20–25), and a "man" who rules over it all (Dan 7:9–13; cf. Gen 1:26–28). Scholars have noted this creational motif.[56] Second, Daniel's vision remains consistent in applying that creational motif, not to everyman, but to one man: the Son of

---

53. Walton, "A Historical Adam: Archetypal Creation View," 89–90.
54. Dempster, *Dominion and Dynasty: A Theology of the Hebrew Bible*, 71–72, 77–78, 147.
55. See also Collins, *Did Adam and Eve Really Exist?*, 66–92.
56. Lacocque, "Allusions to Creation in Daniel 7," 114–31.

Man.[57] To be sure, the rule of the Son of Man results in victory for the saints (Dan 7:27). Nevertheless, the vision still focuses upon an individual as the representative of His people, which is precisely what could be argued for Adam in Genesis 1–3. The Old Testament looks forward to a new Adam.

With this in mind, our Lord fulfills this expectation of the Messiah. His genealogical line extends back to Adam (Luke 3:38). He calls Himself the Son of Man and aligns Himself with the eschatological expectations of Daniel 7 (cf. Luke 21:27). John's portrayal of Jesus as a gardener might also echo Adam in the Garden (John 20:15). Paul famously reiterates Jesus as the Second Adam in Romans (5:14) and 1 Corinthians (15:22, 45). This parallel continues all the way to the very end. In Revelation 20:7–9, Satan goes out to deceive the nations just as he did in the Garden. However, unlike the first Adam who failed, Jesus crushes this attempted subversion, showing that He is the true Son of Man after all (Rev 20:10).

At this point, we can make an important observation. If Genesis 1–3 is truly the story of "everyman," the way the rest of the Scripture develops the storyline does not fit with that paradigm. If Genesis 1–3 was the story of "everyman," then why do inspired writers consistently focus on "one man"? As discussed above, this is not merely found in the New Testament but is grounded in the Old Testament itself. The prophets portray that an individual will assume the role described in Genesis 1:26–28. They claim that the responsibility to reverse the curse begun in Genesis 3 is not for "everyman" but "one man." The New Testament follows in suit.

Such a rationale argues that the biblical writers perceived that Genesis 1–3 is not a story of an archetypical "everyman," but rather the story of one man. How else could we explain why they focus upon an individual as the solution as opposed to something more corporate? Where did such a logic come from? The rationale of the biblical writers demands an individual in Genesis 3 who is the corporate head of humanity.[58] Genesis 1–3 as archetypical simply does not supply that logic. Rather, reading Genesis 1–3 as history makes the best sense of this storyline. In fact, it makes it a part of the storyline, which, as we have seen above, the biblical writers asserted (Neh 9:6; Ps 104) and their logic here presumes.

All of this supports that the "traditional" reading of Genesis 1–3 as history is robustly traditional. It actually starts from Moses and extends all the

57. Collins, "A Historical Adam: Old-Earth Creation View," 171–72; Collins, *Did Adam and Eve Really Exist?*, 66–92.
58. Collins, *Did Adam and Eve Really Exist?*, 66–92.

way through Jesus to the rest of the New Testament. In fact, the rationale of these "traditional" scholars about Genesis 1–3 is embedded in the way they construct the rest of history and a great deal of theology. To change the nature of Genesis 1–3 requires us to shift how we read the entire Bible. This changes how we understand the Old Testament as well as Paul's own logic. As Lamoureux acknowledges, to read Paul apart from a historical Adam "is a very counterintuitive way to read Scripture."[59] That too should give us confidence that our hermeneutical approach is correct. We are seeing the text the way they saw it and thereby our theological rationale is in line with how the rest of Scripture reasons. That is compounding evidence that we understand the text the way the Scripture operates.

CONCLUDING THOUGHTS

We began this chapter with a question of how we ought to read Genesis 1–3. The challenges against a historical reading of Genesis 1–3 are significant and are beneficial, for they force us to reexamine the issue. Upon doing so, we realize that history is not a tertiary issue in Scripture. It is the way theology often is actualized and the grounds for its reality. Furthermore, evidence exists for why Genesis 1–3 fits into this paradigm. Moses confronted ANE myths and ideas with Genesis 1–3. The extreme contrasts between the Creation-Fall account and ANE stories demonstrate that Genesis is not communicating with myth-like tales. Moses argued against those myths with history. This makes sense since later writers view Creation as part of the plotline and history described in Scripture. Moreover, biblical authors, including Moses, David, Daniel, and Paul, seem to view Adam as a historical individual. The logic of their theology depends upon this. In sum, history as grounds for theology is the way the Bible works. It is the way Genesis 1–3 is written. It was the way it was read by the inspired authors. Thus it is the way we should read it.

That being said, in a discussion about the historicity of Genesis 1–3, we cannot lose Moses' intent in discussing history. It is the same intent of all the biblical writers who discuss history. History shows that the theology we believe is real. The question is whether, having defended the historicity of Genesis 1–3, we embrace the reality and repercussions of the theology that was actualized in Creation and the Fall.

---

59. Lamoureux, "No Historical Adam: Evolutionary Creation View," 63.

BIBLIOGRAPHY

Allen, Leslie C. *Psalms 101–150 (Revised)*. Word Biblical Commentary. Dallas: Word Books, 2002.

Barr, James. "One Man, or All Humanity? A Question in the Anthropology of Genesis 1." In *Recycling Biblical Figures: Papers Read at a NOSTER Colloquim in Amsterdam*, 3–21. Leiden: Deo, 1997.

Barrick, William D. "A Historical Adam: Young-Earth Creation View." In *Four Views on the Historical Adam*, edited by Matthew Barrett and Ardel B. Caneday, 197–227. Grand Rapids: Zondervan, 2013.

———. "No Historical Adam: Response from the Young-Earth View." In *Four Views on the Historical Adam*, edited by Matthew Barrett and Ardel B. Caneday, 80–85. Grand Rapids: Zondervan, 2013.

Beale, G. K. *The Temple and the Church's Mission: A Biblical Theology of the Dwelling Place of God*. New Studies in Biblical Theology. Downers Grove, IL: InterVarsity Press, 2004.

Bock, Darrell. *Acts*. Baker Exegetical Commentary on the New Testament. Grand Rapids: Baker, 2007.

Boyd, Steven. "The Genre of Genesis 1:1–2:3: What Means This Text?" In *Coming to Grips with Genesis*, edited by Terry Mortenson and Thane Ury, 163–92. Green Forest, AK: New Leaf Publishing, 2008.

Bruce, F. F. *The Book of the Acts*. Grand Rapids: Eerdmans Publishing, 1988.

Collins, C. John. *Did Adam and Eve Really Exist?: Who They Were and Why You Should Care*. Wheaton, IL: Crossway, 2011.

———. "A Historical Adam: Old-Earth Creation View." In *Four Views on The Historical Adam*, edited by Matthew Barrett and Ardel B. Caneday, 143–75. Grand Rapids: Zondervan, 2013.

Craigie, Peter C. *The Book of Deuteronomy*. New International Commentary on the Old Testament. Grand Rapids: Eerdmans Publishing, 1976.

Davids, Peter H. *The Letters of 2 Peter and Jude*. Pillar New Testament Commentary. Grand Rapids: Eerdmans Publishing, 2006.

Dempster, Stephen G. *Dominion and Dynasty: A Theology of the Hebrew Bible*. New Studies in Biblical Theology. Downers Grove, IL: InterVarsity Press, 2003.

Edwards, James R. *The Gospel According to Mark*. Pillar New Testament Commentary. Grand Rapids: Eerdmans Publishing, 2002.

Enns, Peter. *The Evolution of Adam: What the Bible Does and Doesn't Say about Human Origins*. Grand Rapids: Brazos Press, 2012.

France, R. T. *The Gospel of Mark: A Commentary on the Greek Text*. New International Greek Testament Commentary. Grand Rapids: Eerdmans Publishing, 2002.

Grisanti, M. A. "The Pentateuch." In *The World and the Word: An Introduction to the Old Testament*, edited by M. F. Rooker, M. A. Grisanti, and E. H. Merrill, 163–69. Nashville: Broadman and Holman, 2011.

Gronbaek, Jakob H. "Baal's Battle with Yam—A Canaanite Creation Fight." *Journal for the Study of the Old Testament* 33 (1985): 27–44.

Hallo, W. W., and K. L. Younger. *The Context of Scripture*. Leiden: Brill, 2000.

Hirsch, E. D. *Validity in Interpretation*. New Haven, CT: Yale University Press, 1967.

Knight, George W. *The Pastoral Epistles: A Commentary on the Greek Text*. New International Greek Testament Commentary. Grand Rapids: Eerdmans Publishing, 1992.

Lacocque, André. "Allusions to Creation in Daniel 7." In *Book of Daniel, Volume One*, 114–31. Leiden: Brill, 2001.

Lambert, W. G. "Enuma Elish." In *Anchor Yale Bible Dictionary*, edited by David Noel Freedman, 2:527–28. New York: Doubleday, 1992.

Lamoureux, Denis O. "No Historical Adam: Evolutionary Creation View." In *Four Views on the Historical Adam*, edited by Matthew Barrett and Ardel B. Caneday, 37–65. Grand Rapids: Zondervan, 2013.

Matthews, K. A. *Genesis 1–11:26*. New American Commentary. Nashville: Broadman and Holman Publishers, 1996.

Merrill, Eugene H. *Deuteronomy*. New American Commentary. Nashville: Broadman and Holman Publishers, 1994.

O'Brien, Peter Thomas. *The Letter to the Hebrews*. Pillar New Testament Commentary. Grand Rapids: Eerdmans Publishing, 2010.

Peterson, David. *The Acts of the Apostles*. Pillar New Testament Commentary. Grand Rapids: Eerdmans Publishing, 2009.

Polhill, John B. *Acts*. New American Commentary. Nashville: Broadman and Holman, 1992.

Postell, S. D. *Adam as Israel: Genesis 1–3 as the Introduction to the Torah and Tanakh*. Eugene, OR: Pickwick Publication, 2011.

Pritchard, James B. *Ancient Near Eastern Texts Relating to the Old Testament*. Princeton: Princeton University Press, 1955.

Rogers, Jack Bartlett. *The Authority and Interpretation of the Bible: An Historical Approach*. San Francisco: Harper & Row, 1979.

Schmidt, W. H. "ברא." In *Theological Lexicon of the Old Testament*, edited by Ernst Jenni and Claus Westermann, 1:253–56. Peabody, MA: Hendrickson Publishers, 1997.

Schreiner, Thomas R. *1, 2 Peter, Jude*. Vol. 37. New American Commentary. Nashville: Broadman and Holman Publishers, 2003.

Sparks, Kenton L. *God's Word in Human Words: An Evangelical Appropriation of Critical Biblical Scholarship*. Grand Rapids: Baker, 2008.

Stein, R. H. *A Basic Guide to Interpreting the Bible*. Grand Rapids: Baker, 2001.

Stein, Robert H. "The Benefits of an Author-Oriented Approach to Hermeneutics." *Journal of the Evangelical Theological Society* 44 (2001): 451–66.

Thomas, Robert L. "The Principle of Single Meaning." In *Evangelical Hermeneutics*, edited by Robert L. Thomas, 141–64. Grand Rapids: Kregel, 2002.

Vanhoozer, Kevin J. *Is There a Meaning in This Text?* Grand Rapids: Zondervan, 1998.

Walton, John. "A Historical Adam: Archetypal Creation View." In *Four Views on the Historical Adam*, edited by Matthew Barrett and Ardel B. Caneday, 89–118. Grand Rapids: Zondervan, 2013.

_____. *The Lost World of Genesis One: Ancient Cosmology and the Origins Debate*. Downers Grove, IL: InterVarsity Press, 2009.

_____. "No Historical Adam: Response from the Archetypal View." In *Four Views on the Historical Adam*, edited by Matthew Barrett and Ardel B. Caneday, 66–71. Grand Rapids: Zondervan, 2013.

Waterman, Leroy. "Cosmogonic Affinities in Genesis 1:2." *The American Journal of Semitic Languages and Literatures* 43, no. 3 (April 1, 1927): 177–84.

Zuck, Roy. *Basic Bible Interpretation: A Practical Guide to Discovering Biblical Truth*. Colorado Springs: Chariot Victory Publishing, 2003.

CHAPTER 2

ADAM AND THE ANIMALS

Todd Charles Wood and Joseph W. Francis

INTRODUCTION

Traditional readings of Genesis 1 and 2 recognize Adam and Eve as the first humans, directly created by God, and the natural parents of all other humans.[1] According to Genesis 2, Adam is formed from the "dust" of the ground, and Eve is formed from his side. In contrast to evolution, which posits that an existing "living creature" became human, Genesis 2:7 tells us that the breath of God made the lifeless human a "living creature." The text gives no hint of previous ancestry.

Recognition of Adam and Eve as the created ancestors of all humans is found in apocryphal literature (e.g., Tobit 8:6), the church fathers (e.g., Augustine), the reformers (e.g., Calvin), and early modern scholars (e.g., Ussher, Hale). This perspective is so universally understood that by the eighteenth century, writers often refer to Adam and Eve simply as "our first parents" (e.g., Edwards).[2]

---

1. Barrick, "A Historical Adam: Young-Earth Creation View"; Ryken, "We Cannot Understand the World or Our Faith Without a Historical Adam"; MacArthur, *The Battle for the Beginning*.
2. Augustine, *City of God* XIV, 1; Calvin, *A Commentarie upon the First Booke of Moses Called Genesis*; Ussher, *A Body of Divinitie*, 142; Hale, *The Primitive Origination of Mankind*; Edwards, *The Doctrine of Original Sin Defended*, 224.

Beyond the special creation of Adam and Eve described in Genesis 2, Genesis 1 reveals the uniqueness of humans in at least two ways. First, humans were created in the image of God (Gen 1:26–27). Christians have different ways of interpreting "image," but the most important part of the image for our purposes is its textual contrast with "according to its kind," the phrase applied to the creation of plants and animals in Genesis 1.[3] Whatever else it might mean, "image" functions textually to set humans apart from the rest of the living things in creation.

Second, humans are given "dominion" over all other living things in creation (Gen 1:28). "Dominion" also has different interpretations, but here again, we need only note that dominion distinguishes humans from the rest of creation. No other creatures in Genesis 1 are explicitly given dominion over any others.

Given this biblical emphasis on uniqueness, it might come as some surprise that humans closely resemble animals, sometimes to an exacting degree. For example, every human bone has a counterpart in at least one animal, and important features such as the skull and spine have counterparts in "lower" animals like amphibians and fish.

At the genetic level, we find even more similarity. It is now widely understood that most mammals (humans and fur-bearing vertebrates) have the same basic set of genes and chromosomal segments. These genes and chromosomes are organized differently in different sorts of mammals, but the pieces seem to be essentially the same.[4] Even more astonishingly, a small set of genes can be found in *all* living things.[5]

When we examine primates (those animals that share the most features in common with humans), we find even more similarities. Every bone of the human body is represented by counterparts in the bodies of the great apes: chimpanzees, bonobos, gorillas, and orangutans.[6] At the genetic level, the

---

3. For a review of the image of God, see Gentry, "Kingdom through Covenant: Humanity as the Divine Image."

4. Wienberg and Stanyon, "Comparative Painting of Mammalian Chromosomes."

5. Theobald, "A Formal Test of the Theory of Universal Common Ancestry."

6. Humans and chimps possess some intriguing anatomical differences. For instance, humans have a distinct chin and a white area in the eye which allows us to note the direction of the gaze of other humans. Humans also possess locking knees, legs which are longer than arms, and sweat glands covering the body. Suddendorf also notes the vast difference in mental abilities: "It is our mental capacities that have allowed us to tame fire and invent the wheel. They enable us to construct tools that make us stronger, fiercer, faster, and more precise, resilient, and versatile than any beast. We build machines that speed us from one place to the other, even to outer space. We investigate nature and rapidly accumulate

similarity is most striking of all. The genes of the chimpanzee appear to be almost exact replicas of human genes. In fact, many chimpanzee genes are *exactly* the same as their human counterparts.[7]

We also find an overarching *pattern* of similarity, wherein some creatures resemble humans very closely while others are far more different. In between is every possible degree of similarity. The pattern is complex, since it can be observed for any organism. Whatever the organism, there are always things that are most similar and things that are least similar.

Christians often appeal to a common Creator to explain general features of similarity. After all, human artists and craftsmen are known for their unique styles, which characterize all of their works. Why would we expect God's creation to be any different? In fact, if each type of creature were totally different from every other creature, would we deduce that a single Creator had made us all? Indeed, the unity of creation, exhibited in the similarities of creatures, testifies to the unity of its Creator.

Today, however, some Christians advocate a different interpretation of biology and the Scripture. Since Darwin's *Origin of Species*, the generally accepted explanation for similarity is "propinquity of descent," Darwin's term for closeness of relationship.[8] In this model, the similarity of humans to animals is *not* a consequence of a common designer but arises from common ancestry. In the evolutionary view, modern humans descended from a series of animal ancestors.

This evolutionary view of human origins requires a very different understanding of Scripture, particularly of Adam and Eve, if one wishes to avoid abandoning Christianity altogether. Numerous proposals of what to do with Adam and Eve in light of evolution have recently been proposed and criticized.[9] As young-age creationists, we believe that theological questions surrounding Adam's uniqueness as the first human creation are best answered

---

and share knowledge. We create complex artificial worlds in which we wield unheralded power—power to shape the future and power to destroy and annihilate. We reflect on and argue about our present situation, our history, and our destiny. We envision wonderful harmonious worlds as easily as we do dreadful tyrannies. Our powers are used for good as they are for bad, and we incessantly debate which is which. Our minds have spawned civilizations and technologies that have changed the face of the Earth, while our closest living relatives sit unobtrusively in their remaining forests." Suddendorf, *The Gap*, 2.

7. Wood, "The Chimpanzee Genome and the Problem of Biological Similarity."
8. Darwin, *On the Origin of Species*, 413.
9. Enns, *The Evolution of Adam*; Walton, "Human Origins and the Bible"; Lamoureux, "No Historical Adam: Evolutionary Creation View."

by theologians. In that light, our purpose here is to address the claim that biology exclusively supports the evolutionary interpretation. Specifically, we begin with the assumption that Adam was the first human creation, separate and distinct from all other biological creation and that all other humans are descended from him and Eve by normal generation, with no animal ancestry. From that foundation, we investigate how well the biological evidence fits.

In this chapter we review the concepts and evidences of biological similarity in fossil hominins and comparative genomics.[10] In both cases, we show that the evolutionary interpretation is not the only possible interpretation. Indeed, we will present creationist research into anatomical and genetic differences between humans and animals that confirms the creationist prediction of the uniqueness of humans. We also explore non-evolutionary explanations of biological similarity. Altogether then, our considerations reveal a great deal of nuance and complexity that belies any claim that evolution is the exclusive scientific explanation of human origins.

BIOLOGICAL SIMILARITY: PAST AND PRESENT

Before we discuss the specifics of the hominin fossil record, it is important to review our expectations. If Genesis 1 and 2 are a true, historical record of the origin of humans, what consequences would this have for our understanding of biological similarity? This sounds like a simple question, but it is unexpectedly complicated, since our understanding of the question itself is colored by our experiences as modern Christians. Nowhere is this clearer than when we explore Christian responses to similarity before and after Darwin's *Origin*.[11]

Before the eighteenth century, the relationships of species were envisioned as the *Scala Naturae,* or Great Chain of Being. Aristotle is an early advocate of the Chain in his *Historia Animalium:* "Nature proceeds little by little from things lifeless to animal life in such a way that it is impossible to determine the exact line of demarcation."[12] In Christian versions of the *Scala,* all creation forms a chain from the inanimate elements to God Himself with

---

10. Comparative genomics is the science of comparing genomes from different sources. This can involve gross chromosomal similarities as well as the actual DNA sequences.
11. This section is adapted from Wood, "*Natura Facit Saltum*: The Case for Discontinuity."
12. Thompson, *The History of Animals*, 264.

all possible links on the chain having been created.[13] The Chain was believed to make a perfectly smooth transition, implying that all possible organisms must exist. Early naturalists like Linnaeus and Ray advocated this perspective (and variations thereof).[14]

In the area of human origins, the Chain was invoked to explain how animals could be so similar to human beings. When English anatomist Edward Tyson examined the first chimpanzee known to Western science, he recognized that the chimpanzee was far more similar to humans than any other animal, but he interpreted that similarity in terms of God's Creation. Speaking of the chimpanzee as an "intermediate Link between an *Ape* and a *Man*," Tyson wrote, "This *Climax* or *Gradation* can't but be taken notice of, by any that are curious in observing the Wonders of Creation; and the more he observes it, the more venerable Idea's 'twill give him of the great Creator."[15] In Tyson, we see clearly that observation can be separated from interpretation: Just because an animal is very similar to humans, even to the point of being called an "intermediate link," one need not interpret it as evidence of evolution. For Tyson, an intermediate link between human and animal was evidence of Creation.

The Great Chain of Being fell out of favor in the nineteenth century, but it was the publication of Darwin's *Origin* with its emphasis on gradualism that marked a drastic change in the way people thought about smooth, gradual transitions. In *Origin*, Darwin emphasized that the variations that accumulated to produce new species were extremely slight, thus giving new meaning to the old aphorism *natura non facit saltum* (nature makes no leaps).[16]

The response was striking. Writing just a few months after *Origin* appeared, physician Charles Robert Bree scornfully demanded, "But where . . . I ask Mr. Darwin, are your intermediate forms?"[17] Other evolution skeptics were similarly unconvinced. In 1930, creationist Dudley Joseph Whitney lamented, "A few links might be missing without discrediting the theory, but the trouble is that virtually *all* the links are missing."[18] Long gone were celebrations of intermediate

---

13. Lovejoy coined the "principle of plenitude" to describe the expansion of the concept developed by Aristotle in the *Scala Naturae*, namely that all the forms of life which can exist do exist. Lovejoy, *The Great Chain of Being*.
14. Linnaeus, *Philosophia Botanica*; Ray, *Methodus Plantarum Nova*.
15. Tyson, *Orang Outang*, 5.
16. Darwin, *Origin*, 194.
17. Bree, *Species Not Transmutable*, 60.
18. Whitney, "Evolution and Uniformitarian Geology."

links as evidence of God's Creation. Instead, discontinuity between organisms was now seen as the true evidence of Creation. On the subject of discontinuity, biologist Frank Lewis Marsh wrote, "It really appears that it is more sensible to assume that the ancestors of our modern groups were not evolved but created."[19]

Why should it matter that Christians once accepted perfect continuity as evidence of God's Creation? As creationists, it would be easy for us to simply assert that the Bible teaches that humans were created physically distinct from all other creatures. Such a claim would be well in line with the claims of many other creationists, but when we look into the history of the church and see other faithful creationists claiming just the opposite, that should give us pause. What exactly does the Bible teach about the physical distinctions between humans and animals? As scientists, we are uncomfortable answering a question that is so far outside of our expertise, but what we can do instead is test the creationist claim that humans and apes are physically distinct. If we could verify that claim, it would be an important confirmation of modern creationist scholarship.

THE FOSSIL RECORD

Look at modern humans and apes, even casually, and you can easily compile a long list of characteristics that are very different between the two. If all we had to explain were living creatures, it would be relatively easy to argue for a substantial physical distinction between humans and animals, but reality is not that simple. Since the 1850s, many fossils have been discovered that possess attributes found in modern humans *and* apes. These fossils are collectively referred to as "hominins" after the scientific subfamily Homininae, and they represent the chief challenge to our quest to identify a physical distinction between humans and apes.

Neandertals

The first to be discovered were the Neandertals, which are generally considered to be a separate species[20] classified within our own genus *Homo*.[21] Of all

---

19. Marsh, *Evolution, Creation, and Science*, 230.
20. We should note here that when a paleoanthropologist designates something as a separate species, this merely refers to a certain set of characteristics that set those individuals apart from all others. Fossil "species" should not be thought of as something separately created from other species. It is possible that a fossil "species" could have descended from another created species.
21. Jurmain, et al., *Introduction to Physical Anthropology*, 378–93.

hominins, Neandertals resemble modern humans most closely. Distinguishing characteristics of the Neandertal face include a heavy brow ridge, low forehead, and protruding nose. Unlike human jaws, which have a bony chin, Neandertal jaws slope back with no chin at all. The size of their skull cavity (where their brains were) is bigger than that of the average modern human, and the back of their skulls were expanded in a structure called an "occipital bun."

Geographically, Neandertals have only been found in Europe, the Middle East, and central Asia. By conventional estimates, Neandertals lived contemporaneously with modern humans and died out comparatively recently. They are believed to have buried their dead, and they were adept at making sophisticated stone tools, which modern scientists call Mousterian tools. More recent discoveries have shown that Neandertals made bone tools and even pigmented ornaments.

Homo Erectus

In 1891, Eugène Du Bois discovered another important fossil hominin on the Indonesian island of Java. Today scientists call Du Bois's discovery *Homo erectus*.[22] Additional specimens of *Homo erectus* have been recovered from numerous locations around the world. In Africa, *erectus*-like fossils go by the name *Homo ergaster*, and from Africa we get our most complete view of a *Homo erectus*. The "Nariokotome Boy," a nearly complete skeleton of a juvenile *Homo ergaster*, was discovered in Kenya in 1984.

The skeleton of Nariokotome Boy is very similar to those of modern humans, but the *Homo erectus* skull exhibits several differences. Like Neandertals, *Homo erectus* skulls have low foreheads and heavy brow ridges, and their jaws lack a pronounced chin. They have an enlarged area in the rear of their skulls, but in *Homo erectus* this projection (the "nuchal torus") is a thickening of bone instead of an enlargement of the brain cavity, as it is in Neandertals. *Homo erectus* had smaller brains than modern humans, and there is currently no evidence of intentional burial. Based on characteristics of their teeth, we infer that *Homo erectus* cooked food, and we know that they made stone tools (the Acheulian tools).

Australopithecus

In 1924, anthropologist Raymond Dart discovered a new hominin in a shipment of fossils excavated from Taung, South Africa. The "Taung Child"

---

22. Ibid., 341–64.

consisted of a partial skull and "brain cast" that was dubbed *Australopithecus af-ricanus*.[23] Since 1924, important *Australopithecus* discoveries in east Africa have considerably expanded our understanding of this group. Near Hadar, Ethiopia, at least one hundred different specimens representing at least sixty individuals have been recovered from the same fossil deposit. These east African forms are called *Australopithecus afarensis* and include the famous "Lucy" skeleton.

Australopithecus skulls are quite distinct from those of modern humans. Their faces were sloped with protruding muzzles. The teeth and jaws are often larger than modern humans', and the brain cavities are much smaller. *Aus-tralopithecus* forearms are proportionally quite long when compared to the forearms of modern humans. All of these characteristics appear to resemble modern apes more than modern humans. Why are they considered homi-nins? Hominins are distinguished from other species because they habitually walk on two legs rather than all fours. In technical terms, they are bipedal.[24]

---

23. Ibid., 322–35.
24. Several evidences support the habitual bipedality of *Australopithecus* as described in Jur-main, et al., *Introduction to Physical Anthropology*, 312–16. Four such evidences can be mentioned briefly:
(1) The foramen magnum of bipeds is angled directly under the skull. The foramen mag-num is the opening in the base of the skull where the spinal cord meets the brain. In mod-ern apes, the foramen magnum is angled toward the back, but in modern humans, the foramen magnum is perpendicular to the base of the skull, because our faces need to be perpendicular to the axis of our bodies. In *Australopithecus* skulls, the foramen magnum is perpendicular as it is in modern humans.
(2) The pelvis (the hip bone) is shaped differently in bipeds and quadrupeds. Chimpan-zees have a flat pelvis, but the modern human pelvis is bowl-shaped. The shape supports our internal organs that hang straight down toward our feet. In *Australopithecus*, pelvis bones are bowl-shaped.
(3) The thigh bone (femur) articulates at a noticeable angle in bipeds. The human thigh bones angle inward, to keep our lower legs directly beneath the main axis of our bodies. This angle can be detected in the way the long bone meets other bones in the knee and hip. In modern chimps, the femur comes out straight from the pelvis and meets the knee with no angle at all. This allows chimps to keep their back feet apart, giving them stability in their quadrupedal stance. In *Australopithecus*, we find angles characteristic of a biped rather than a quadruped.
(4) Fossil trackways found at the Laetoli site in Tanzania preserve multiple footprints of biped-al hominins. Since these are trace fossils rather than direct remains of an organism, the iden-tification as *Australopithecus* is inferential; nevertheless, the size of the prints and the stride is much smaller than those of modern humans. The way the feet compress the substrate suggests something other than a modern human foot also. Although some creationists classify these prints as human, we cautiously follow paleontologists in attributing them to *Australopithecus*. Even though these four lines of evidence support the bipedality of *Australopithecus*, this does not mean that they walked around on two legs *just like we do*. Computer analysis of the gait of *Australopithecus* indicates that they would have walked noticeably differently from modern hu-mans. DeSilva, et al., "The Lower Limb and Mechanics of Walking in *Australopithecus sediba*."

When considered in the context of human similarity to apes, the similarity of *Australopithecus* to modern humans and apes surely represents something important. From the waist up, *Australopithecus* resembles modern apes more than modern humans, but the legs and features associated with bipedal walking make *Australopithecus* more similar to modern humans than modern apes. How we ought to interpret *Australopithecus* in the context of human origins is a separate question from what *Australopithecus* was actually like. We will deal with that important question in the next section.

Other Species

In addition to these well-known groups of hominins, there are many other "species" that are known from only a few fossils, some of which are extremely fragmentary. In the *Australopithecus* group, besides the well-known *A. africanus* and *A. afarensis*, we have the fragmentary *A. anamensis*[25] and the recently discovered *A. sediba*.[26] In the genus *Homo* (our genus), we find the controversial *Homo floresiensis*, which is purportedly a late offshoot of *Homo erectus*[27] and a catch-all group colloquially known as "early *Homo*."

In the context of "early *Homo*," two somewhat controversial skulls—known by their museum codes KNM-ER 1470 and KNM-ER 1813—illustrate disagreements among paleoanthropologists caused by the scarcity of fossils.[28] Initially, both skulls were classified in the same species, *Homo habilis*, but the skulls are quite different. Consequently, later researchers proposed two different names: *Homo habilis* for 1813 and *Homo rudolfensis* for 1470. Since there were only these two skulls, paleoanthropologists had difficulty deciding whether they were the same or different species, but newly discovered skulls that resemble *H. rudolfensis* may help resolve the matter.[29] Skull 1813 (*H. habilis*) lies outside of the range of variation seen in these new skulls and probably represents a separate species.

With lots of specimens (as in the case of Neandertals), we can be confident about species identifications, because there are many examples for comparison.

---

25. Leakey, et al., "New Four-Million-Year-Old Hominid Species from Kanapoi and Allia Bay, Kenya."
26. Berger, et al., "*Australopithecus sediba*: A New Species of *Homo*-like Australopith from South Africa."
27. Brown, et al., "A New Small-Bodied Hominin from the Late Pleistocene of Flores, Indonesia."
28. For more on early *Homo*, see Jurmain, et al., *Introduction to Physical Anthropology*, 333–35.
29. Leakey, "New fossils from Koobi Fora in northern Kenya confirm taxonomic diversity in early *Homo*."

In the case of early *Homo*, fragmentary specimens guarantee that conclusions will be tentative and that experts will disagree. Uncertainty over individual fossils should therefore be reflected in our uncertainty over their place in the larger scheme of human origins, whether we advocate a creationist or evolutionary model of human origins. Some things are just intrinsically uncertain, and no one should be faulted for uncertainty that is beyond our control.

Perhaps the best illustration of the importance of uncertainty in the hominin fossil record is found at Dmanisi in the Republic of Georgia. Located in southern Georgia near the Armenian border, Dmanisi has yielded a surprising array of five very complete skulls. Some researchers classify these skulls in a new species called *Homo georgicus*, while others argue that they belong in the *Homo erectus/Homo ergaster* group. What makes them interesting is not the species names, but the wide variation all from the same locality. Skull 4 resembles Neandertals or early *Homo sapiens*, while Skulls 2 and 3 look more like *Homo erectus*. Skull 5 is very different, much more like early *Homo*. Skull 5 has a lower forehead, a projecting muzzle, and a bigger jawbone than the other Dmanisi skulls.[30] If these fossils had been found in different parts of the world or in different layers of rock, they would have been classified as different species, but here at Dmanisi, they probably came from a single species.

The final chapter to the Dmanisi story has yet to be written, and experts are still working on interpreting the fossils from that site. We can nevertheless be certain that extremely different forms of *Homo* that would otherwise be placed in different species and relegated to different conventional time periods all lived contemporaneously at Dmanisi. This should make us wonder if we really understand how to recognize hominin species in the first place.

WHERE DID THESE HOMININS COME FROM?

Paleontologists agree almost without exception that these fossils reveal the gradual evolution of humans from ape-like ancestors, even as they disagree over the details. Precisely how each fossil species relates to the others is still a matter of intense research, but generally speaking, modern humans are thought to have evolved from an ancestral species that lived in Africa about 150,000 years ago. Those early *Homo* fossils probably arose from some mem-

---

30. Lordkipanidze, et al., "A Complete Skull from Dmanisi, Georgia, and the Evolutionary Biology of Early *Homo*."

ber of the *Australopithecus* group, possibly something similar to *A. sediba* or *A. africanus*. Other *Homo* and *Australopithecus* species represent side branches on the main trunk of our evolutionary tree. Neandertals are a close cousin to modern humans, and the "robust" *Australopithecus* species are much more distant relatives. All of this evolutionary innovation happened within the last five million years. Such is the conventional view.[31]

Evangelical literature denying the historical Adam gives the impression that there is no possible way to interpret this evidence other than in favor of human evolution. Yet, as we read such claims, it is hard to avoid the conclusion that these individuals who are so confident that there is no explanation other than evolution do not try very hard to *develop and test* explanations other than evolution. There seems to be a contentment with the standard human evolution model, which precludes any serious quest to find other answers. It therefore falls to creationists to develop and test alternative models.

Detecting Discontinuity

Previously in this chapter, we suggested that we could begin this task simply by testing the creationist claim that humans and animals are physically distinct, and not merely distinct in trivial ways but fundamentally different in their anatomy. Testing this requires development of a whole new methodology to study species. Evolutionary methods are not sufficient, because evolutionists assume that all things are related to a common ancestor and therefore the only question that remains is *how* they are related. Since creationists ask a different question altogether—are humans really related to other fossil hominins?—we cannot use methods that simply assume common ancestry.

There are other ways of thinking about the similarity and difference between species, however, and one such way is statistical baraminology. The term *baramin* was coined by Frank Lewis Marsh, based on the biblical Hebrew terms *bara* (create) and *min* (kind). According to Marsh, modern species are descended from original "created kinds" or baramins that God made during Creation week.[32] Modern statistical baraminology builds on Marsh's ideas using a set of mathematical techniques for detecting clusters of species that are separated from other clusters by discontinuity.[33] In statistical baraminology studies,

---

31. Jurmain, et al., *Introduction to Physical Anthropology*.
32. Marsh coined *baramin* in Marsh, *Fundamental Biology*, 100.
33. Wood and Murray, *Understanding the Pattern of Life*; Wood, "Baraminic Distance, Bootstraps, and BDISTMDS."

a cluster of species that significantly differs from other species is interpreted as unrelated to other species and probably descended from a single created kind.[34]

Before we discuss the outcome of statistical baraminology research on hominins, it is valuable to review what sort of information was examined. Frequently in statistical baraminology, researchers use sets of characteristics originally compiled for evolutionary analysis. We think there is an important advantage to using such data: We can avoid being accused of "cherry picking" data or compiling some biased set of characteristics. If anything, the characteristics used in statistical baraminology should be biased *against* creationist conclusions.

On the other hand, using someone else's data can lead to a very limited perspective on the species we want to analyze. We might actually learn more about the data compilers' ability to compile data than we learn about the species being investigated. A possible remedy for this is evaluating sets of characteristics compiled by different evolutionary experts. In a previous study, five sets of hominin characteristics compiled by different researchers were examined using statistical baraminology.[35]

Human Baraminology

For each set of characteristics where clustering could be detected, modern humans did not cluster with chimpanzees or most *Australopithecus* species. Instead, modern humans clustered with species like Neandertals and *Homo erectus*. Two sets of characteristics did not show any clustering, but when there was clustering, humans never clustered with *Australopithecus* or other species that are clearly apes (like chimpanzees). The exception to this trend is the one analysis that showed that *Australopithecus sediba*, the most human-like of the *Australopithecus* species, clustered with modern humans rather than other *Australopithecus* species. It is possible that this single set of characteristics was biased in some unknown way, thus leading to a false clustering. It is also possible that *Australopithecus sediba* is just an unusual-looking human. Either interpretation of *A. sediba* would still be consistent with the creationist claim that humans are distinct from animals.

---

34. We admit that there are challenging problems with statistical baraminology; nevertheless, at this time, statistical baraminology is the only method creationists have for rigorously analyzing created kinds based on fossil remains. When used with caution and care, therefore, we need not be overly suspicious of statistical baraminology results.
35. Wood, "Baraminological Analysis Places *Homo habilis*, *Homo rudolfensis*, and *Australopithecus sediba* in the Human Holobaramin."

That is the most important result from the statistical baraminology study. Creationists have claimed for years that humans are readily distinguishable from animals. Statistical baraminology supports that contention. In addition, statistical baraminology results confirm other creationist opinions about fossil hominins. Creationists generally agree that Neandertals and probably *Homo erectus* are human descendants of Adam and Eve.[36] The statistical baraminology analysis supports that. In addition, creationists contend that *Australopithecus* is not human, and for most species, statistical baraminology agrees. These confirmations of creationist claims about hominins are the most significant results of the statistical baraminology studies.

How then do we interpret the trends of the fossil record in the context of a creationist worldview? We affirm that the category of *humanity*—defined as the natural descendants of Adam and Eve—is broader than modern *Homo sapiens*. Minimally, Neandertals and *Homo erectus* are also human. It is possible that other species, such as early *Homo* or *Australopithecus sediba*, should also be counted as human, but since creationists disagree on these species, we will not be dogmatic on that point.

Although Neandertals and *Homo erectus* are part of the human family, we also recognize that these groups are currently extinct and have been for some time. When did they live? Given the near-unanimous consensus of creationists that all hominin fossils are post-Flood, we would infer that Neandertals and *Homo erectus* represent populations of humans that dispersed from Babel immediately after the confusion of languages. In that light, we note with much interest that the fossil locality with the most diverse range of hominin (probably human) fossils is Dmanisi, which is remarkably close (in a global sense) to the putative region of Ararat and Babel. At some time very shortly after the tower of Babel, one family dispersed and dominated others that had already dispersed. This family gave rise to "modern humans" (*Homo sapiens*). Through a combination of inbreeding and conflict, *Homo sapiens* came to be the only humans left.

But What about the Similarity?

Though we have seen very important differences between humans and apes, a persistent theological question remains: Why create animals so

---

36. See a summary of other creationist opinions in Wood, "Baraminological Analysis Places *Homo habilis, Homo rudolfensis*, and *Australopithecus sediba* in the Human Holobaramin."

similar to humans at all? After all, if God wanted humans to appear distinct from other creatures, He could have done so by not creating great apes at all. He could have expanded that distinctiveness even more by not creating any mammals at all. Humans resemble birds and reptiles much less than we resemble our livestock or furry pets.

We suggest that the purpose of this similarity could be rooted in our responsibility to have dominion over creation and be good stewards.[37] That responsibility is facilitated by our resemblance to other creatures. We see this reflected in the popularity of some endangered species. The public reacts strongly to the giant panda and its plight, but snails, salamanders, and other species that are more threatened than the giant panda do not enjoy such celebrity. Why? They are less similar and less relatable. Evidently, we best exercise stewardship over those creatures that we resemble most.

To put it in other terms, similarity facilitates relationship. Think about relationships between people. Making and sustaining friendships is easier with people who share something in common—a job, a neighborhood, or a hobby—than with people who have little in common. So too with creation. Humans naturally seek and build "relationships" with the world around us, and especially with creatures that we can relate to because we share features in common. We suggest that this is part of God's design. Since God seeks to build relationships with us, we as the image of God do the same with the rest of creation. So God makes us similar to animals to help us develop relationships, which in turn makes us good stewards of creation.

Additionally, recent and historical creationist work in theology suggests that the similarity between animals and humans is often used in the Bible for instruction in prophecy, the sacrificial system, and human behavior.[38] For instance, the bear described in Daniel 7 has ribs in his teeth and devoured much flesh. These common anatomical structures that humans share with animals helps our understanding of the prophecy. In other passages, humans are compared and distinguished from the vulgar aspects of some animals, and thus similarity is also used to emphasize unique human attributes consistent with the uniqueness of humans as God's image-bearer.

---

37.   Francis and Chou, "Does Biblical Similarity Inform Biological Similarity?"
38.   Ibid.; also, Topsell, *The Historie of Foure-Footed Beasts*.

Hominin Genomes

In the last half century, a new line of evidence—the human genome—has provided new information relevant to the question of human origins. According to several evangelical evolutionists, the human genome sequence was a kind of tipping point, beyond which maintaining a belief in a traditional creation account was no longer possible. In his *Evolution of Adam*, Peter Enns wrote, "The Human Genome Project, completed in 2003, has shown beyond any reasonable scientific doubt that humans and primates share common ancestry."[39] Similarly, Francis Collins wrote, "The study of genomes leads inexorably to the conclusion that we humans share a common ancestor with other living things."[40] In other words, the human genome makes the evidence of human evolution irrefutable.

To fully understand and appreciate the evidence of the human genome, we need first to understand the genome itself. Genomes are composed of deoxyribonucleic acid (DNA). DNA is the chemical of inheritance. It contains the blueprints for building proteins, which in turn are the workhorses of human cells. Working together, the proteins specified by the DNA contribute to visible attributes. The color of our eyes, the texture of our hair, our height, our bones, our internal organs, and every other aspect of our bodies is in some way specified by these proteins. As the material of inheritance, DNA is passed from parent to child, and that makes DNA a living record of our family history. Why do you have your dad's nose or your mom's eyes or your grandpa's hair? You inherited their DNA.

DNA itself is a chemical with a structure very much like beads on a string. The beads of DNA are called bases, and they come in four varieties: adenine, guanine, cytosine, and thymine. The order of the bases spell out genes, which code for proteins, much in the same way that letters spell out words that stand for ideas. A single inheritable piece of DNA is called a chromosome. All the DNA of a cell, or all its genes, or all its chromosomes, are collectively called a genome.

The human genome is organized into forty-six different chromosomes. There are twenty-two matching pairs of chromosomes called autosomes and a final pair of X and Y sex chromosomes. Human cells also contain many copies

---

39. Enns, *Evolution of Adam*, ix.
40. Collins, *The Language of God*, 133–34.

of a small mitochondrial chromosome that is stored in a separate compartment from the rest of the chromosomes.

A typical human chromosome is a long, linear molecule of DNA, and only part of those DNA bases spell out genes. Typically, less than five percent of the nucleotide bases of a human chromosome are actually part of genes that code for proteins. Another forty-five percent is composed of repetitive sequences called *transposable elements*, sequences which are capable of replicating and moving around the genome independently of the normal genome replication process. The other fifty percent is poorly understood.[41]

There are fewer than 25,000 human genes in the human genome,[42] and their structure is surprisingly complicated. Scientists like to make analogies between DNA sequence and written language, in order to emphasize how DNA codes for protein, but that analogy breaks down when we look at the peculiar structure of a human gene. Like a sentence, human genes have a start and a stop (a base where the code begins and another where the code ends), but unlike sentences, only some of the bases in between the start and stop are part of the code. The DNA of genes is divided into two groups, called introns and exons. Exons are the parts of the genes that actually code for the protein, while introns are intervening sequences that are left out. Imagine if to read a sentence correctly, you were only supposed to read one word in ten. That would be similar to how human genes are structured.

Why introns exist is something of a mystery. We know that introns allow for something called *alternative splicing*, where a single gene can code for multiple proteins by putting together different sets of exons. Not all human genes undergo alternative splicing, though.[43] We also know that some introns contain sequences that regulate genes and control how genes are turned on and off. But these control sequences are often quite small, while introns typically constitute the vast majority of the DNA sequence of a gene. If one includes both introns and exons in the size of genes, then human genes actually occupy about twenty-five percent of the DNA sequence in the human genome.

---

41. International Human Genome Sequencing Consortium, "Initial Sequencing and Analysis of the Human Genome."
42. Recent estimates place the number around 21,000 or 22,000. Pertea and Salzberg, "Between a chicken and a grape: estimating the number of human genes."
43. But most do. See Pan, "Deep Surveying of Alternative Splicing Complexity in the Human Transcriptome by High-throughput Sequencing."

Transposable elements are segments of DNA capable of moving around the genome, often copying themselves or being copied. The copies are then inserted back into the same genome, which causes a long-term increase in the copy number of transposable elements. Consequently, many thousands of copies of transposable elements can be found throughout the human genome, and a few transposable elements exceed 100,000 copies. A staggering 1.09 million copies of the *Alu* transposable element are currently known.[44]

Comparing Human and Chimpanzee DNA

Evolutionary biologists have long had an interest in comparing genomes from different species. For humans, the most obvious candidate for comparison is the chimpanzee. In the earliest days of examining DNA and proteins, molecular biologists King and Wilson noted with a great deal of surprise that human and chimpanzee proteins were very often identical. There were no differences at all. Since humans and chimpanzees are so obviously different, how could they possibly have identical genes? King and Wilson proposed that the control elements, the parts of the DNA that turned genes on and off, were the real source of the difference between humans and chimpanzees.[45]

In 1983 the first chimpanzee DNA sequences were published, and the human and chimpanzee DNA sequences for a blood protein called alpha globin were found to be 99.5% identical.[46] Next to the alpha globin gene on the same human chromosome, researchers found a second copy of the alpha globin gene that appeared to have been "disabled" by a mutation. The second copy could not be activated and function like the real alpha globin gene, and the disabled gene was called a "pseudogene." On the chimpanzee chromosome, the same pseudogene was found at the same location. The pseudogenes were ninety-eight percent identical. Since that time, many other examples of pseudogenes have been found,[47] and humans and great apes almost always have the same pseudogenes. The interpretation of all pseudogenes is generally the same: once there were two functional copies of the gene, but one was damaged by a mutation.

---

44. International Human Genome Sequencing Consortium, "Initial Sequencing and Analysis of the Human Genome."
45. King and Wilson, "Evolution at Two Levels in Humans and Chimpanzees."
46. Liebhaber and Begley, "Structural and Evolutionary Analysis of the Two Chimpanzee Alpha-globin mRNAs."
47. For just one example, consider olfactory receptor pseudogenes: Olender, et al., "Update on the Olfactory Receptor (OR) Gene Superfamily."

In 1986, pseudogene researcher Edward Max published a paper explaining what came to be known as the "plagiarized error" argument.[48] According to Max, we can think about pseudogenes in the same way we might think about plagiarism. While it might be reasonable to expect a certain bit of identical wording between two different written documents, if you found identical grammatical or spelling errors along with the identical wording, then you would know that one was copied from the other. Likewise with pseudogenes, which could be considered shared "errors" in the human and chimpanzee genomes. Shared errors do not originate by chance, and Max argued that the only possible explanation was that the human and chimpanzee pseudogenes descended from a pseudogene originally possessed by a human/chimpanzee common ancestor.

While detailed studies of human and chimpanzee DNA sequences were happening, other scientists were trying to take a broader view of the human and chimpanzee genomes. One such attempt involved studying chromosomal banding patterns. Banding patterns are distinctive striped patterns that appear on chromosomes when they wind up during cell division. Banding patterns can be photographed under a regular microscope, and so are easy to study.

When researchers compared the banding patterns of chimpanzee and human genomes, they found that most human chromosomes had nearly identical matching pairs among the chimpanzee chromosomes. Some had rearranged parts, where one segment was in the opposite order in the two species. Human chromosome 2 corresponds to two different, smaller chimpanzee chromosomes. Overall, however, the chromosomes looked amazingly similar under the microscope.[49]

Other researchers tried to "melt" DNA in order to study the similarity of chimpanzee and human chromosomes. The melting point of DNA depends on base "pairing," whereby bases on opposite strands of DNA stick to each other. If you mix human and chimpanzee DNA strands, the base pairing will be off, since not all bases are the same in the two species. These mismatched bases destabilize the DNA and cause the melting point to go down. The reduction in melting point should be related very closely to the percentage of bases that differ between the two species. In 1976, researchers found that the

---

48. Max, "Plagiarized Errors and Molecular Genetics: Another Argument in the Evolution-Creation Controversy."
49. Yunis and Prakash, "The Origin of Man: A Chromosomal Pictorial Legacy."

human genome was more than ninety percent identical over its entire length to the chimpanzee genome.[50]

What have we learned from these studies? The first and most important thing that we learned is that the human genome is full of DNA that we do not yet understand. That fact alone should inspire humility and caution in our claims about what genomes do or do not show. The second thing we learned is that parts of the human genome *appear to be* leftovers from well-known mutational processes. These parts include pseudogenes and transposable elements, and most of these sequences are shared almost exactly with great apes. Finally, we've confirmed that the human genome is highly similar to ape genomes: chimpanzee is most similar, followed by gorilla and orangutan, in that order.[51]

Interpreting Hominin Genomes

Once the complete human and chimpanzee genome sequences were published,[52] did we discover new, irrefutable evidence of human evolution from animals? Not really. Mostly, we only increased the number of examples of all of the previously well-known observations and arguments. We can now estimate with great precision the differences between human and chimpanzee genomes, and they are surprisingly similar. That similarity extends well beyond the genes to the transposable elements, pseudogenes, and even the large fraction of DNA that is poorly understood. In no sense has the human genome "sealed the deal" or made us *certain* about a previously *tentative* conclusion by providing qualitatively new evidence. Genomic arguments in favor of human evolution are the same sort of arguments developed in the decades prior to the human and chimpanzee genome projects.

Interpreting Genome Similarity

A favorite evolutionary argument goes something like this: "Since there's no creationist explanation of this similarity, the evolutionary explanation must be correct." We think you can see the problem with this line of reasoning: To com-

50. Deininger and Schmid, "Thermal Stability of Human DNA and Chimpanzee DNA Heteroduplexes."
51. Regardless of how we measure the similarity, these claims remain true.
52. International Human Genome Sequencing Consortium, "Initial Sequencing and Analysis of the Human Genome"; Chimpanzee Sequencing and Analysis Consortium, "Initial Sequence of the Chimpanzee Genome and Comparison with the Human Genome."

pare two theories, you actually need two theories. At this time, creationists have some ideas about what similarity might mean, but they can hardly be called a full "theory of similarity." In this chapter, we presented the idea that similarity facilitates relationship, but we recognize that this would not apply to DNA similarities, which are not observable by the average person. Others have proposed functional reasons for similarity, and we might also explain similarity in organisms the same way we explain similarity in words of the same language. God used language to create, and that language is directly reflected in His creation.

Even though we find all of these creationist ideas intriguing, none of them alone could be counted as a full "theory of similarity." Consequently, the best evolutionary argument is only that the similarity of human and ape genomes *appears* to be explained by common ancestry. No one can truly say that the creationist explanation has been falsified, since there is not yet a creationist explanation. An evolutionist might respond by claiming that there is no *imaginable* alternative to evolution, but that seems to be more a lack of imagination than an argument.

Evidence of History

Another question that arises about genomes and evolution is the observation of what appear to be remnants of past transposable element activity, mutations that produce pseudogenes, and other "debris." The number of transposable elements in the human genome suggests a long history of mutation and change, especially since we share almost all of the same evidence of mutation and change as chimpanzees. Since these elements are generally thought to contribute little functionality to the genome, they are collectively referred to as "junk" DNA.[53] How could they be explained in a creationist scenario?

We can imagine a number of responses to the junk DNA argument. Beginning with a very obvious response, we note that young-age creationists challenge the notion that junk DNA is functionally unimportant.[54] Discovering that a large fraction of the human genome was functionally important

---

53. We acknowledge the importance of carefully defining "junk" and "function." See recent papers on the ENCODE project: Niu and Jiang, "Can ENCODE Tell Us How Much Junk DNA We Carry in Our Genome?"; Doolittle, "Is Junk DNA Bunk? A Critique of ENCODE"; Eddy, "The ENCODE Project: Missteps Overshadowing a Success"; Eddy, "The C-Value Paradox, Junk DNA and ENCODE"; Graur, et al., "On the Immortality of Television Sets: 'Function' in the Human Genome according to the Evolution-Free Gospel of ENCODE"; Hurst, "Open Questions: A Logic (or Lack Thereof) of Genome Organization."
54. E.g., Carter, "The Slow, Painful Death of Junk DNA"; Williams, "Astonishing DNA Complexity Demolishes Neo-Darwinism"; Woodmorappe, "Junk DNA Indicted."

would pose a very serious challenge to the models of population genetics upon which much of the junk DNA argument is built.

We can also imagine several creationist scenarios that would explain why such a large fraction of the human genome appears to be functionally unimportant. One possibility is that God foresaw the coming corruption of creation due to sin, especially the potentially damaging effects of mutation, and so to counteract mutational damage, He created a large "buffer zone" of functionally unimportant DNA around the functionally important parts. Random mutations would then occur mostly in the functionally unimportant parts of the genome, leaving the functionally important features intact. In this scenario, it is the functional unimportance of the genome that *is* the wise design.

Another possibility is that only the *current* human genome contains a large portion of functionally inert DNA. Perhaps this portion was rendered inactive as part of the curse on creation, or perhaps this DNA will become functional at some future point. Perhaps both could be the case. Junk DNA could be part of the groaning of creation that awaits future reactivation in the coming kingdom.

We admit that these are all speculative ideas, but our point is not to endorse one explanation over the other. Our point is that even if the human genome turns out to be mostly nonfunctional, that would still not be incompatible with a creationist or design perspective. We also note that none of these arguments address the question of similarity. Even in the most extreme case, if the majority of the genome turns out to be functionally important, that would still not explain the high degree of similarity to great ape genomes. Consequently, we favor developing a creationist model of genome design that would explain the similarity itself, which we believe would provide a framework to explain the purported junk DNA as part of the design of similarity.[55]

Is There Anything Different about Human and Ape Genomes?

After all this discussion of similarity, we might wonder whether there is any evidence of significant differences between the human and ape genomes. Or is all this talk about creationist explanations of similarity just talk? In other words, outside of a prior commitment to creationism based on the Bible, is there any reason to suspect that separate origins might be a viable explana-

55. Wood, "The Chimpanzee Genome and the Problem of Biological Similarity."

tion? In a recent article, one such factor was reported as possibly signaling separate creation: transversion/transition ratios.[56]

The simplest mutations that can occur are point mutations, the substitution of one base for another. Point mutations come in two types, transitions and transversions. When we examine the frequency of these two types of mutations, we find that transitions are much more common than transversions. Although the terms "transition" and "transversion" are defined as a type of mutation, we can also think of them in purely observational terms. For example, when we find a difference between a chimpanzee and human sequence, we could classify that difference as a transition or transversion, regardless of whether the difference resulted from an actual mutation.

Creationist research has shown that when we compare human DNA to other human DNA, we find a very characteristic ratio of transversions to transitions (about ten transitions for every one transversion), but when we compare human and chimpanzee DNA, the ratio is significantly different (about fifteen to one). In an evolutionary model, this difference could be the result of a phenomenon called saturation, whereby the ratio of transversions and transitions fluctuates substantially when there are few mutations. At the point of saturation, fluctuations in the ratio stop. However, if that were the explanation, we should observe a different ratio when comparing very different human DNA sequences, but we do not. Instead, we find the same transversion/transition ratio that we find when comparing very similar humans to each other. In other words, there appears to be no change that we usually observe as sequences approach saturation. This could be a clue that evolution does not adequately explain human and ape genomes, but we need to do further research before we draw any firm conclusions.

Conclusion

Our objective here has been to evaluate a single claim, is evolution the *only* explanation for the similarity of humans and animals? In the area of anatomy, we found that recent creationist research has confirmed a distinction between humans and even the most similar apes, *Australopithecus*. This result is important because it confirms a long-standing creationist claim that different

---

56. Wood, "Ancient mtDNA Implies a Nonconstant Molecular Clock in the Human Holobaramin."

"created kinds" can be distinguished. Additional work is necessary to confirm these preliminary results, but we are optimistic that future research and even new fossil discoveries will continue to be consistent with a creationist perspective. In comparative anatomy, then, we cannot sustain the claim that evolution is the *only* explanation.

In the area of genomics, we found much more uncertainty regarding the interpretation of the human and chimpanzee genomes. Most importantly, we found uncertainty on both sides of the discussion. Evolutionary claims tend to be overstated, and creationist responses are currently underdeveloped. This is easily one of the most exciting and open areas of creationist research, and creationists have many different avenues of fruitful study as we explore the meaning of genomes. Once again, we cannot sustain the claim that evolution is the *only* explanation of the similarity of human and ape genomes.

If our discussion has not inspired readers to adopt a creationist understanding of human origins, we should at least recognize all of our uncertainty as we try to understand God's creation. Claiming that evolution is the only explanation and that creationism has no explanation is at best hyperbole. Christians engaged in the debate over the historical Adam should therefore use this opportunity to exercise godly humility as we all try to answer important scientific questions in a context of faithfulness to Christ, to His body the Church, and to each other as brothers and sisters in Christ.

BIBLIOGRAPHY

Barrick, William D. "A Historical Adam: Young-Earth Creation View." In *Four Views on the Historical Adam*, edited by Matthew Barrett and Ardel B. Caneday, 197–227. Grand Rapids: Zondervan, 2013.

Berger, Lee R., et al. "*Australopithecus sediba*: A New Species of *Homo*-like Australopith from South Africa." *Science* 328 (2010): 195–204.

Bree, Charles Robert. *Species Not Transmutable*. London: Groombridge and Sons, 1860.

Brown, P., T. Sutikna, M. J. Morwood, R. P. Soejono, Jatmiko, E. Wayhu Saptomo, and Rokus Awe Due. "A New Small-Bodied Hominin from the Late Pleistocene of Flores, Indonesia," *Nature* 431 (2004): 1055–61.

Calvin, John. *A Commentarie upon the First Booke of Moses Called Genesis*. London: John Harison and George Bishop, 1578.

Carter, Robert W. "The Slow, Painful Death of Junk DNA." *Journal of Creation* 23 (2009): 12–13.

Chimpanzee Sequencing and Analysis Consortium, "Initial Sequence of the Chimpanzee Genome and Comparison with the Human Genome." *Nature* 437 (2005): 69–87.

Collins, Francis. *The Language of God*. New York: Free Press, 2006.

Darwin, Charles. *On the Origin of Species*. London: John Murray, 1859.

Deininger, Prescott L., and Carl W. Schmid. "Thermal Stability of Human DNA and Chimpanzee DNA Heteroduplexes." *Science* 194 (1976): 846–48.

DeSilva, Jeremy M. K. G. Holt, S. E. Churchill, K. J. Carlson, C. S. Walker, B. Zipfel, and L. R. Berger. "The Lower Limb and Mechanics of Walking in *Australopithecus sediba*." *Science* 340 (6129):1232999 (2013).

Doolittle, W. Ford. "Is Junk DNA Bunk? A Critique of ENCODE." *Proceedings of the National Academy of Sciences USA* 110 (2013): 5294–300.

Eddy, Sean R. "The C-Value Paradox, Junk DNA and ENCODE." *Current Biology* 22 (2013): R898.

_____. "The ENCODE Project: Missteps Overshadowing a Success." *Current Biology* 23 (2013): R259–61.

Edwards, Jonathan. *The Doctrine of Original Sin Defended*. Boston: J. Johnson and Co., 1766.

Enns, Peter. *The Evolution of Adam*. Grand Rapids: Baker, 2012.

Francis, J., and A. Chou. "Does Biblical Similarity Inform Biological Similarity?" *Journal of Creation Theology and Science Series B: Biological Science* 1 (2011): 20–21.

Gentry, Peter J. "Kingdom through Covenant: Humanity as the Divine Image." *Southern Baptist Journal of Theology* 12 (2008): 16–42.

Graur, Dan, Y. Zheng, N. Price, R. B. R. Azevedo, R. A. Zufall, and E. Elhaik. "On the Immortality of Television Sets: 'Function' in the Human Genome According to the Evolution-Free Gospel of ENCODE." *Genome Biology and Evolution* 5 (2013): 578–90.

Hale, Matthew. *The Primitive Origination of Mankind*. London: Shrowsbery, 1677.

Hurst, Laurence D. "Open Questions: A Logic (or Lack Thereof) of Genome Organization." *BMC Biology* 11 (2013): 58.

International Human Genome Sequencing Consortium. "Initial Sequencing and Analysis of the Human Genome." *Nature* 409 (2001): 860–921.

Jurmain, Robert, Lynn Kilgore, Wenda Trevathan, and Russell L. Ciochon. *Introduction to Physical Anthropology*. Belmont, CA: Wadsworth, 2012.

King, Mary-Claire, and A. C. Wilson. "Evolution at Two Levels in Humans and Chimpanzees." *Science* 188 (1975): 107–16.

Lamoureux, Denis O. "No Historical Adam: Evolutionary Creation View." In *Four Views on the Historical Adam*, edited by Matthew Barrett and Ardel B. Caneday, 37–65. Grand Rapids: Zondervan, 2013.

Leakey, Maeve G. "New fossils from Koobi Fora in northern Kenya confirm taxonomic diversity in early *Homo*." *Nature* 488 (2012): 201–4.

_____, C. S. Feibel, I. McDougall, and A. Walker. "New Four-Million-Year-Old Hominid Species from Kanapoi and Allia Bay, Kenya." *Nature* 376 (1995): 565–71.

Liebhaber, S.A. and K.A. Begley. "Structural and Evolutionary Analysis of the Two Chimpanzee Alpha-globin mRNAs." *Nucleic Acids Research* 11 (1983): 8915–29.

Linnaeus, Carolus. *Philosophia Botanica*. Translated by S. Freer. Oxford: Oxford University Press, 2003.

Lordkipanidze, David, M. S. Ponce de León, A. Margvelashvili, Y. Rak, G. P. Rightmire, A. Vekua1, and C. P. E. Zollikofer. "A Complete Skull from Dmanisi, Georgia, and the Evolutionary Biology of Early *Homo*." *Science* 342 (2013): 326–31.

Lovejoy, Arthur. *The Great Chain of Being*. Cambridge, MA: Harvard University Press, 1936.

MacArthur, John. *The Battle for the Beginning: The Bible on Creation and the Fall of Adam*. Nashvillle: Thomas Nelson, 2001.

Marsh, Frank Lewis. *Evolution, Creation, and Science*. Washington, DC: Review & Herald Publishing, 1947.

_____. *Fundamental Biology*. Lincoln, NE: Self-published, 1941.

Max, Edward E. "Plagiarized Errors and Molecular Genetics: Another Argument in the Evolution-Creation Controversy." *Creation/Evolution* XIX (1986): 34–46.

Niu, Deng-Ke, and Li Jiang. "Can ENCODE Tell Us How Much Junk DNA We Carry in Our Genome?" *Biochemical and Biophysical Research Communications* 430 (2013): 1340–43.

Olender, Tsviya, D. Lancet, and D. W. Nebert. "Update on the Olfactory Receptor (OR) Gene Superfamily." *Human Genomics* 3 (2008): 87–97.

Pan, Qun. "Deep Surveying of Alternative Splicing Complexity in the Human Transcriptome by High-throughput Sequencing." *Nature Genetics* 40 (2008): 1413–15.

Pertea, Mihaela, and Steven L. Salzberg. "Between a chicken and a grape: estimating the number of human genes." *Genome Biology* 11 (2010): 206.

Ray, John. *Methodus Plantarum Nova.* London: Impensis Henrici Faithorne & Joannis Kersey, 1682.

Ryken, Philip G. "We Cannot Understand the World or Our Faith without a Historical Adam." In *Four Views on the Historical Adam,* edited by Matthew Barrett and Ardel B. Caneday, 267–79. Grand Rapids: Zondervan, 2013.

Suddendorf, Thomas. *The Gap: The Science of What Separates Us from Other Animals.* New York: Basic Books, 2013.

Theobald, Douglas L. "A Formal Test of the Theory of Universal Common Ancestry." *Nature* 465 (2010): 219–22.

Thompson, D'Arcy Wentworth. *The History of Animals.* Oxford: Clarendon, 1910.

Topsell, Edward. *The Historie of Foure-Footed Beasts.* London: William Iaggard, 1607.

Tyson, Edward. *Orang Outang, sive Homo sylvestris: or, the Anatomy of a Pygmie Compared with that of a Monkey, an Ape, and a Man.* London: Thomas Bennet, 1699.

Ussher, James. *A Body of Divinitie.* London: Downes and Badger, 1645.

Walton, John H. "Human Origins and the Bible." *Zygon* 47 (2012): 875–89.

Whitney, Dudley Joseph. "Evolution and Uniformitarian Geology." *The Bible Champion* 36 (1930): 259–63.

Wienberg, Johannes and Roscoe Stanyon. "Comparative Painting of Mammalian Chromosomes." *Current Opinion in Genetics & Development* 7 (1997): 784–91.

Williams, Alex. "Astonishing DNA Complexity Demolishes Neo-Darwinism." *Journal of Creation* 21 (2007): 111–17.

Wood, Todd Charles. "Ancient mtDNA Implies a Nonconstant Molecular Clock in the Human Holobaramin." *Journal of Creation Theology and Science Series B: Life Sciences* 2 (2012): 18–26.

_____. "Baraminic Distance, Bootstraps, and BDISTMDS." *Occasional Papers of the BSG* 12 (2008): 1–17.

_____. "Baraminological Analysis Places *Homo habilis*, *Homo rudolfensis*, and *Australopithecus sediba* in the Human Holobaramin." *Answers Research Journal* 3 (2010): 71–90.

_____. "*Natura Facit Saltum*: The Case for Discontinuity." In *Genesis Kinds: Creationism and the Origin of Species*, edited by Todd Charles Wood and Paul A. Garner, 113–27. Eugene, OR: Wipf and Stock, 2009.

_____. "The Chimpanzee Genome and the Problem of Biological Similarity." *Occasional Papers of the BSG* 7 (2006): 1–18.

Wood, Todd Charles and Megan J. Murray. *Understanding the Pattern of Life*. Nashville: Broadman and Holman, 2003.

Woodmorappe, John. "Junk DNA Indicted." *TJ* 18 (2004): 27–33.

Yunis, Jorge J. and Om Prakash. "The Origin of Man: A Chromosomal Pictorial Legacy." *Science* 215 (1982): 1525–30.

GENETICS OF ADAM

Todd Charles Wood and Joseph W. Francis

Evangelical scholars who question the historicity of Genesis 1–11 often accept human evolution from animals as God's mechanism of creation. "Human evolution" itself evokes the popular imagery of the brutish "cave man," with his hairy body draped in animal skins and a blank stare on his ape-like face. Even though these images are imaginative, the fossil record reveals the existence of apes that possess some traits that today are found only in humans. Evolutionary biologists and even some evangelical Christians claim such fossils as evidence of human evolution from animal ancestors. As we reviewed in our previous chapter, these fossils are distinct from humans and are consistent with creationist claims of the distinct creation of humans.

In the past thirty years, however, the argument for human evolution has itself evolved. A whole new kind of evidence has emerged from a number of large-scale genetics surveys. In these sorts of arguments, comparisons of humans and animals are not central features. Instead, our genome[1] alone supposedly shows that we could not have descended from a single ancestral couple.

---

1. The "genome" is a general term that describes all the genes and genetic material of a single individual or species.

Some evangelical scholars accept these arguments and question the traditional belief in Adam and Eve as the first parents of humanity.[2] Others attempt to retain a belief in a representative or covenantal Adam and Eve, who were not necessarily the ancestors of all modern humans.[3] In both cases, such scholars reject or at least question traditional belief in Adam and Eve as the first human ancestors.

As in our previous chapter, our goal here is *not to critically evaluate evolution itself but rather to evaluate the claim that only evolution can make sense of human genetic diversity.* Consequently, we shall explore possible creationist explanations of the same data presented as evidence of evolution. Our main question is whether human genetic diversity should force us to adopt an evolutionary view of Creation. In other words, are there meaningful ways that a historical view of Genesis could interact with the genetic data?

Basic Genetics

For a basic introduction to DNA and the content of genomes, consult our previous chapter. Since we now want to contemplate human genetic diversity, we need to consider how genetic variations arise and how they are passed along to future generations. In the context of the subject of this chapter, we need to understand the basics of inheritance to be able to explain how human genetics today could arise from a single ancestral pair.

The process of making a copy of a genome to pass on to offspring is called replication.[4] Replication is complex and extremely accurate, but like any copying process, it is possible to copy imperfectly. Errors can creep into the copies. Any permanent change in a DNA sequence is called a "mutation."

As mutations arise and get passed along to offspring, they make variant copies of genes and chromosomes that can tell us something about the family tree. For example, we might infer that very similar DNA sequences represent close relatives, while less similar sequences come from more distant relatives. If we know how often DNA changes, we can even estimate how many generations or years separate individuals from their ancestor.

2. Enns, *Evolution of Adam*; Lamoureux, "No Historical Adam: Evolutionary Creation View."
3. Collins, *Did Adam and Eve Really Exist?*
4. Information on DNA metabolism and basic genetics is available from any textbook on genetics, cell biology, or biochemistry. E.g., see Voet and Voet, *Biochemistry*, 1136–1211.

Remember that we are only comparing humans to humans, so this ancestor is just another human being.

A second important process, called *recombination*, can also contribute to modern human variation. As we noted in the previous chapter, human chromosomes come in matching pairs that are numbered one through twenty-two.[5] During the formation of sperm and egg cells, these matching pairs undergo a process called crossing over. First, the chromosomes literally cross over, forming an X structure. The crossing chromosomes then break and reattach, allowing parts of the chromosomes to be essentially scrambled in a very orderly fashion. The result is two chromosomes of equal length, which are rearranged pieces of the original pair of chromosomes. This process is called "recombination." After many generations of recombination, chromosomes end up as "quilts" of pieces of chromosomes inherited from many different ancestors. The most important consequence of this process for our purposes is that different parts of the human genome can have different histories. This is easiest to understand when we think in terms of family trees.

In the 1850s, Calvin Wood moved from New York to a farm in southern Michigan. Five generations later, his great-great-great-grandson would co-author this article. Even though Todd Wood bears Calvin's family name, he only has about three percent of Calvin Wood's genome. Why? Since Calvin Wood was five generations back on Todd Wood's family tree, he was one of thirty-two different individuals who would become Todd's great-great-great-grandparents, all of whom contributed (roughly equal) parts of Todd's genome. Without recombination, Todd Wood could only receive whole chromosomes from his ancestors, and at five generations distant, it is possible that he might not have *any* DNA from the man who gave him his family name. Because of recombination, though, three percent of Calvin Wood's genome is scattered around all through Todd Wood's genome. If we had access to Calvin Wood's genome, we could even run tests to determine which parts of Todd Wood's genome came from Calvin.

How could we see which parts of Todd's genome came from Calvin from so many generations ago? Since human DNA is very similar, the DNA that came from Calvin Wood should be very similar to the DNA that came from Calvin's wife (Todd's great-great-great-grandmother). How could we

---

5. The twenty-third pair of chromosomes consists of the X and Y sex chromosomes. They are quite different and are not considered to be a matching pair.

tell one from another? All human DNA is indeed very similar, but when we look at DNA variation within a species, we need to focus on the differences. Places on chromosomes that are highly variable between members of the same species are called "genetic markers." If we want to compare the DNA of two individuals from the same species—for example by doing a paternity test—we would examine their markers and see how many match. Since we know a lot about markers, we could calculate how likely it would be that two randomly chosen individuals could share that many markers in common.

What is true for Calvin Wood's genome is true for any other ancestor as well. If we had access to ancient human genomes, we could recognize the parts of our modern genomes that came from those ancestors, even if we do not know exactly how we are related. We can also model recombination rates and use those models to figure out how many generations separate us from those ancestors (assuming the models are correct). The way we do that is by looking at the size of the ancestral DNA segments still in our modern genomes. As recombination proceeds over many generations, the pieces of DNA inherited from our ancestors get smaller and smaller. If we find segments matching an ancient genome that are very small, we can infer that they must be very remote ancestors. Likewise if the segments are large, then they must be very recent ancestors.[6]

One important thing about these models we need to keep in mind is that they depend on assumptions, just like any other scientific model. The assumptions needed to model population genetics include things like mutation rates, recombination rates, reproductive output, and mortality. When scientists find that a model poorly predicts modern genetics, they rarely throw out the entire model. Instead, they might simply adjust one or more of the assumptions and see if it fixes the problem.

Modeling Human History

Simple Ancestor

With these basic ideas in mind, we can now turn to some of the recent claims about the history of humanity based on studies of modern human ge-

---

6. This is a well-known property of *linkage disequilibrium*. See Hedrick, *Genetics of Populations*, 525–96.

netic diversity. The first of these is the oldest and most famous, "mitochondrial Eve." This theory was introduced in a paper published in the journal *Nature* in 1987,[7] and although there was much initial debate over the details of the theory, the conclusions are generally accepted today.[8] According to the theory, the most recent common female ancestor of all modern humans lived in Africa about 150,000 years ago.[9]

Before we discuss how scientists came to these conclusions, we need to discuss mitochondrial DNA, which differs from the other human chromosomes in important ways.[10] Mitochondrial DNA is found inside a cell's mitochondria, which are little compartments responsible for converting some of the food you eat into most of the usable energy. Unlike the larger linear chromosomes, which are found in a cell's nucleus, the mitochondrial DNA is a very small, circular chromosome. For example, the smallest human chromosome is forty-eight million bases, while the mitochondrial DNA is only sixteen thousand bases. Mitochondrial DNA is also not inherited like the other chromosomes.[11] The other chromosomes are inherited equally from each parent, twenty-three from the father and twenty-three from the mother. Mitochondrial DNA comes exclusively from the mother.[12] The maternal inheritance of mitochondrial DNA explains why the name "mitochondrial Eve" became popular—the original ancestor of all modern human mitochondria must have been a woman.

Why do scientists conclude that mitochondrial Eve was African? When we compare mitochondrial DNA from many different modern humans, the sequences that are most different from all others come from southern African tribes, such as the San or Bushmen.[13] Recall that a large number of differences between two sequences indicates that a great amount of time has elapsed

---

7. Cann, et al., "Mitochondrial DNA and Human Evolution."

8. E.g., see Stringer and Andrews, *The Complete World of Human Evolution*, 178–79.

9. We are here summarizing the conventional mitochondrial Eve theory, even though as young-age creationists we do not accept the date estimate.

10. Pakendorf and Stoneking, "Mitochondrial DNA and Human Evolution."

11. International Human Genome Sequencing Consortium, "Initial Sequence and Analysis of the Human Genome," Table 8; Anderson, et al., "Sequencing and organization of the human mitochondrial genome."

12. The reason you only inherit mitochondrial DNA from your mother is that during human reproduction when the egg and sperm unite, the much larger egg has a lot of mitochondria, but the much smaller sperm injects primarily only its nuclear DNA into the large egg. Seldom do any mitochondria get injected into the egg from the sperm.

13. E.g., Ingman, et al., "Mitochondrial genome variation and the origin of modern humans."

since the original ancestor. Since these tribes are the most different from all other humans, scientists infer that the mitochondrial DNA of these African tribes diverged from the rest of modern humans at the earliest point on the human family tree. In other words, on the human mitochondrial DNA family tree, the southern African tribes are on the earliest branch. They are everyone else's most distant cousins. If that is the case, then it makes sense that the earliest human ancestor lived in Africa.

Why do scientists conclude that mitochondrial Eve lived 150,000 years ago? As we mentioned previously, the number of differences between two DNA sequences is related to the time they have been independently mutating. That gives us a relative measure of how closely or distantly two individuals might be related. How do we turn that into an actual measurement of time? In the early days of studying mitochondrial DNA, scientists used a "molecular clock" calibration method to try to estimate how old mitochondrial Eve was. These methods would try to estimate the rate at which DNA base differences accumulate in a population over time. That rate was then used to calibrate a "clock," which could in turn tell something about the dates of ancestors who lived at an unknown time.

In modern DNA studies, scientists use a collection of methods called "coalescent models."[14] These models attempt to work backwards from the present genetic diversity to a generation at which there was no diversity (that is, the generation in which there was only one type of mitochondrial DNA). These coalescent models can account for other factors like population size that might influence the frequency of a genetic variant in a population. Coalescent models are therefore preferred over simple molecular clock techniques, which can be fooled by a large number of complications.

Like the mitochondrial DNA, there is a portion of the human genome that is passed only from fathers to sons: the Y chromosome. Since the Y chromosome is the male sex-determining chromosome, it can only be passed from fathers to sons. A survey of human Y chromosomes might tell us something about the original male ancestor of the human Y chromosome, dubbed "Y chromosome Adam."

Studies indicate a "recent" common ancestor for Y chromosome Adam ("recent" in the sense of tens of thousands of years).[15] These studies are consistent with the mitochondrial Eve results, even though they are not exactly the same. Taken together, studies of the Y chromosome and mitochondrial DNA

---

14. See Hein, Schierup, and Wiuf, *Gene Genealogies, Variation and Evolution*.
15. Hammer, "A recent common ancestry for human Y chromosomes."

both indicate that the most recent male and female ancestors of humanity were Africans who probably lived less than 200,000 years ago.

Other Ancestors

A word of caution is in order at this point. With names like "Y chromosome Adam" and "mitochondrial Eve," it is tempting for a creationist to celebrate the vindication of the Bible by modern science. When we examine these studies more carefully, however, we find a number of reasons to be cautious about equating these genetic ancestors with Adam and Eve. The most important reason is that different parts of the human genome can have different histories because of recombination. That means that Y chromosome Adam is properly understood as the ancestor of the Y chromosome only. Because his other chromosomes have not been considered in this analysis, we cannot say he represents the ancestor of all humanity. Likewise, mitochondrial Eve is considered an ancestor based on only an analysis of the mitochondria, and because all of her chromosomes have not been analyzed we cannot say for sure that she is the mother of all humanity.

Since the mitochondrial DNA and the Y chromosome together account for less than two percent of the entire human genome, we ought to wonder about the ancestors of the other ninety-eight percent. It is possible that the rest of the genome could be consistent with the mitochondrial DNA ancestor, and therefore be consistent with a recent ancestral pair (like the biblical Adam and Eve), but we cannot say for sure until we look at the other ninety-eight percent of the genome. Scientists emphasize this uncertainty by claiming that mitochondrial Eve and Y chromosome Adam need not have been the only humans alive at the time.[16] That raises a related question: Can we find out how many people were alive at the time of mitochondrial Eve and Y chromosome Adam?

Modern statistical genetics give us several methods of estimating ancient population sizes.[17] For example, imagine if you could analyze variations from many locations in the human genome. For each location, you can evaluate the number of variations present in the modern human population and how frequent those variations are. Generally speaking, variations that are common in the current living population are probably older than variations that are rare or restricted to one particular people group.

16. E.g., see Stoneking, "Mitochondrial DNA and Human Evolution," 242.
17. Gattepaille, Jkobsson, and Blum, "Inferring Population Size Changes with Sequence and SNP Data: Lessons from Human Bottlenecks"; Park, "Linkage Disequilibrium Decay and Past Population History in the Human Genome."

How does that provide information about the size of the human population long ago? Some coalescent methods work generation by generation. For example, they might look at the frequency of variations at a particular genomic location and ask how likely it would be for the previous generation to have no variation. Remember that these studies are examining multiple locations. If a lot of locations have lots of variation, then the population must be fairly large. If only a few locations are variable, the population could be much smaller.

To put all this in simpler terms, higher genetic variability in a modern population could be explained either as a longer time since a single common ancestor or a bigger population, or a combination of both. Current studies indicate that the modern human genome is consistent with a recent, explosive population growth. In less than a thousand generations, humans grew from just a few thousand individuals to the seven billion that occupy the planet today. Looking back to 5,000–10,000 generations ago (around 75,000–200,000 years ago), genetic models predict relatively small population sizes, on the order of thousands. Even though these are relatively small population sizes, modern genomes have a diversity that is difficult to reconcile with just a single ancestral pair only a few hundred generations ago (5,000–10,000 years ago).[18]

Based on these results, we can see why some evangelical scholars have argued that Adam and Eve could not have existed as the created ancestors of all humans. Even if we do not compare humans to animals, there is still evidence in our own genomes that indicates that we did not come from a single pair of individuals. After reviewing this evidence, evolutionary creationist Dennis Venema concluded, "The hypothesis that humans are genetically derived from a single ancestral pair in the recent past has no support from a genomics perspective, and, indeed, is counter to a large body of evidence."[19]

NEANDERTALS AND THE REST OF THE FAMILY

How then should creationists approach the diversity of human genomes? Creationists start with a number of assumptions that differ from other scientists. We

---

18. Gronau, et al., "Bayesian Inference of Ancient Human Demography from Individual Genome Sequences"; Li and Durbin, "Inference of Human Population History from Individual Whole-Genome Sequences"; Tenesa, et al., "Recent Human Effective Population Size Estimated from Linkage Disequilibrium."
19. Venema, "Genesis and the Genome: Genomics Evidence for Human-Ape Common Ancestry and Ancestral Hominid Population Sizes," 175.

believe that all humans today and in the past really did descend from Adam and Eve, and we believe that our original ancestors lived comparatively recently, only thousands of years ago. Based on evidence reviewed in our previous chapter, we also recognize other humans besides just modern *Homo sapiens* as true descendants of Adam and Eve. Consequently, surveys of human genetic variability that only look at *Homo sapiens* may not have anything to tell us about Adam and Eve.

This is an important creationist response to those who question the existence of Adam and Eve based on estimations of ancient population sizes. If we view Adam and Eve as the earliest ancestors of just *modern* humans, we are looking in the wrong place. In other words, if we want to understand the ancestors of all humans, we have to examine *all* humans. Consequently, as we develop our young-age creationist response to genome variability, we need to take an important detour to consider Neandertals and other descendants of Adam and Eve, which have been largely ignored by evolutionary creationists.[20]

Neandertals are one of the best studied and characterized ancient humans, and they provide a rich set of genetic data to study. Over the past fifteen years, there have been multiple efforts to sequence DNA from Neandertal fossils.[21] The methods involved in recovering ancient DNA are not foolproof, but the potential sources of error are known well enough that we can have some measure of confidence in the Neandertal DNA sequences that have been published.

Neandertal genetic studies started out as a handful of short sequences from the mitochondrial DNA but now have expanded to much larger samples of the entire nuclear genome. The specimens that have been studied come from the entire geographic range where Neandertals are found, including the Iberian Peninsula, south central Europe, and the Caucasus region. This range of samples is important to help establish what kind of variation existed within the Neandertal population.

Mitochondrial DNA

One important discovery is that Neandertal mitochondrial DNA tends to be fairly similar to mitochondrial DNA of other Neandertals.[22] The fact that all

---

20. "Evolutionary creationist" is a new term used by some "theistic evolutionists" to indicate their beliefs.
21. Krings, et al., "DNA Sequence of the Mitochondrial Hypervariable Region II from the Neandertal Type Specimen"; Green, et al., "A Complete Neandertal Mitochondrial Genome Sequence Determined by High-Throughput Sequencing"; Briggs, et al., "Targeted Retrieval and Analysis of Five Neandertal mtDNA Genomes"; Green, et al. "A Draft Sequence of the Neandertal Genome."
22. Briggs, et al., "Targeted Retrieval and Analysis of Five Neandertal mtDNA Genomes."

the samples of DNA from fossilized Neandertal bones are fairly similar tells us we are probably looking at authentic Neandertal DNA that has not been subject to modern contamination or degradation that has altered the DNA sequence.[23]

The next important discovery about Neandertal mitochondrial DNA is that it is quite different from the mitochondrial DNA of modern humans. For the entire mitochondrial DNA (about 16,000 bases), the two most different modern humans yet sequenced differ by about eighty bases, about half a percent. In contrast, the average Neandertal differs from the average modern human by about 180–190 bases, which is more than twice the number of differences between the two most different modern humans. To put those differences in perspective, the mitochondrial DNA from humans and Neandertals differ from modern chimpanzees by an average of ten percent.[24]

At this point, you might be wondering what this has to do with Adam and Eve. Could these differences between humans and Neandertals actually fit into the range of modern humans? Could there be some kind of variability that could account for how Neandertals *appear* to be so different from modern people? Or are we dealing with something really different from modern humans, and if so, what does that mean?

One possibility is that Neandertal differences are not real differences. How does that work? Say you compare one nucleotide base at one particular position in the human mitochondrial genome. You find that Neandertals have the same base as some modern humans but a different base than other modern humans. Should that count as a difference between Neandertals and humans or as a similarity? Since we have lots of mitochondrial DNA from modern humans and several Neandertal samples, we can ask: How many bases are different between modern humans and Neandertals where all the modern human samples are the same and all the Neandertal samples are the same? We refer to these differences as *fixed differences*.

Looking only at fixed differences, we find that Neandertal mitochondrial DNA differs from modern human mitochondrial DNA at 104 positions.[25] So even when we take into account variability among modern humans and among Neandertals, we still find that the mitochondrial DNA of Neandertals

---

23. Wood, "Ancient mtDNA Implies a Nonconstant Molecular Clock in the Human Holo-
    baramin."
24. Ibid. Notice that this is the mitochondrial DNA only, which is typically ten times more
    divergent than the DNA of other chromosomes.
25. Ibid.

is different from that of modern humans. To account for Neandertals in any creationist model, we must account for these differences.[26]

The Rest of the Genome

The complete Neandertal genome was published only a few years ago, and it was obtained from three different bones from the Vindija cave in Croatia. This initial genome sequence was an extremely rough draft, with lots of pieces missing and an error rate one hundred to one thousand times higher than the modern Human Genome Project.[27] More recently, a much more complete and accurate version of a Neandertal genome has been published, which largely corroborates the results of analyses from the initial draft genome sequence.[28]

The Neandertal genome revealed a very interesting and important pattern. Recall that we said that because of recombination, genomes are patchworks of ancestors, and if we knew the genome sequence of one of our ancestors, we could pick out their genetic markers in the genomes of their descendants. With the Neandertal genome, scientists were able to examine markers present in Neandertals and ask whether the same markers were present in any modern human populations. The initial study looked at markers found in Europeans, Asians, and southern Africans. They found that Neandertals shared a surprising number of markers with modern Europeans and Asians that were not found in southern Africans. Scientists interpreted this result as evidence of hybrid offspring between Neandertals and the ancestors of modern Europeans and Asians.[29]

Since Neandertals had a Eurasian distribution, it makes sense that Neandertal markers would be passed on to Europeans and Asians but not southern Africans. Neandertals probably never had any contact with southern Africans. More recently, scientists wondered if there could be any Neandertal markers in people from northern Africa. Since Neandertals ranged as far south as Israel, perhaps they encountered and interacted with *Homo sapiens* tribes from northern Africa. A search for Neandertal markers in northern Africans turned

26. Even though the DNA is different between extant humans and Neandertals, the differences are small compared to the differences between humans and animals, and it is important to continually keep in mind that Neandertals are human in their anatomy (with some slight differences) and in their practice of culture.
27. Green, et al., "A Draft Sequence of the Neandertal Genome."
28. Prüfer, et al., "The Complete Genome Sequence of a Neanderthal from the Altai Mountains."
29. Green, et al., "A Draft Sequence of the Neandertal Genome."

up evidence of hybridization there as well.[30] As far as we know now, the only modern humans that lack Neandertal markers are from southern Africa.

Is it possible that we could explain these shared markers by some other mechanism? Is it possible that ancient *Homo sapiens* did not have conjugal relationships or intermarry with Neandertals, but acquired similar markers by some other means? We can test for two possibilities. First, Neandertals and modern Eurasians could have inherited these markers from a distant ancestor (like Adam himself). Because of the multiple generations that would have elapsed, the genetic markers would be small. Second, Neandertals and Eurasians could share the markers because of intermarriage. Since that would have been more recently, the markers would be larger. Researchers found that the size of the Neandertal regions in Eurasian genomes was most consistent with recent hybridization.[31]

Still More Humans

In addition to Neandertals, we now know about a different population of ancient *Homo* first found in the Denisova cave in Siberia. Since all we know of the fossil record of this population is a tooth and a finger bone, scientists have not given them a formal name. Instead, they are known simply as Denisovans.[32]

Denisovans are strikingly different from Neandertals and modern humans. Based on the mitochondrial DNA, the average Denisovan differs by about 370 bases from the average modern human. That's about 2.4% of the mitochondrial DNA that is different. Counting only fixed differences, there are 255 between Denisovans and modern humans. Comparing Denisovan and Neandertal mitochondrial DNA, we find an average of 355 base differences and 349 fixed differences.[33]

Since the Denisovan mitochondrial DNA is so different from both Neandertals and modern humans, we might expect that the Denisovans are a branch of our family tree that diverged much earlier than Neandertals and modern hu-

---

30. Anchez-Quinto, et al., "North African Populations Carry the Signature of Admixture with Neandertals."
31. Sankararaman, et al., "The Date of Interbreeding between Neandertals and Modern Humans."
32. Krause, et al., "The Complete Mitochondrial DNA Genome of an Unknown Hominin from Southern Siberia."
33. We should note that the number of fixed differences is likely to go down, since there were only two Denisovan mitochondrial chromosomes analyzed in that study. When we have a better sample of Denisovans, we will be better able to identify bases that are variable within the Denisovan population and therefore not fixed differences from modern humans or Neandertals. Wood, "Ancient mtDNA Implies a Nonconstant Molecular Clock in the Human Holobaramin."

mans. Remember, though, that different parts of the genome can have different ancestries, so we should ask whether the rest of the Denisovan genome would be consistent with what we see in the mitochondrial DNA. Shortly after the initial Neandertal draft genome was published, scientists also published a draft of the Denisovan genome.[34] In contrast to the mitochondrial DNA, the full Denisovan genome implies that Denisovans are more closely related to the Neandertals than to modern humans. If we drew a family tree, Neandertals and Denisovans might be "siblings," while modern humans are just "cousins" to both.

Since the Neandertal genome revealed evidence of hybridization with ancestors of some modern humans, scientists surveyed modern humans for Denisovan markers, which might indicate that hybridization occurred between ancient *Homo sapiens* and Denisovans. Denisovan markers were identified in the genomes of modern Melanesians, especially from tribes on the island of New Guinea. Thus, it appears as if the ancestors of Melanesians had children with these Denisovans.[35]

In 2013, a new study of bones and DNA recovered from a cave in Spain has added a new wrinkle to the Denisovan story.[36] The bones from the cave have characteristics of both Neandertals and another *Homo* species called *Homo heidelbergensis*. Paleoanthropologists believe that *Homo heidelbergensis* was an earlier species than Neandertals, and some suspect that they might have been ancestral to Neandertals. The mitochondrial DNA sequenced from these Spanish fossils is most similar to that of the Denisovans. Could this indicate a connection between *Homo heidelbergensis* and the Denisovans? At this point, we cannot be certain about what these newly discovered DNA sequences mean, but we expect future discoveries will help clarify the relationship between Denisovans, Neandertals, *Homo heidelbergensis*, and modern humans.

CREATIONIST INTERPRETATIONS

Our objective here is to evaluate whether or not genetics studies of modern and ancient humans are inconsistent with a belief in a single ancestral pair from whom all humans descended (i.e., Adam and Eve). Is this really an archaic, faulty belief, or can we explain how genetic evidences support the ex-

34. Reich, et al., "Genetic History of an Archaic Hominin Group from Denisova Cave in Siberia."
35. Ibid.
36. Meyer, et al., "A Mitochondrial Genome Sequence of a Hominin from Sima de los Huesos."

istence of Adam and Eve? We have already argued that the human family tree extends beyond just modern *Homo sapiens*. We have long-extinct cousins now known only from the fossil record. Consequently, creationists can affirm that mitochondrial Eve, Y chromosome Adam, and most ancestral population size estimates might tell us about the emergence of *modern* humans but not the emergence of *all* humans.

This brings up a very important question: can we be sure that Neandertals and other *Homo* species are really descended from Adam and Eve? We argued previously that young-age creationists mostly agree that Neandertals and *Homo erectus* are humans too, but what exactly does that agreement mean? Could the consensus be wrong? The statistical baraminology studies also do not conclusively prove that Neandertals and other *Homo* species are human.[37] How can we be sure that *Homo sapiens* is the only human species?

With these recent studies of Neandertal and Denisovan DNA, we have a new way to address this question. Specifically, we can appeal to the inference of hybridization between Neandertals and ancestors of modern Eurasian humans and between Denisovans and ancestors of modern Melanesians. If Denisovans and especially Neandertals were animals rather than human, then we would have to conclude that evidence of hybridization is evidence of bestiality. What would this mean for theology? Do half-human, half-animal offspring have a soul? Do they have the image of God? Are they responsible for their sin? Culturally, what would this mean for the offspring's cognitive functions? How could half-human, half-animal offspring find mates in order to pass their animal genes along to the human populations that now possess Neandertal and Denisovan genes? All of these thorny problems can be resolved completely by affirming the humanity of Neandertals and Denisovans. They are also descendants of Adam and Eve, and any "hybrid" children would also be fully human.[38]

If that is the case, if Neandertals and Denisovans are human, can we fit them into the much shorter chronology that creationists advocate? Could they have descended from Adam and Eve in a few generations? Remember that Neandertals and Denisovans are long extinct, and in the creationist chro-

---

37. We indicated in our previous chapter that creationists can use a technique called statistical baraminology to determine the groupings of the original created kinds, but we acknowledge that this method is not infallible and could be wrong.

38. Wood, "Who were Adam and Eve? Scientific reflections on Collins's *Did Adam and Eve Really Exist?*"

nology, probably died out very soon after the Flood. So only fifteen to twenty generations separate the Neandertals and Denisovans from their common ancestor. Is this possible?

We do not have a good answer to that question yet, but we can make some observations. Initial creationist studies using simple molecular clocks show that putting Neandertals and Denisovans in the human family tree is not easy. Recall that Neandertals and Denisovans differ from modern humans by hundreds of fixed differences in the mitochondrial DNA alone. Because of this difference, we cannot use conventional molecular clocks to fit them into a model of humanity arising from Adam and Eve over the last six thousand years.

What could this mean? One possibility is that the ancestors of Denisovans, Neandertals, and modern humans experienced much higher mutation rates. Another possibility is that the ancestors of just one of these populations experienced higher mutation rates. If humanity has experienced higher mutation rates in the past or on particular branches of the human family tree, this could mean that we humans really could have descended from Adam and Eve just as the Bible says; however, more work needs to be done by creationists to show this for sure.

For now, we can definitely emphasize that ancient population size estimates support a rapid population growth within less than one thousand generations. That would be less than twenty thousand years ago, which indicates that even under the conventional population genetics model, most of the genetic variation in the human population is very recent. Another important observation about estimating population size is that these are *estimates* only, and different methods estimate different population sizes. Since the estimates could prove to be wrong, it would be inappropriate to claim that they *completely* rule out a historical Adam and Eve, especially when so much of modern variability is so young.

We have explored possible young-age creationist interpretations, but what about old-earth or progressive creationism? Some progressive creationists also believe in Adam and Eve as the original progenitors of the human race.[39] Could progressive creationism better explain the genetic data?

Progressive creationists Hugh Ross and Fazale Rana insist that Adam and Eve were human and lived between 50,000–100,000 years ago. Consequently, they view Neandertals (and presumably Denisovans) as nonhumans. This perspective leaves them in the awkward position of having to explain the ap-

---

39. Rana and Ross, *Who Was Adam?*

pearance of both Neandertal and Denisovan genetic markers in modern humans. Since these genetic markers appear quite young (because of their size), the difficulty is not easily resolved without endorsing bestiality. Thus, while progressive creationism might better explain the gradual buildup of human genetic variability, it has its own unique problems.[40]

We set out in this chapter to evaluate claims that modern genetic studies of humans alone have ruled out the possibility that we all descended from a real Adam and Eve. Is human evolution the only possible explanation of human genetics? We cannot deny that the genetic evidence presents challenges, but we prefer to view them as opportunities. Over the past fifty years, creationist research has been surprisingly fruitful, and we have no reason to think it will not continue to provide unexpected insights into our study of Creation. As a result, we prefer to continue exploring genetic models of human history within the young-age creationist paradigm.

The Story Thus Far...

Creation

At this point, some readers might be wondering if we could put all of these ideas and evidences into a single story, some kind of framework or model for our understanding of Adam, Eve, and their descendants. To do so, we begin with our basic scriptural commitment and what we can logically deduce from it. Adam and Eve are the first humans, since Eve is the "mother of all living" (Gen 3:20). Consequently, all other humans, no matter what they looked like, have descended from them. Since we have no record of God creating other humans, we infer that humans descended from Adam and Eve by natural means, which we can now investigate through the science of developmental biology and genetics. As a result, we affirm the basic process of population genetics used to draw conclusions about our human ancestors is valid when applied to humans. We also note that any such conclusions drawn are tentative, since no science is infallible.

What can we say about Adam and Eve? As modern humans, we find it easy to imagine that Adam and Eve looked like us. In Sunday-school artwork, they are depicted as anatomically modern. Often, they are depicted as Cau-

---

40. Wood, "Who were Adam and Eve? Scientific reflections on Collins's *Did Adam and Eve Really Exist?*"

casians, and Adam has a short-cropped haircut. Such depictions and conceptions reflect more about us than they do about Adam and Eve. The truth is
that we know very little about what Adam and Eve would have looked like.
We creationists recognize that they were human like us, but their skin col-
or, hairstyle, and many other attributes are largely matters of conjecture. We
would be wise to put aside childish depictions and think more carefully about
Adam and Eve's appearance, especially in light of the hominin fossil record.

Whatever they looked like, they had a long lifespan (Gen 5:5) in which
to have "sons and daughters" (Gen 5:4). Today, we know that mating between
close relatives is bad. Such pairing leads to offspring that have undesirable and
even harmful traits. This phenomenon is called "inbreeding depression."[41] Since
Adam and Eve's children were the only people around, is it possible that they
could have married each other and produced healthy offspring? We think this is
easily resolved since inbreeding depression results from the presence of harmful mutations in the human genome. Presumably at this early date, harmful
mutations had not yet occurred, and there would have been no bad results from
inbreeding. Furthermore, the cultural taboo against incest would also not have
existed. We therefore see no problem with marrying siblings at this point in human history, although later it was expressly forbidden (Lev 18:8–18).[42]

As the population of humans increased, so too did their sinfulness (Gen
6:5).[43] As a result, God destroyed the earth and all humans except for Noah,
his three sons, and their wives. From these eight then the earth was re-
populated. In the context of genetics, these eight would be our most recent
common ancestors, not Adam and Eve. We can therefore conclusively reject
identifying the current mitochondrial "Eve" candidate with the biblical Eve.
At best, she might have been Noah's wife or one of his daughters-in-law.[44]

---

41. Charlesworth and Charlesworth, "Inbreeding Depression and Its Evolutionary
    Consequences."
42. We note here that identifying Cain's wife as his sister is a very old tradition in the church.
    See John Chrysostom, *Homilies on Genesis* XX, 3; Augustine, *City of God* 15.16.
43. We recognize that interbreeding with the "sons of God" might also have biological conse-
    quences, but the Bible and church tradition give us little guidance in understanding this
    difficult passage. Since we cannot do much beyond speculating, we here acknowledge
    without comment this episode in human history. See Newman, "The Ancient Exegesis of
    Genesis 6:2, 4."
44. Mitochondrial Eve as identified as one of Noah's daughters-in-law would ultimately be re-
    lated to Eve. However, since there is randomness in the inheritance of mitochondria, each
    daughter-in-law of Noah could have different mitochondrial DNA and therefore not pre-
    cisely reflect Eve's mitochondrial DNA. See Wood, "Four Women, a Boat, and Lots of Kids."

Because we know how Y-chromosomes are inherited, we can say for certain that Y-chromosome "Adam" was Noah.[45]

After the Flood

The period between the Flood and Babel was a time of great upheaval. We infer this from other fields of creationist research, especially geology.[46] Biologically, creationists think that created kinds underwent a process of diversification at this time.[47] This diversification rapidly generated new species and very quickly ceased.[48] In the chronology of Genesis 11, we place this period of upheaval during the first three centuries after the Flood.[49] Combining the geological and biological upheaval, we find an explanation for what appear to be fossils documenting the evolution of some mammal groups, like horses.[50] These fossils document the rapid diversification within created kinds, and the geological upheaval immediately after the Flood gives opportunity for these transient species to be preserved as fossils.

In this context of geological and biological upheaval, we place extinct humans known only from the fossil record. The earliest humans in the fossil record (*Homo erectus*) appear almost simultaneously in Asia, Africa, and the Indonesian island of Java, but the Bible records no intentional global dispersal of humans after the Flood and prior to the tower of Babel (Gen 11:8). We therefore infer that all fossils of true humans must have been deposited after the tower of Babel.

Where do other forms of humans come from? Presumably, humans were also undergoing a process of diversification like all created kinds. Perhaps we do not observe quite the same variety of humans because humans remained in a single population at Babel for so long. The dispersal of organisms, especially land animals, across the globe after the Flood provided many opportunities for isolated populations to develop interesting new traits. With no such dispersal in the human family, any newly developed traits would be part of the entire population at Babel and would not be isolated from other populations of humans.

---

45. We are not saying that Noah is not related to Adam here. Since Noah represents a single human from the lineage of Adam, our estimates lead back to Noah but are not good enough to go back further in time.
46. Wise, *Faith, Form, and Time*, 179–225.
47. It is possible that similar biological diversification within created kinds occurred before the Flood, but we cannot say for certain.
48. Wood and Murray, *Understanding the Pattern of Life*, 169–85.
49. Wood, "The AGEing Process: Rapid Post-Flood Intrabaraminic Diversification Caused by Altruistic Genetic Elements (AGEs)," 5–9.
50. Cavanaugh, et al., "Fossil Equids: A Monobaraminic, Stratomorphic Series."

Nevertheless, the varieties of humans found at Dmanisi fit remarkably well with the scenario described here. If we are correct about the tower of Babel and the diversification and dispersal of humans, then we would expect to find the most diverse populations of humans at locations nearest Babel. Based on conventional dating, Dmanisi is one of the earliest locations of human fossils known, and the fossils found there are more diverse than fossils found at any other single location. Of all the earliest fossil sites that preserve ancient humans, Dmanisi is the closest to the Middle East site of the tower of Babel.

What could explain the preservation of animals like *Australopithecus* just before humans appear in the fossil record? This pattern appears to be explained by the evolution of humans from *Australopithecus*. Once again, the young-age-creationist answer appears to be the tower of Babel. Since the animals began dispersing around the world prior to Babel, we should expect to find animal fossils prior to human fossils, which is exactly what we find.[51]

How could humans and animals diversify? No one can say for certain, but we conclude (with other young-age creationists) that diversification must have been caused by some kind of genetic changes in the genomes of created kinds.[52] Recent studies of mitochondrial DNA indicate that these changes included individual base changes in the DNA sequence.[53] In other words, the period of diversification was also a period of increased mutation rate.

Because Neandertals and Denisovans differ significantly from modern humans, we argued that they cannot easily fit into a creationist chronology without assuming that there was an increased mutation rate at a time in human history before Neandertals and *Homo sapiens*.[54] Now we can see that an increased mutation rate fits right in with our larger understanding of the biological upheaval after the Flood, which includes rapid, mutational changes in animals. Consequently, we should be surprised if Neandertals and Denisovans were *not* substantially different from modern *Homo sapiens*.

Is there any biblical evidence for this period of rapid biological change? We think that the rapid drop in lifespan seen in the patriarchs of Genesis 11:10–25 is a consequence of this rapid change. Some creationists have speculated that

---

51. Wise, "Lucy Was Buried First."
52. Wood, "A Review of the Last Decade of Creation Biology Research on Natural History, 2003–2012."
53. Wood, "Mitochondrial DNA Analysis of Three Terrestrial Mammal Baramins (Equidae, Felidae, and Canidae) Implies an Accelerated Mutation Rate near the Time of the Flood."
54. Wood, "Ancient mtDNA Implies a Nonconstant Molecular Clock in the Human Holobaramin."

environmental changes account for the decreased lifespan, but this is extremely unlikely. To change a lifespan by a factor of ten requires a genetic change,[55]
which is consistent with our model of rapid genetic change after the Flood.

Modern Humanity

The dispersal from Babel also offers an explanation for cultural differences
between *Homo sapiens* and other extinct human groups. In our previous
chapter, we noted that evidence of advanced culture is scant in humans other
than *Homo sapiens*. Neandertals and *Homo erectus* are known to have used
stone tools[56] but otherwise were very technologically limited. Neandertals left
evidence of intentional burial.[57] Interpreted outside the context of biblical history, we might interpret these patterns as gradual evolution of humanity from
nonhuman or subhuman ancestors.

Within biblical history, we might wonder why these early people groups are
not more technologically advanced. After all, the post-Flood human culture is
capable of building cities and towers (Gen 11:4–5), which is no small technological feat. We admit that the Babel culture was technologically advanced, but
God's shattering of that culture by confusing their language (Gen 11:7–9) surely
had other important cultural consequences. We might expect that some of the
new language groups lacked individuals with certain technological skills. Perhaps then, we can understand the "primitive" *Homo erectus* or Neandertals as
groups that merely had few if any individuals with advanced technological skills.

At some point, one family of humans that possessed the genetic and anatomical traits of modern *Homo sapiens* began to disperse and dominate other
humans. Could this group have come from African humans, which conventional anthropologists believe? While that is a possibility, it is also possible
that the earliest branches of the *Homo sapiens* family migrated to southern
Africa and stayed there, even though they originated somewhere else. In either case, the pattern of global *Homo sapiens* dispersal inferred from genetic
data[58] is consistent with what we would expect if *Homo sapiens* dispersed

---

55. Wieland, "Decreased Lifespans: Have We Been Looking in the Right Place?"
56. At least one group of Neandertals is also known to have used bone tools. See Soressi, et al.,
    "Neandertals Made the First Specialized Bone Tools in Europe."
57. The recently reported *Homo naledi* is also believed to have buried its dead. See Dirks,
    et al., "Geological and Taphonomic Context for the New Hominin Species *Homo naledi*
    from the Dinaledi Chamber, South Africa."
58. van Oven and Kayser, "Updated Comprehensive Phylogenetic Tree of Global Human Mi-
    tochondrial DNA Variation."

from the Middle East. The earliest branches of the human family tree migrated to Africa, Europe, and Asia, followed by migration to Australia, North and South America, and across the Pacific islands.

Wherever they came from, *Homo sapiens* were far more successful in technology, dispersal, and reproduction than any of other humans alive at the time. Based on the evidence of hybridization among Neandertals and Denisovans, we can see that these other groups were not simply driven to extinction by the migration of *Homo sapiens*. Instead, the other human groups were absorbed by tribes of *Homo sapiens* entering their territory. Genes of those extinct humans still exist in modern humans today, and some ancient humans appear to have provided *Homo sapiens* with beneficial genetic traits.[59]

In regard to the extinction of ancient humans like Neandertals, we also note the interesting Old Testament references to "giants" (e.g., Deut 2:20–21, 3:11). Whatever these giants were, they were evidently different enough from other people to warrant special mention. These might represent other, yet unknown forms of humans now extinct or early hybrids between *Homo sapiens* and other, extinct humans. The persistence of these forms of human through the time of the Exodus implies that the elimination of human forms that were distinct from *Homo sapiens* was not a sudden but a gradual replacement.

CONCLUSION

Considered superficially and in isolation from the young-age-creationist model of history, the genetic evidence against Adam and Eve might seem conclusive. Indeed, the current debate over the historical Adam was inspired at least in part by genetic studies that supposedly support the evolution of humans from animal ancestors. However, we believe that the young-age-creationist model of human history taken as a whole provides a satisfying framework for understanding the genetic evidence. There is undoubtedly much work left to do on the young-age-creationist model, but we can certainly say, as we concluded in our previous chapter, that evolution is not the only possible way of reading genetic evidence.

---

59. Ding, et al., "Neanderthal Introgression at Chromosome 3p21.31 Was Under Positive Natural Selection in East Asians."

Bibliography

Anchez-Quinto, Federico, L. R. Botigué, S. Civit, C. Arenas, M. C. Ávila-Arcos, C. D. Bustamante, D. Comas, and C. Lalueza-Fox. "North African Populations Carry the Signature of Admixture with Neandertals." *PLoS ONE* 7 (2012): e47765.

Anderson, S., et al. "Sequence and organization of the human mitochondrial genome." *Nature* 290 (1981): 457–65.

Briggs, Adrian W., et al. "Targeted Retrieval and Analysis of Five Neandertal mtDNA Genomes." *Science* 325 (2009): 318–21.

Cann, Rebecca L., Mark Stoneking, and Allan C. Wilson. "Mitochondrial DNA and Human Evolution." *Nature* 325 (1987): 31–36.

Cavanaugh, David P., T. C. Wood , and K. P. Wise. "Fossil Equids: A Monobaraminic, Stratomorphic Series." In *Proceedings of the Fifth International Conference on Creationism*, edited by Robert Ivey, 143–53. Pittsburgh, PA: Creation Science Fellowship, 2003.

Charlesworth, D. and B. Charlesworth. "Inbreeding Depression and ITS Evolutionary Consequences." *Annual Review of Ecology and Systematics* 18 (1987): 237–68.

Collins, C. John. *Did Adam and Eve Really Exist?* Wheaton, IL: Crossway, 2011.

Ding, Qiliang, et al. "Neanderthal Introgression at Chromosome 3p21.31 Was Under Positive Natural Selection in East Asians." *Molecular Biology and Evolution* (2013), doi:10.1093/molbev/mst260 (accessed February 16, 2014).

Dirks, Paul, et al. "Geological and Taphonomic Context for the New Hominin Species *Homo naledi* from the Dinaledi Chamber, South Africa." *eLife* 4 (2015): e09561

Enns, Peter. *The Evolution of Adam*. Grand Rapids: Baker, 2012.

Gattepaille, L. M., M. Jakobsson, and M. G. B. Blum. "Inferring Population Size Changes with Sequence and SNP Data: Lessons from Human Bottlenecks," 110 (2013): 409–19.

Green, Richard E., et al. "A Complete Neandertal Mitochondrial Genome Sequence Determined by High-Throughput Sequencing." *Cell* 134 (2008): 416–26.

_____, et al. "A Draft Sequence of the Neandertal Genome." *Science* 328 (2010): 710–22.

Gronau, Ilan, M. J. Hubisz, B. Gulko, C. G. Danko, and A. Siepel "Bayesian Inference of Ancient Human Demography from Individual Genome Sequences." *Nature Genetics* 43 (2011): 1031–35.

Hammer, Michael F. "A recent common ancestry for human Y chromosomes." *Nature* (1995): 376–78.

Hedrick, Philip W. *Genetics of Populations.* Sudbury, MA: Jones and Bartlett, 2005.

Hein, Jotun, Mikkel H. Schierup, and Carsten Wiuf, *Gene Genealogies, Variation and Evolution.* Oxford: Oxford University Press, 2005.

Ingman, Max, et al. "Mitochondrial genome variation and the origin of modern humans." *Nature* 408 (2000): 708–13.

International Human Genome Sequencing Consortium. "Initial Sequencing and Analysis of the Human Genome." *Nature* 409 (2001): 860–921.

Krause, Johannes, et al. "The Complete Mitochondrial DNA Genome of an Unknown Hominin from Southern Siberia." *Nature* 464 (2010): 894–97.

Krings, Matthias, et al. "DNA Sequence of the Mitochondrial Hypervariable Region II from the Neandertal Type Specimen." *Proceedings of the National Academy of Sciences USA* 96 (1999): 5581–85.

Lamoureux, Denis O. "No Historical Adam: Evolutionary Creation View." In *Four Views on the Historical Adam*, edited by Matthew Barrett and Ardel B. Caneday, 37–65. Grand Rapids: Zondervan, 2013.

Li, Heng, and Richard Durbin. "Inference of Human Population History from Individual Whole-Genome Sequences." *Nature* 475 (2011): 493–96.

Meyer, Matthias, et al. "A Mitochondrial Genome Sequence of a Hominin from Sima de los Huesos." *Nature* 505 (2014): 403–06.

Newman, Robert C. "The Ancient Exegesis of Genesis 6:2, 4." *Grace Theological Journal* 5 (1984): 13–36.

Pakendorf, Brigitte, and Mark Stoneking. "Mitochondrial DNA and Human Evolution." *Annual Review of Genomics and Human Genetics* 6 (2005): 165–83.

Park, Leeyoung. "Linkage Disequilibrium Decay and Past Population History in the Human Genome." *PLoS ONE* 7 (2012): e46603.

Prüfer, Kay, et al. "The Complete Genome Sequence of a Neanderthal from the Altai Mountains." *Nature* 505 (2014): 43–49.

Rana, Fazale, and Hugh Ross, *Who Was Adam?* Colorado Springs: NavPress, 2005.

Reich, David, et al. "Genetic History of an Archaic Hominin Group from Denisova Cave in Siberia." *Nature* 468 (2010): 1053–60.

Sankararaman, Sriram, et al. "The Date of Interbreeding between Neandertals and Modern Humans." *PLoS Genetics* 8 (2012): e1002947.

Soressi, Marie, et al. "Neandertals Made the First Specialized Bone Tools in Europe." *Proceedings of the National Academy of Sciences USA* 110 (2013): 14186–90.

Stoneking, Mark. "Mitochondrial DNA and Human Evolution." *Journal of Bioenergetics and Biomembranes* 26 (1994): 241–49.

Stringer, Chris, and Peter Andrews. *The Complete World of Human Evolution*. London: Thames & Hudson, 2012.

Tenesa, Albert, et al. "Recent Human Effective Population Size Estimated from Linkage Disequilibrium." *Genome Research* 17 (2007): 520–26.

van Oven, Mannis, and Manfred Kayser. "Updated Comprehensive Phylogenetic Tree of Global Human Mitochondrial DNA Variation." *Human Mutation* 29 (2008): E386-E394.

Venema, Dennis R. "Genesis and the Genome: Genomics Evidence for Human-Ape Common Ancestry and Ancestral Hominid Population Sizes." *Perspectives on Science and the Christian Faith* 62 (2010): 166–78.

Voet, Donald, and Judith G. Voet. *Biochemistry*. Hoboken, NJ: John Wiley, 2004.

Wieland, Carl. "Decreased Lifespans: Have We Been Looking in the Right Place?" *Creation Ex Nihilo Technical Journal* 8 (1994): 138–41.

Wise, Kurt P. *Faith, Form, and Time*. Nashville: Broadman & Holman, 2002.

_____. "Lucy Was Buried First." *Answers*, July-September, 2008, 66–68.

Wood, Todd Charles. "A Review of the Last Decade of Creation Biology Research on Natural History, 2003–2012." In *Proceedings of the Seventh International Conference on Creationism*, edited by Mark Horstemeyer. Pittsburgh, PA: Creation Science Fellowship, 2013.

_____. "Ancient mtDNA Implies a Nonconstant Molecular Clock in the Human Holobaramin." *Journal of Creation Theology and Science Series B: Life Sciences* 2 (2012): 18–26.

_____. "Four Women, a Boat, and Lots of Kids." *Answers*, July-September, 2008, 70–74.

_____. "Mitochondrial DNA Analysis of Three Terrestrial Mammal Baramins (Equidae, Felidae, and Canidae) Implies an Accelerated Mutation Rate near the Time of the Flood." In *Proceedings of the Seventh International Conference on Creationism*, edited by Mark Horstemeyer. Pittsburgh, PA: Creation Science Fellowship, 2013.

_____. "The AGEing Process: Rapid Post-Flood Intrabaraminic Diversification Caused by Altruistic Genetic Elements (AGEs)." *Origins* 54 (2002): 5–34.

_____. "Who were Adam and Eve? Scientific reflections on Collins's *Did Adam and Eve Really Exist?*" *Journal of Creation Theology and Science Series B: Life Sciences* 2 (2012): 28–32.

Wood, Todd Charles and Megan J. Murray. *Understanding the Pattern of Life*. Nashville: Broadman & Holman, 2003.

CHAPTER 4

GENESIS 3—A MAP OF MISREADINGS

Grant Horner

So saying, her rash hand in evil hour
Forth reaching to the Fruit, she pluck'd, she eat:
Earth felt the wound, and Nature from her seat
Sighing through all her Works gave signs of woe,
That all was lost....

Paradise Lost, Book 9, John Milton, 1667

THE TURNING AWAY

We do not meditate nearly enough on what it means that Paradise has indeed been lost. The first three chapters of Genesis are the most important and momentous words ever written. Everything else one believes about the Bible and Christian theology and practice depends ultimately on this brief, dense, rich packet of profound language. It strikes at the core of everything that matters. If we have a natural tendency to misread the beginning of Genesis, and I will argue that we do, then we are faced with a serious problem, in fact the double problem of misreading our own origins *and* misreading our misreading. Errors are most serious when we are unaware of our entanglement.

These opening chapters of Genesis present, in simplest terms, two things: the Creation of everything out of nothing, and the turning away. God made everything out of nothing. It was seen and said to be good. Then—the highest and greatest and most perfect thing He made—Man bearing His incomparably lovely image—chose, instead of facing God at all times, *the turning away*. Imagine being rejected by your mirror.

No other text tells readers so clearly how they came to be in the desperate condition they are in. No other text tells you so clearly why you tend not to read that text rightly. How in the world did Adam and Eve's cosmos turn into our chaos? The way that story is told—and how we believe it to be told—is as important as the fact of its telling. I believe that the way many humans misread Genesis is simply a continuation of *the turning away*.

I am not, nor could I pretend to be, a trained theologian. I am a literary and cultural theorist. I work with stories, ideas, and images: literature, philosophy, art, and film. I teach students to think theologically and biblically about the culture in which they find themselves as believers. Like most people, then, I am no professional "expert" in the Bible or theology. I often have far more questions than answers, I still work hard to understand many parts of the Bible, and I struggle with temptations of all kinds. I have wonderful friends who patiently answer my questions about the Bible, advise me when I need counsel, and correct me when I am in the wrong. I am pretty sure I am just a normal Christian, wishing I were much better than I am, and hoping only in God's promise of grace.

All I bring to a reading of the early chapters of Genesis is a deep reverence for the Scripture and a soul sensitized to how texts work on people. This comes from much reading of both the Bible as well as mere human literature. I am very interested in how reading "works" on humans. I was converted while completely alone and reading the Bible—the Gospel of John to be particular. My Word-based conversion has guided my entire subsequent life and has left me convinced of the Bible's supernatural origins, nature, and effects. Over three decades of reading Scripture and comparing it to human thought and wisdom has convinced me of the absolute uniqueness and miraculous power of the Scriptures in the lives of those who place their trust in their beautiful message.

What you will *not* find in this essay, nestled among a number of other chapters written by my colleagues, is a technical, linguistic, scientific, or professional-theological reading of "what happened in the Garden." Instead, I propose to think through the story-logic of the Temptation and Fall in terms of its results in the lives of those who read the story. *Genesis 3 is the story that tells you how you came to be so unable to read the story being told.*

Here is why: The last thing that we fallen humans really want to understand is our true nature; our desperate condition; and how we are, without the work of the Holy Spirit, utterly unable to rightly understand the narrative of our Fall. We are, as Martin Luther observed, *incurvatus in se*—"curved into ourselves." This curvature functions as a deep blindness about our own human architecture. If you have ever wondered why there are so many varying —and opposed—interpretations of Genesis 3, I would like to suggest to you that Genesis 3 is not the problem.

It is the explanation.

Story, Plot, Sense: A Literary Perspective on Genesis 3

Our Reading within the Narrative

I have had the unusual experience of spending many years studying and thinking about how texts work, how stories are told, and how these artifacts affect our minds. For many years I have taught courses on the history of varying conceptions of the interpretive processes; we read and talk through thinkers from Plato to Kant, from Aristotle to Nietzsche, and from Longinus to the Romantics of the eighteenth and nineteenth centuries. We study formalism and deconstruction, linguistic theories and aesthetics, conceptions about genre, and even theories about theories. There are almost as many theories of how to read as there are texts to read. Everyone has a different view on what interpretation is and how it works. Disagreements in this academic field are fierce and hard-fought; in fact, one could say that the more obscure the intellectual point, the fiercer the fighting. Yet, all who write about interpretation desire and expect readers to take their own words seriously, work through the language, and come to a conclusion about what the author meant. Even those arguing vociferously for an absolute indeterminacy of language *always make that argument in a form that makes some sort of sense.* Everyone expects their readers to be uncurved, as it were.

Philosophical discourse may be difficult to grasp due to its abstract nature, but most of us can read a story and understand the flow of the narrative. While it may indeed be difficult to grasp the deeper literary "meaning" of something like *Moby Dick* or *Hamlet*, it is not uncommon to be able to follow the plot, and recognize it as fiction that imitates life.

The story told in Genesis 3 is incredibly simple. It reads almost with a fairy tale's simplicity, though it would be wrong to read it as such. (Not to mention, it would be the saddest fairy tale of them all.) Genesis 3 reads much like Genesis 1 and 2, as well as the rest of Genesis—and Exodus for that matter. *It tells a story*: This happened first; then that happened; then these other things happened. Things happen *in order*; they are *related*; together, they all have an *aggregate meaning*. But most importantly, these stories are narratives—a series of events involving people. And stories have the fascinating property of teaching you how to read them.

The first time someone reads a play by Shakespeare, a novel by Tolstoy, or a poem by Coleridge, there is always a level of blindness to much of what is going on. Repeated readings of individual works or particular authors train the mind to perceive more fully, more richly, what is brought forth by the text. If you read thirty-six of Shakespeare's plays, and have read most of them several times, you will be a competent reader of the Bard. If you then come for the first time to your thirty-seventh play, let us say the fairly obscure but utterly marvelous late romance called *The Winter's Tale* (1611), you will be able to quickly read, enjoy, and understand that play better than another first-time reader, even a more intelligent or better-educated one, who has never read any Shakespeare. Experience builds competency, because you learn the rules.

Have you ever read a certain book more than once? twice? ten times? Is it not amazing how wonderful a powerful text can be, not in spite of but because of its familiarity? Complex chains of references, systems of ideas, and webs of images slowly combine over time through multiple readings to enrich the reader's experience and interpretive acumen. In a certain sense you never read the same novel twice because each reading is informed by the earlier ones, which serve to help the present reading and strengthen your understanding and appreciation. Additionally, we bring a store of new life experiences to later readings and this can have a significant impact on later interpretations, even of the Bible.[1] Over time we begin to grasp how a text,

---

1. Augustine produced several commentaries on Genesis during his lifetime—a total of five if we include his writings on Moses in the last three books of *Confessions* and books 11–14 in *City of God*. His earliest commentary was deeply and purely allegorical: *On Genesis against the Manichees*. This early work is often cited by Christians who do not hold to the literal-historical hermeneutic of Genesis, as "proof" that the greatest teacher of the early church did not hold to the "conservative" view but rather the "liberal" one—as if that should settle the issue. But the issue is far from settled for those who value Augus-

how all texts, *work*, and how they work on us. This is incredibly theologically significant, because the Lord reveals Himself in the written Scriptures, and by His Living Word, Jesus of Nazareth.

Every text teaches us how to read the text at hand. No one reads *The Lord of the Rings* and then tries to book a flight to Middle Earth; it is understood to be fiction. Conversely, when we read a narrative about a historical event, one replete with dates, names, locations, causes, aftereffects, and eyewitness sources—all the markers of history writing—we understand that the events actually happened, though all historians will naturally have some errors and some biases in their accounts and interpretations. When looking at any kind of text at all, allegories, imaginative fictions, and symbolic or figurative elements are usually more or less obvious. This is not to say that historical narratives never have allegorical or symbolic significance, but rather that the history in a narrative is not therefore necessarily suspect. One could present in a sermon the political tactic of Hitler-appeasement by many nations of Europe as a metaphoric picture, showing us what happens when we do not deal strongly with our own sin. However, that does not mean the preacher is saying that the history itself is a fiction.

Similarly, Genesis (and many other parts of Scripture) may indeed have elements that are symbolic, allegorical, and figurative. The Apostle Paul recognizes allegory in Old Testament narrative, but argues from literality far more often. In Galatians 4:21–31 he clearly states that the Old Testament story can be read with a layered meaning (historical narrative X points to current spiritual truth Y), but there are two important distinctions to make in Paul's use of the concept of allegory. First, Paul does not say that his understanding of a symbolic/allegoric level in Galatians 4 negates the historical truth of the events recorded in Genesis. In fact,

---

tine's opinion, the present author included. For this was only Augustine's first writing on Genesis. As he matured he wrote several more works commenting on it extensively. The last one presents a very different opinion; in fact, it is an *explicit retraction of his youthful views.* Here Augustine insists on the literal historicity of Genesis while also claiming that there are spiritual and even allegorical truths that can be gleaned from the true history as recorded by Moses. In other words, years of studying Scripture changed his earlier opinion (that Genesis was allegorical) to his final view (that it was first and foremost literal history). See *De genesi ad litteram* (401–15), available in translation as *The Literal Meaning of Genesis*, Vol. 1; Ancient Christian Writers, vol. 41, translated and annotated by John Hammond Taylor, S.J. (New York: Paulist Press, 1982). Augustine's example is telling, as is how some scholars cite him: Critics of the literal reading often cite his early commentary in their defense—the later work is, unsurprisingly, not mentioned.

his use of allegory seems to depend on the historicity of the people and plot points. [2] Second, in other Scriptures where a parallel structure (the core mechanism of symbolism and allegory) is part of his argument, such as Romans 5:12–21, he does not use the word "allegory" at all, though it would seem to fit even better here than in Galatians.[3] Nor does he call Adam a symbol. Symbolism is a single parallel structure; allegory is a tight and extended structure of correspondences.[4] The Adam of Paradise and the Second Adam of the Gospels and Paul's theology form a clean, natural, simple parallel. Paul does not suggest, either directly or indirectly, that the first Adam was not a real individual who lived in the Garden, who really disobeyed God, and who really fell into depravity. His entire point about the Second Adam entering history to obey the Father and save mankind is built upon the historical life and literal Fall of the first one (1 Cor 15:45, 47–49).[5]

That being said, a text does not simply become allegory just because some readers call it that. As other writers in this volume attest, there is abundant reason to read the opening chapters of Genesis literally and historically, though I believe that no amount of evidence will convince someone predetermined to consider this as unsophisticated.

To be direct: Do we think God is trying to deceive us with his text about the Garden of Eden? Is he "hiding" a "deeper meaning" behind the appearance of a simple story? Is God stashing an allegory behind what would appear

---

2. For example, Paul tells the Galatians, who are highly susceptible to legalistic bondage, that they are free because they were not born/reborn into slavery but freedom, just like Isaac: "Now you, brothers, like Isaac, are children of promise." In verse 28 his entire point is that the current Galatians (who are real people with real freedom in Christ) are "like" Isaac (a real person with real freedom compared to Ishmael). Isaac is the child of promise. If his life and freedom were not historically real, then neither is theirs.

3. It is important to note that Adam being referred to as a "type" (prefiguring element) pointing forward to the promised Messiah (cf. Gen 3:15), the Second Adam, does not imply that Adam was not historically real as an individual. Again, the stronger reading is that the historical Christ is a full reiteration of the original perfect man, and that the first man's historicity, in his life and his fall, are the necessary prerequisites of the entire gospel.

4. A pair of examples may clarify this: A "black sheep" may stand symbolically for an individual who shames his family; Bunyan's *Pilgrim's Progress* (1678) is a long narrative with numerous symbolic parallels that imitate a life of spiritual struggles. The symbols form an overarching structure of correspondences that help us recognize Bunyan's "fiction" as a viable picture of reality.

5. There is nothing here like a claim that this clear parallel is an allegory which reduces Adam to a non-real symbolic phantasm; the first Adam is as real as the second, and Adam's death is as historically real and grievous as Christ's resurrection is real and glorious.

even to a child to be a straightforward historical narrative? Is not this very much what Satan says to Eve—suggesting an alternative meaning to a situation, a piece of fruit, and to God's clear language, as opposed to the one most simple, most likely, and most plain?

Our Reading in Light of the Greater Narrative

The Greek philosopher Aristotle famously defined "plot" as a narrative series of events with a beginning, a middle, and an end.[6] A story is an organically linked, causal chain of entailment—this happens, which leads to that event, and then this other thing results. All these eventually lead to yet another thing, a final thing. Even the most mind-bending, plot-twisting novels and movies always have an internal logic that is coherent, stable, and which can be followed. A story that makes no sense at all is nonsense. At the end of *Macbeth*, Shakespeare's lead character comes to see life as meaningless. He says, "It is a tale / Told by an idiot, full of sound and fury / Signifying nothing" (Act 5, Scene 5, lines 26–28). These memorable lines speak to my point: Everyone knows that a tale that makes no sense—has no ordered chain of connected moments—is meaningless. It signifies nothing, like a tale of gibberish sputtered forth by a person of extremely limited intellect, someone Macbeth calls "an idiot."

The story of how God works in the universe is also a narrative, one that follows certain rules, as all narratives do. The rules are not complex, but many readers of that story, not satisfied intellectually with its lovely simplicity, have always endeavored to "problematize," "complexify," or "demythologize" the story. These impressive sounding bits of academic jargon often boil down to simple unbelief in almost every case, an unwillingness to accept the story on its own terms. If the foundation of Christianity is the bodily resurrection of Jesus, understood as actual history, then why should we think of Paradise, Adam, the Temptation, and the Fall as symbolic-allegorical, ahistorical non-events? In any case other than a literal historical reading of the opening of Genesis, the cohesion of the gospel narrative simply collapses. You cannot consistently claim faith in a literal historical Jesus if you build that belief upon the sandy foundation of "problematizing" or "demythologizing" Genesis—a book Jesus quotes with great seriousness.[7] You can

---

6. Aristotle, *Poetics*, Book 7.
7. In addition to Christ himself, every single New Testament author quotes or alludes to

overemphasize the claims of science (to the detriment of God's truth), you can apply your trendy literary theories (to the denial of God's Word), and you can demythologize all you like (to the denigration of the miraculous gospel). But in the end it always comes down to a question of authority: Do you believe what you read in the text, or do you choose to explain it away by arguing that the text is not saying what it is clearly saying?

Now, I read for a living, and I study the history of varying conceptions of interpretation, from texts to visual art to film to philosophy. I will be the first to tell you that there are different kinds of texts and different kinds of stories, and there are many genres and many figures of speech. But narratives remain essentially consistent *within themselves*. They have to or they will not be read. No one in their right mind would read J. R. R. Tolkien's *Lord of the Rings* trilogy and claim that the first novel is fantasy fiction, the second book an accurate historical account of real life, and the third a collection of poetry about ethics blended with technical information about microbiology. You can say that if you like, but no one will take you seriously because you do not take the text seriously, following the text's own implicit rules. The text is consistent; it coheres; it makes sense. You may not *like* fantasy; personally, I am not much of a fan of the genre. But I cannot claim that Tolkien's masterpiece is really about racism in the National Hockey League, just because Gollum is too hard to believe in.

Reading narrative makes little sense unless you apply a reasonably charitable degree of common-sense understanding of language as you yourself use it every day. The history of much biblical interpretation has been the history of a drawn-out series of attempts to make the Scriptures say what they do not say. Some scholars will claim Christian faith in the resurrection, or the historicity of Jesus, or the reliability of the book of Acts; then they will turn around and deny the narrative clarity of the opening chapters of Genesis. This simply makes no sense, especially in light of

---

Genesis, totaling five dozen references. Matthew 22:15–22, Mark 12:13–17, and Luke 20:20–36 all refer back to the concept of the image of God being owned by God in Genesis 1:26–27. Jesus also quotes Genesis 1:27 and 2:24 to discuss the inviolability of marriage. In Matthew 11:23–24 Capernaum is compared to Sodom, which was judged by the Lord in Genesis 18–19. In Luke 17:26–29 Jesus warns that the end of days would be like the times of Noah in Genesis 6–8. In John 8:33–41 Jesus compares the Pharisees negatively with Abraham, and also compares his own eternal existence with Abraham in verse 58. It is hard to quote Genesis more seriously than in that last case!

the fact that these interpreters expect us to read *their* texts for what they clearly say about the Bible not saying clearly what it clearly says.

THE REAL PROBLEM

Our Curvedness and Curved Reading

So why then are there so many varying interpretations (and therefore misinterpretations) of Genesis 3? I would like to suggest to you again that the text of Genesis 3 is not the problem. *It is the explanation.*

What do I mean when I say that misinterpreting Genesis 3 is explained by Genesis 3? The answer is simple. The Fall so deeply affected Adam and Eve and all their descendants that we have not only lost our ability to know God—we have lost our ability *to know that we have lost our ability*. Our spiritual blindness, for which we traded away the perfect vision of Eden, leaves us so blind that we think we see. We are blind in a labyrinth that has no end.[8] So the position we must adopt when approaching Scripture (and this certainly includes the opening of Genesis) is a posture of abject humility. We do not instruct the text; it instructs us. We do not critique the text; it critiques us. And in a certain sense, we do not interpret the text; it interprets us. It tells us the truth about ourselves, without which we will remain in the state of postlapsarian (after the Fall) blindness-in-the-labyrinth.

My thesis is therefore simple: Our tendency to explain away, dehistoricize, and misread Genesis 3 is a direct result of the very thing the narrative describes in such absolutely clear terms—a literal, historical account of a Fall into spiritual blindness. We suffer from an inability to read our own story of how we fell into our habit of misreading what God says so clearly. Our history of many misreadings shows that the text is exactly what it appears to be to any simple-hearted reader—history, a sort of genealogy of how we became misreaders of our very origins. The irony is palpable—if you are willing to see it.

Martin Luther, the great sixteenth-century reformer, had a phrase he often used about the depth of our fallenness, which is particularly evocative for

---

8. John Calvin makes extensive use of this metaphor to great effect. His often-used Latin phrase *in se descendere* points to a view of the self that perfectly encapsulates our miserable position: we descend into ourselves in order to "find ourselves" or "find God" or "find meaning / peace / satisfaction." But our utter depravity entraps us in our own minds and we became the labyrinth of ourselves, unable to escape.

the present argument: Man is *incurvatus in se*—curved inward into himself. We are unable to look accurately beyond ourselves, to really see either God or His world. All we see is ourselves; our view is selfish in every sense.

Furthermore, that inward view of ourselves is distorted, as our perverse fallen minds create a self-image that is irreducibly inaccurate (Jer 17:9).[9] An arresting image that may clarify this admittedly abstract notion is a hollow mirrored ball—with the mirrored surface on the inside. No light can get in; nothing is reflected but the mirror, and there is nothing to be seen; all is darkness and vacuity, a reflection of a reflection in the dark. That is what we are like after the Fall. Only God can provide the light necessary to truly see ourselves, the glorious world, and His perfect beauty.

Multiple misreadings of Genesis 3 will thus be the most natural thing in the world, *if the story is true*. Especially if it tells us exactly who and what we now are. We do not much like that story. The details are not very flattering. Willingness to accept that story on its own terms (which is always the first step towards a correct reading)—agreeing that it says what it says and that what it says is absolutely true—is to deny our own condition as good, right, and unbroken. We are not good after the Fall in Genesis 3, nor are we right; we are dashed to pieces, shattered like a mirrored ball that has fallen among sharp rocks from a great height.

The Tree: An Example of Curvedness

Christians and nonbelievers alike talk about "temptation" all the time. We see temptation in a piece of chocolate cake, a vacation or car we desire but cannot afford, a beautiful woman we are not married to, or the raging desire for retaliation when we have been wronged. Most of us quite naturally think of temptation in terms of something outside us coupled with a feeling of desire within us. The desired object (or action) is generally recognized as wrong, and we are torn between our knowledge of what is right and our desire for what we know is not. The New Testament has many passages on temptation; among the most familiar is this one: "Let no one say when he is tempted, 'I am being tempted by God,' for God cannot be tempted with evil, and he himself

---

9. Cf. John Calvin: "Again, it is certain that man never achieves a clear knowledge of himself unless he has first looked upon God's face, and then descends from contemplating him to scrutinizing himself. For we always seem to ourselves righteous and upright and wise and holy—this pride is innate in all of us—unless by clear proofs we stand convinced of our own unrighteousness, foulness, folly, and impurity.... For, because all of us are inclined by nature to hypocrisy, *a kind of empty image* of righteousness in place of righteousness itself abundantly satisfies us." *Institutes of the Christian Religion*, 1.2.2 (emphasis added).

tempts no one. But each person is tempted when he is lured and enticed by his own desire. Then desire when it has conceived gives birth to sin, and sin when it is fully grown brings forth death" (Jas 1:13–15).

The Temptation of First and Second Adam

The major problem we have is that we often improperly apply the James passage and many other New Testament passages to what happened in the Garden. The first thing we must recall is the distinction between Adam's original state (sinless perfection as the *imago dei*) and his fallen state (sinful imperfection overwriting and partly obscuring the *imago dei*). The nature of the Second Adam, Christ, is beyond the scope of this essay, but He was perfect in all His ways (Heb 4:15; 7:26; 9:14; 1 Pet 2:22; 1 John 3:5; 2 Cor 5:21; John 8:46), just like Adam was before the Fall. Jesus was indeed tempted in the wilderness (Matt 4:1–11; Mark 1:12–13; Luke 4:1–13). But His temptation was *temptation as a human*, as the Second Adam. He was entirely human but for one thing: He had no sinful nature as Adam and his descendants did and do have after the Fall. So He was tempted[10] like Adam. What does that mean? It means that His temptation did not arise from some interior predisposition to sin (Jesus had no such sinful core); it arose from an exterior object and/or force that was *trying to get inside and change His nature*. Satan suggesting the forbidden fruit is an analogue to Satan offering Jesus opportunities to use His Divine power for His own mere human benefit. But Jesus' divine powers were not provided for His human benefit—they were to glorify God by obedience unto death in procuring human salvation.

Thus we can say that for Adam, temptation was *singular* and *exterior*: One thing was forbidden; all else was permissible. For Jesus, who had no sinful nature, temptation was also exterior, and though it was in one sense singular—to obey the command of the Father: "My food is to do the will of him who sent me and to accomplish his work" (John 4:34)—it was also infinite. There were innumerable ways, conceivably at least, that He could have failed to obey the Father and accomplish His work. And this exteriorized temptation, so different from our own, was always trying to get inside Him to change His nature, just as

---

10. Matthew, Mark, and Luke, the synoptic Gospels, all mention Christ's temptation. The Gospel of John, which focuses on His divine nature, does not. His human nature as the Second Adam was tempted as the first Adam was; His divine nature was not.

Satan aimed to recreate man in *his* image. The chief fallen angel, of course, does not go after Adam directly; his initial target is Eve, and his temptation could not be more subtle. It has very little to do with the fruit, in fact. It is indirectly about the nature of God, and very indirectly about the nature of Eve. He has to make her doubt what God says, and make her feel that God is a liar who is jealous that she might gain something, which in turn *suggests that Eve lacks something good.* Simply put, Satan must convince Eve that she is not what she is (perfect and complete) in order to make her become what she is not (broken and empty). The irony is as heartbreaking as it is wickedly symmetrical.

Our Temptation

Now that all of Eve's children are symmetrically wicked, we need to understand what post-lapsarian temptation is and how its mechanism works. The first mistake we make—a mistake that is itself a result of the Fall—is that we do not understand the machinery of our own temptation. We are not entirely like either the first (at least before the Fall) or Second Adam. Neither had a sinful nature—an internal prompting towards disobedience. Adam's initial temptation was *singular* and *exterior*—the tree—and Christ's was *exterior* and *infinite* (Heb 4:15)—He had to keep the whole Law and he was tempted by Satan himself. His infinite power as the Lord presented Him with an infinite possibility of temptations as a man—imagine what He could have done if such power had turned to evil! But He never wavered and He obeyed impeccably.[11] He is utterly beautiful beyond comprehension; His mastery over all things can only leave us in awe.

Unlike Christ, though, here we stand. Our temptation is *internal* and *infinite*. There exists no thing that could not serve as a temptation to someone, somewhere. The human soul, now broken, depraved, and laden with vain graspings, can be tempted by anything and everything. And the temptation is internal, as James makes clear. The location of temptation is important to understand, as it is a rallying point both *against* external legalism and *for* internal holiness. Do not look at an evil world filled with evil things and say, "I'd better be careful! Temptation is out there, everywhere!" No, it is not. Temptation is now *inside you*, courtesy of an invitation made by Satan and accepted by humanity in the person of Adam. You have been invaded and conquered and are now ruled by a tyrant within, unless the true King redeems you from bondage.

---

11. I use this term deliberately, as it has a long theological history in the discussions of the temptation of Jesus.

Rethinking the Forbidden Tree

This brings us back to what happened in the Garden of Eden. Was there something in the fruit? Was God's aim simply to prevent Adam and Eve from gaining something from the fruit that was good that He did not want them to have? Was God actually jealous in that way? Or was He protecting them from something bad in the fruit itself? In other words, was it somehow "poisonous" and therefore warned against, or was the fruit good but forbidden out of jealousy?

If you look at what Satan suggests to Eve, you may notice that he subtly allows for both possibilities in his words. If the fruit is poisonous, that would be a good reason to forbid it—to protect Eve from something harmful. Eve is already wary of the fruit, and even adds to God's words by saying she is not even allowed to touch it. But why would God forbid something without a *reason*? Now this of course is not at all the case; God forbade the fruit, but not because it would kill them if they ate it. Everything God made was good.

Here is another disturbing question, one Christians rarely think about: Why was the tree placed in the middle of the garden if it was forbidden? Was God tempting Adam and Eve in any way at all? Could He not have put it out of reach, hidden it, built a fence? Why did He not, then? There must be some reason—a spiritual reason—that God would forbid something and then put it, not just within reach but within easy reach. Yet Scripture teaches clearly that God does not tempt, nor does He secretly want man to disobey. He requires absolute holiness and total obedience.

Let us think about this differently. Pre-lapsarian (before the Fall) man had no sinful nature, no predisposition towards disobedience. Perhaps the tree was *put in the middle* of the Garden *because it was forbidden.*

If we think about it this way, everything changes. We should not be tempted to think of the tree as a temptation from God. *God does not tempt.* Think about this: If *we* want to forbid something, we hide it away and make it hard to get to—liquor, guns, money, secret plans, or our daughters, perhaps. But if we put something out in a central, visible location, it is not necessarily because we are providing access *per se*; sometimes we put things in a central, visible location so its presence *reminds* us about something important. Think about street signs, stoplights, warnings, trophies, crosses on steeples, and baby pictures hanging on walls. These serve as reminders—they are signs pointing to something else, something important to be kept in mind. I believe the tree with the forbidden fruit was just such a reminder.

The forbidden tree is in some ways the analogue of another "tree"—the cross. Both are often misread signs. One looks promising but brings death; the other looks like failure but brings new life. The cross is not a magic trick that saves, any more than the tree had magic fruit that would in and of itself make you able to know the difference between good and evil. The cross was the sacrifice by which God satisfied His justice and made us right with Him, while maintaining His absolute standard of justice. Similarly, the forbidden tree was primarily a sign to remind Adam and Eve—even in their dominion over Paradise—to reject any idea of independence from God. Perfect lords over creation though they were, they were not lords over God. The tree was not only a sign, of course; it was a thing that, if partaken of disobediently, would bring death. But it was not designed to bring death like a guillotine, a gun, or a bomb; everything the Lord made *was* *good*. The tree was a good thing. It was not designed to kill. It was designed to keep the heart of man turned towards a Lord who was a greater Lord than man.

We should *not* think of the Garden like this: "Okay, Adam, you have rule over all this other stuff, from kumquats to armadillos, from the deep blue sea to lovely Eve, but you cannot eat the fruit because it has the power of knowledge which God is jealously withholding from you." Rather we should think of the Garden this way: "Adam, you have unimaginable freedom, *and* one centrally located and very simple reminder that your freedom operates under God's ultimate rule—you are lords but he is THE LORD." The tree had a positive function, not a negative one; it was not a mere prohibition but a reminder functioning as a prohibition. This shows God is not merely some jealous forbidder but a gracious Lord.

The problem is not that the narrative is unclear. The problem is our curvedness—which resulted from what the narrative describes so clearly.

The End of the Matter

Less than a quarter of the way through John Calvin's masterpiece *Institutio Religionis Christianae* (*The Institutes of the Christian Religion*, 1559), the Reformer steps outside of his long argument about the knowledge of God and the knowledge of man, and in the following astounding passage he summarizes the entire previous three hundred pages of biblical theology:

> The whole human race perished in the person of Adam. Consequently that original excellence and nobility which we

have recounted would be of no profit to us but would rather redound to our greater shame, until God, who does not recognize as his handiwork men defiled and corrupted by sin, appeared as Redeemer in the person of his only begotten son. The natural order was that the frame of the universe should be the school in which we were to learn piety.…But after man's rebellion, our eyes—wherever they turn—encounter God's curse. This curse…must overwhelm our souls with despair… we cannot by contemplating the universe infer that he is father. Rather, conscience presses us within and shows in our sin just cause for his disowning us. Dullness and ingratitude follow.…And as all our senses have become perverted, we wickedly defraud God of his glory. This magnificent theater of heaven and earth, crammed with innumerable miracles, Paul calls the "wisdom of God." But because we have profited so little by it, he calls us to faith of Christ, which, because it appears foolish, the unbelievers despise. Therefore, although the preaching of the cross does not agree with our human inclination, if we desire to return to God our Author and Maker…we ought nevertheless to embrace it humbly.[12]

Calvin rightly brings us back to the beginning—God as author and maker, and everything that entails, including the Fall in Genesis 3—and then bridges it forward to the cross. The gospel is not divided. *You simply cannot take the cross and the resurrection seriously if you do not take the Creation and Fall seriously.* The internal story-logic of redemption does not work that way. Christ's death as the second Adam reverses ours in the first Adam. The first Adam fell; the second was lifted up (John 12:32–33).

The end of the story is organically related to the beginning. Genesis tells us of *the turning away.* The Gospels tell us of God's turning away from Jesus on the cross—something unimaginable to our puny, self-incurved minds. The rest of the apostolic writings tell us of God turning His heart toward us, and His turning of our hearts back to Him.

We need to be turned back to Him because we have lost our ability to read the world He has made, including ourselves. The frame and architecture

---

12. Calvin, *Institutes of the Christian Religion,* 2.6.1.

of the universe, all of God's creation and everything in it, was designed to declare His glory and serve as tutors to show perfect humankind His ways. All of the objects, structures, systems, laws, and ideas in His world—which was an embodiment of His wisdom (1 Cor 1:21; Rom 1:19–20)—were created to prepare and equip us for immortality in the Garden, to keep us at once glorified and humble. All of this was to remind man in his perfect state that he was still under the Lord's absolute rule.

A crucial part of that system, the perfect original school of Christ, was the forbidden tree—a simple, central, visible reminder that man, perfect as he was, *was not God*. It was not a curse; it was a blessing. It was not a negative; it was a positive. It was a prohibition, yes—but much more than that, *it was an opportunity to obey*. And obedience to God is the most beautiful thing there is. And the simpler, the better.

So, Genesis 3 is a story. It is densely theological of course, but it is narrative theology and theological narrative. It tells us how we came to be so very stubborn regarding the story of our own origins as fallen readers who misread God, His world, and even His own shattered image in ourselves. It is a story, and stories themselves teach us how they are to be read. This story begins the entire journey to restore the fragments of Paradise lost.

How we read this story matters.

I'll be very direct: If you do not think the text of Genesis, including early Genesis, does the following things:

1. Tells a story,
2. Tells it simply and clearly,
3. Means, literally and historically, exactly what it says, and

Finally, while not denying the possibility of allegorical and typological readings in Genesis as they may be specified in later Scriptures, presents...

4. That Genesis 3 presents by and through divine inspiration an accurate, inerrant, straightforward literal/historical narrative of exactly what happened in the Garden of Eden, an interpretation which is the topmost, primary, and most immediately correct and relevant way to understand how God is speaking in Genesis 1–3,

Then why do you believe the gospel?

The gospel is a story. It has some surprising, even some rather hard-to-believe elements. It is the story of an unspeakably lovely world lost by one perfect man—but recovered by another perfect Man. Life was exchanged for death in Paradise by the first Adam. Death was exchanged for life by the second Adam in Bethlehem; in Nazareth; in Galilee; at the tomb of the fierce men possessed by demons; in the synagogue at Capernaum; at a well with a miserable outcast woman; at a dead little girl's bedside; at the tomb of four-days-dead Lazarus; in Jerusalem; in the Temple, which had become a den of thieves and hypocrites; in the Upper Room; in Gethsemane; before Pilate and the High Priest; along the *via dolorosa*; on that hill like a skull; and in the newly cut grave. And finally, in the presence of a pleased Father who accepted the sacrifice of an obedient Son. "Although he was a son, he learned obedience through what he suffered" (Heb 5:8).

You did not see these things happen; ultimately *you have only the text that tells you they did.*

So my question is: What are you going to do with Genesis 3? It comes down to this. It does not matter if you have an eighth-grade education or a PhD, whether you're doctor or a landscaper, a waitress or a seminary professor. You might know half a dozen languages or you may be barely able to read one. The question is: Do you believe what the Bible says in Genesis 3, or do you not? The gospel does not begin in Matthew 1; it begins in Genesis 3.

It is almost as if the forbidden tree—the sign of obedience and the fruit of remembrance in the Garden of Eden—points right back to the very text of Genesis 3, to which it can be likened: *Both text and tree remind us that we are not God and must obey His clear and simple Word*, which is always only meant for our good.

If you believe the story this tree-text tells, then you have recognized that the narrative of the Fall of Adam in Paradise ultimately points to you, to your condition, and to God's gracious remedy. If you do not—then perhaps you are simply demonstrating the truth of the divine text even while denying the turning away.

BIBLIOGRAPHY

Aristotle. *Poetics.* Aristotle Volume XXIII, Loeb Classical Library 199. Translated by Stephen Halliwell. Cambridge, MA: Harvard University Press, 1995.

Augustine. *On Genesis: Two Books on Genesis against the Manichees; and, On the Literal Interpretation of Genesis, an Unfinished Book.* The Fathers of the Church: A New Translation (Patristic series), Vol. 84. Translated by Roland J. Teske. Washington, DC: The Catholic University of America Press, 1990.

Calvin, John. *Institutes of the Christian Religion.* Translated by Ford Lewis Battles. Louisville: Westminster John Knox Press, 1960.

Currid, John D. *Genesis Volume 1.* Evangelical Press Study Commentary. Darlington, UK: Evangelical Press, 2003.

Hamilton, Victor P. *The Book of Genesis: Chapters 1–17.* New International Commentary on the Old Testament. Grand Rapids: Eerdmans Publishing, 1990.

Kidner, Derek. *Genesis.* Tyndale Old Testament Commentaries. Downers Grove, IL: InterVarsity Press Academic, 2008.

Ross, Allen. *Creation & Blessing.* Grand Rapids: Baker, 1997.

Wenham, Gordon J. *Genesis 1–15.* Vol. 1. Word Biblical Commentary. Nashville: Thomas Nelson, 1987.

PART 2:

THEOLOGICAL RAMIFICATIONS
OF THE CREATION AND FALL

CHAPTER 5

GENESIS 3 AND ORIGINAL SIN

Paul R. Thorsell

O Adam, what have you done? For though it was you who sinned, the fall was not yours alone, but ours also who are your descendants.[1]

Can. 2. If anyone asserts that Adam's transgression injured him alone and not his descendants, ... he will do an injustice to God, contradicting the Apostle....[2]

This is what theologians call the doctrine of "Original Sin," by which they mean that the results of Adam's sin, both legal and moral, have been transmitted to Adam's posterity....[3]

L ike every good story, the biblical narrative contains a plot with a protagonist and an antagonist. The opening sentences of Genesis identify the protagonist (God), and a first reader might wonder who could or would dare stand

---

1. 4 Ezra 7:118; cited from Charlesworth, *Old Testament Pseudepigrapha*, 1:451.
2. Second Council of Orange (529), cited from *Enchiridion Symbolorum*, §175.
3. Whitelaw, "Biblical Conception of Sin," 3:16.

against the powerful and good Creator. The antagonist, God's great enemy introduced in chapter 3, is not the serpent—a relatively minor character—but sin, that ill-defined yet powerful threat against God's good purpose for His creation. Chapter 3 is where sin "takes the stage" and the biblical plot "thickens."

Until the modern era, Christians read Genesis 3 not as fiction with universalistic overtones (as perhaps Homer's *Odyssey* or Shakespeare's *Hamlet*) but as a narrative of actual events explaining the way things are.[4] The narrative was an etiology, that is, a story explaining the cause of present circumstances.[5] Christians reading Genesis 3 through the lenses of Romans 5 and 1 Corinthians 15 recognized a doctrine of "original sin"—that the sin of the first couple set loose a cascade of consequences—including moral corruption, physical death, and divine condemnation—on the human race.[6]

The modern era called this reading into question. The new science of evolutionary biology and the rise of naturalistic criticism worked to thwart attempts to derive any doctrine of original sin from Genesis 3. The former denied that the narrative reflected actual events by precluding a real first couple or a real beginning of human death.[7] The latter suggested that the narrative was a post-exilic synthesis of traditions, similar to other ancient Near Eastern stories, redacted by Judean priests. Therefore, the narrative is not about the origin of human sin and death but about the importance of remaining obedient to YHWH's Law in order to retain a toehold in their corner of the Persian Empire. Consequently, "the traditional Christian doctrine of the Fall of Man, and the associated doctrine of Original Sin, cannot be found in the Hebrew Old Testament or cannot be supported by a reasonable interpretation of chapter 3 of Genesis."[8]

I intend to argue the contrary—that the narrative of Genesis 3 does teach a rudimentary doctrine of original sin consistent with the main lines of Chris-

---

4. The Gnostics were the exception. They interpreted the Creation story not as "*history with a moral* [but] as *myth with meaning*" (italics original); Pagels, *Adam, Eve*, 64.
5. I use "etiology" here not in the critical sense of a story *invented* to explain present circumstances, but in the causative sense of a story of *actual events* determining present reality. By definition, etiology is a text that explains a state of affairs by reference to a past event, irrespective of whether that event is historically reliable or mythical. See Lohfink, "Genesis 2–3," 18–34.
6. That Adam's sin brought evil consequences on the human race "is part of the faith of the whole Christian world," but the nature, extent, and ground of those consequences "have ever been a matter of diversity and discussion." Hodge, *Systematic Theology*, 2:192.
7. The Pelagian heresy was a harbinger of modern theology because, though acknowledging a real first couple, it denied that human death commenced with Adam's sin; Augustine of Hippo, *De gestis pelagii*, 23.
8. Fitzpatrick, *Fall and Ascent*, xv.

tian theology. I proceed, in counter-historical order, first to sketch the main lines of the Christian doctrine of original sin. With this definition in hand, I examine Paul's teaching of the nature and consequences of Adam's transgression to determine if original sin is part of his thought. Turning from Paul to the Old Testament, I consider the implications of those allusions to Genesis 3 outside of the Pentateuch. Finally, I scrutinize Genesis 3 within its Pentateuchal context to determine whether the text itself teaches the doctrine of original sin.

The Church's Doctrine of Original Sin

What does the church mean when it speaks of "original sin"? The word "original" refers not to Adam's sin in the Garden but to that sin each individual receives from Adam by way of origin.[9] Original sin therefore is transmitted sin—what Adam transmits to his posterity. Christians from virtually all theological traditions have embraced some form of the doctrine of original sin—both Protestant and Roman Catholic, both western evangelicalism and Eastern Orthodoxy.[10] Though it is construed variously among the traditions, virtually all have affirmed that Adam's primal act of disobedience fundamentally altered the character of human existence in relation to God.

The Church before Augustine

The doctrine of original sin has been regarded by some, at least since the Enlightenment, as the creation of Augustine of Hippo.[11] In his writings we do meet the first systematically presented doctrine of original sin. But if we had only Genesis and Romans, these would be enough to rebut the notion that Augustine invented original sin out of whole cloth. Belief in universal human solidarity in Adam prevailed throughout the ancient church before Augustine. Bishop Melito of Sardis wrote (c. 170):

---

9. Augustine, *De peccato originali*, 1–3; Anselm of Canterbury, *De conceptu virginali*, 1–2.
10. Some argue that eastern Christianity did not teach this doctrine. However, they can do this only by unreasonably restricting what counts as "original sin" to the western Augustinian form of the doctrine; Kelly, *Early Christian Doctrines*, 350.
11. Voltaire contended that the doctrine can be found neither in Genesis, nor anywhere in the Bible, nor the earliest church writings. It sprang from "the warm and romantic brain of an African debauchee and penitent, Manichæan and Christian, tolerant and persecuting—who passed his life in perpetual self-contradiction." S.v. "Original Sin," in *Philosophical Dictionary*. See also Pagels, "Politics of Paradise."

> When [Adam] had become prolific and very aged and had
> returned to the earth on account of his eating from the tree,
> he left an inheritance for his children…not chastity but adul-
> tery, not incorruption but corruption, not honor but dishon-
> or, not liberty but slavery, not kingly rule but tyranny, not life
> but death, not salvation but perdition.[12]

Melito, dependent on Genesis and Paul, evidences a notion of racial solidarity
cast in terms of inherited moral corruption. Irenaeus (c. 185) argued for the
necessity of the incarnation on the basis that the many had become sinners and
lost life through Adam's disobedience.[13] Adam made Christ's work necessary.
Yet Irenaeus gave no specifics about *how* all participate in Adam and his sin.

Origen, in the third century, spoke of racial unity in the first man as the
cause of humanity's death and exile from paradise.[14] But this idea did not
preclude him from speculating about a pre-conception fall.[15] In the West, Tertullian (c. 205) construed human solidarity in Adam by way of transmitted
sin. Tertullian's view that the souls of infants derived from their parents easily
allowed him to conceive the solidarity of all in Adam's sin: "Every soul, then,
by reason of its birth, has its nature in Adam until it is born again in Christ."[16]

Athanasius (c. 360) defended the necessity of the incarnation by invoking
the unity of the human race in Adam—"Death…gained from that time forth
a legal hold over us [i.e., the race of men]."[17] Connection with Adam's transgression produced a regression from an original supernatural state to a mortal state.[18] But inherited guilt goes unmentioned. Perhaps the closest we get
to an Augustinian description of original sin is from the pen of Augustine's
teacher, Ambrose of Milan (c. 379): "In Adam I fell, in Adam I was cast out of

---

12. *De pascha* 49; quoted from Norris, *Christological Controversy*, 29–30. Beatrice contends that
     Melito did not embrace original sin, 172–73. But he considers that what counts as a doctrine
     of original sin must include the teaching that Adam's sin renders all liable to damnation and
     that it is transmitted via concupiscence. By this narrow definition, he excludes many early
     texts supporting solidarity in the sin of Adam. See 260–61.
13. *Adversus haereses*, 3.18.7. Similarly, in 5.16.3 with reference to Adam's sin he remarked, "It
     was by these things that we disobeyed God," and "We were debtors to none other but to
     Him whose commandment we had transgressed at the beginning."
14. Beatrice, *Transmission of Sin*, 180–81; Tennant, *Sources of the Doctrines*, 302–305.
15. Origen famously embraced the Platonic view of the preexistence of human souls. These souls,
     he explained, were punished for spiritual sins by being united with bodies; *De principiis*, 2.9.5–6.
16. *De anima*, 40.
17. *De incarnation*, 6.
18. Ibid., 4–5.

Paradise, in Adam I died; how shall the Lord call me back, except He find me in Adam; guilty as I was in him, so now justified in Christ. If, then, death be the debt of all, we must be able to endure the payment."[19]

Augustine's Doctrine

Racial solidarity in Adam's sin and its consequences pervaded the faith of the pre-Augustinian church.[20] Augustine's contribution is found both in how he explained this solidarity and the conclusions he drew from it. First, Augustine explained that our sharing in the consequences of Adam's sin showed that we also shared the *guilt*.[21] Every individual is a part of the "mass of sin" or "mass of damnation" in Adam until cut off and united with Christ. Humans are part of this "mass" by their origin, not choice. Consequently, even infants without personal sin are doomed unless they receive the grace of Christ in baptism.

Second, Augustine maintained that in the fallen world the libido involved in sexual relations was the vehicle by which original sin was transmitted. Human procreation or the sexual act was itself not evil.[22] Both were part of the pre-Fall world and both were necessary to transmit human nature. But the libido accompanying every sexual act since the Fall corrupted that nature and so passed Adam's sin along with it.[23]

Third, part of the penalty inherited from Adam was a morally corrupted nature that disabled the human will. Augustine affirmed that the human will was free even after the Fall but this will was free only to do evil, not good.[24] Due to this inability, no one could be saved without prevenient grace.[25]

Developments in the Medieval and Reformation Church

During Augustine's lifetime, several local councils made pronouncements on the doctrine of original sin, some of which were approved at the Council of

---

19. *De excessu fratris sui Satyri,* 2.6.
20. Beatrice, Transmission of sin, 58, notes evidence in Augustine's early writings prior to his controversy with Pelagius.
21. *Opus imperfectum,* 1.47.
22. These notions would contradict his belief in the original goodness of Creation and the text of Genesis in which God commanded humanity to reproduce; Augustine, *De civitate dei,* 13.14.
23. This implied that there was no libido before the Fall. The sexual act would take place as a choice without passion. Consequently, the inability for the libido to be bridled in the fallen world was, for Augustine, the clearest evidence of original sin; Augustine, *De civitate dei,* 13.13; 14.24. See Pagels, "Politics of Paradise," 80–83.
24. *Contra duas epistolas Pelagianorum,* 2.9.
25. That is, grace that precedes any human good will or act.

Ephesus (431).[26] The most decisive dogmatic pronouncement generally recognized in the Western church was promulgated at the Council of Orange
(529). Augustine's emphases on the transmission of Adamic guilt, the moral
corruption of every human, and the necessity for prevenient grace were reaffirmed at Orange and, ten centuries later, at the anti-Protestant Council of
Trent.[27] The most significant omission from these dogmatic statements concerned Augustine's notion of *how* original sin was transmitted; neither Orange nor Trent repeated his contention that the libido is the vehicle by which
Adam's sin is transmitted.

The Eastern and Western churches parted ways on the notion of inherited
guilt. Anselm of Canterbury in the West continued the Augustinian notion of
inherited guilt with the implication that children are born with a moral debt.
"For this reason it seems necessary for human nature to be born in infants
with the obligation of making satisfaction for the first sin ... as well as the obligation of having original justice."[28] Thomas Aquinas maintained Augustine's
view while incorporating some Aristotelian distinctions.[29] In the East, however, theologians were averse to speaking of the guilt of original sin.[30] By virtue
of racial solidarity, every human possessed a nature prone to evil and death;
yet all still possessed freedom to do good. Guilt was never incurred except by
personal acts.[31] Yet both East and West affirmed a unity in Adam, a corporate
solidarity involving all in the shared death and corruption of the one.

When the Reformation broke out, the principals initially took vastly different positions on the subject of original sin. Martin Luther affirmed the traditional Western position. Original sin involved both the corruption of will
and an inherited guilt.[32] Not so with the earliest Reformed theologians. Ulrich

---

26. *Enchiridion Symbolorum*, §§129–30.
27. Ibid., §§787–91.
28. *De conceptu virginali 2.* Peter Abelard, a contemporary of Anselm, was one of those who
    dissented from the basic Augustinian structure. He rejected the transmission of guilt
    from Adam and so approached the eastern understanding of original sin as contagion.
    Abailard's Ethics, 27–28.
29. *Summa Theologiae* I–II q. 82, art. 3. Thomas defined original sin in the formal sense as
    the privation of original justice but in the material sense as concupiscence. Both incurred
    guilt and punishment before God.
30. So John of Damascus, *De fide orthodoxa* 3.1.
31. Pelikan, *Spirit of Eastern Christendom*, 260; Clendenin, *Eastern Orthodox Christianity*,
    132–33.
32. Althaus, *Theology of Luther*, 157–58; Lohse, *Luther's Theology*, 251–53. Philip Melanch-
    thon continued Luther's basic position; "Loci communes theologici," 1–3, cited from *Mel-
    anchthon and Bucer*, 30–33. See also *Augsburg Confession*, art. 2.

Zwingli, leader of the Reformation in Zurich, rejected the Augustinian notion that original sin included the guilt of Adam's sin.[33] John Calvin at Geneva held a mediating position that Adam's posterity is not guilty of Adam's sin. They become guilty by way of receiving a corrupt nature.[34] Some rationalistically inclined radicals rejected entirely the doctrine of original sin.[35] But apart from these radicals, Catholics and non-Catholics alike embraced original sin.

Modern Developments

The Reformed churches took two trajectories after the sixteenth century. On the one hand, Reformed scholastics expounded original sin in line with the increasingly prominent covenantal structure of Reformed theology. The *Formula Consensus Helvetica* (1675) explained original sin in light of the covenant of works.[36] The dominant scheme saw an *immediate* imputation of Adam's guilt to his posterity by way of federal headship and the *mediate* transmission of Adam's corrupt nature by way of generation.[37] Many of the free churches followed.[38] But dissidents reacted against this construal in Reformed theology.[39] What often marked the method of these dissidents was an increasing dependence on human reason.

This dependence on rationality would become the hallmark of eighteenth century theology and spur the rise of Neology in Germany and the New Divinity in the American colonies.[40] Liberal Protestant theology continued this direction in the nineteenth century. Original sin, even loosely conceived, was jettisoned

---

33. "Of Baptism," in *Zwingli and Bullinger*, 153.
34. *Institutes of the Christian Religion*, 2.1.8; see also his *Romans and Thessalonians*, 111–12. The *Belgic Confession* of 1561 (art. 15), though ambiguous, continued Calvin's perspective. The Anglican *Thirty-nine Articles* of 1571 preserves an Augustinian view of original sin in that Adam's posterity inherits both the fault and corruption of Adam (art. 9).
35. See the *Racovian Catechism* (c. 1605) influenced by Faustus Socinus, 325–30.
36. Canons 9–12.
37. *Westminster Shorter Catechism*, qq. 16–18.
38. So the *Savoy Declaration* (1658), arts. 6–7. This is sometimes the case even without reference to the covenant of works; *London Baptist Confession of Faith* (1644), arts. 4–5.
39. This is true both of the Remonstrants in the early seventeenth century and the school of Saumur later in the century. Arminius himself was uneasy with the notion that Adam's guilt was inherited. Simon Episcopius, who became the leader of the Remonstrant party after Arminius's death, eventually denied both universal guilt and universal corruption from Adam's sin. Ellis, *Episcopius' Doctrine*, 76–79, 150–52, 158–60. Josué de la Place of the school of Saumur became noteworthy for his advocacy of the theory of the mediate imputation of Adam's guilt; Hoekema, *Created in God's Image*, 156–57.
40. Karl Barth argued that eighteenth-century theology trimmed dogma to fit "what was thought to be secured as the rational truth of religion." Augustine's doctrine was rejected "because he had so little understood that man is fundamentally good." *Protestant Theology*, 130.

as inconsistent with what humans know of God and irreconcilable with the religious reality found in the Christian consciousness.[41] Protestant conservatives resisted these trends so that original sin became a mark of evangelical theology.[42]

The anti-Protestant and anti-rationalist polemics within Roman Catholic theology partially immunized it from rationalistic tendencies in the nineteenth century.[43] Its understanding of original sin remained traditional into the twentieth century. But the Church needed to address the challenges from evolutionary biology. Pius XII was a transitional figure. Acknowledging that humans might have non-human ancestors, he refused to concede that there might never have been an individual, historical Adam:

> [T]he faithful cannot embrace that opinion which maintains that either after Adam there existed on this earth true men who did not take their origin through natural generation from him as from the first parent of all, or that Adam represents a certain number of first parents. Now it is in no way apparent how such an opinion can be reconciled with that which the sources of revealed truth and the documents of the Teaching Authority of the Church propose with regard to original sin, which proceeds from a sin actually committed by an individual Adam and which, through generation, is passed on to all and is in everyone as his own.[44]

After the pontificate of Pius XII, the Church has been less resistant to such tendencies. Original sin was reaffirmed in confessional statements but only

41. Friedrich Schleiermacher rejected both the imputation of Adam's sin and the possibility that one sin could change human nature; *Christian Faith*, §72.3–4 (pp. 298–301). The American theologian, Horace Bushnell (*Christian Nurture*, 52–53) took a similar approach. Karl Barth commented that Enlightenment theology commenced its criticism of traditional theology not with the Trinity, Christology, or miracles but with the dogmatic assertions on the guilt and enslavement of sin; *Church Dogmatics*, 4.1.479.
42. Whitelaw, "Biblical Conception," 9–24. The view prevailed among conservative theologians—even among those who embraced some form of theistic evolution—that the text of Genesis and the NT references to Adam demanded that Adam was a specific individual and that the narrative of Genesis 3 recorded actual events. See, for instance, Strong, *Systematic Theology*, 1:vii–viii; 2:472–78, 583. Non-conservative theologians, by way of contrast, took the early chapters of Genesis as describing not actual events but the nature of humanity and sin by way of myth. So Clarke, *Christian Theology*, 224–25, 241–42.
43. Schoof, *Catholic Theology*, 30–37.
44. *Humani generis* 37 (1950).

in ambiguous language able to accommodate those who were dubious about one biological ancestor.[45]

The history of the church evidences a virtual unanimity that humanity at large was somehow connected to a personal Adam, his sin, and its consequences. The notable exceptions to this virtual unanimity—ancient Gnosticism, Pelagius, and modern liberal theology—prove the rule. This is not to deny significant diversity in how this racial solidarity in Adam was conceived. The Augustinian formula of transmitted guilt, vitiated nature, and disabled will dominated Western theological tradition until the modern era. The East eschewed notions of inherited guilt and disabled will to focus on death and moral corruption from Adam. But racial solidarity was a theological axiom based on the Genesis narrative and Paul's theological conclusions on that narrative.

Paul on Genesis 3

Paul's construal of Genesis 3 contributed most of the major elements for the church's doctrine of original sin. The Canons of Orange accused opponents of original sin of "contradicting the Apostle."[46] Paul's view of racial solidarity and the nature of his Adam-Christ comparison are hotly debated among scholars. The limits of this chapter preclude a detailed analysis of these issues. My intention is more modest, namely, to show good grounds for the church's doctrine of original sin in Paul's interpretation of Genesis 3.

Paul shared with his Jewish contemporaries an interest in the events of Genesis 3. He observed, as they did, a primordial event with universal consequences.[47] Their assumption of corporate solidarity was also his.[48] Judaism

---

45. *Catechism of the Catholic Church*, §§386–90 (1994); *Gaudium et spes*, 13 (1965). This reaffirmation did not reject the notion of biological evolution as an explanation for human origins (*Catechism*, §§281–85). The *Catechism* interpreted Genesis 3 to affirm in figurative language "a primeval event, a deed that took place *at the beginning of the history of man*" (§390; italics original). The language is ambiguous, giving leeway for those who affirm the Fall of man and original sin as existential truth rather than historical fact.

46. Can. 2.

47. See Sandmel, *Judaism and Christian Beginnings*, 186–91, and Oesterley, *Jews and Judaism*, 165–74. N. T. Wright argues convincingly that before his encounter on the Damascus road, Paul, like second temple Judaism, knew that there was a problem connected with Adam. But after his encounter with Christ, Paul concluded from Genesis 3 that the problem was deeper and the solution more radical than he had thought before. *Paul and the Faithfulness of God*, 2:749–54.

48. For instance, in second temple Judaism, punishment and reward fell on a man's descendants for what he had committed. See Moore, *Judaism in the First Centuries*, 1:475–76;

knew of a problem with humanity from Genesis 3, though estimates differed significantly. Sirach 25:24 blamed Eve instead of Adam; Wisdom 2:24 made the devil the primary culprit. Some writings linked human corruption to the influence of malicious angels recorded in Genesis.[49] Fourth Ezra and 2 Baruch blamed Adam for his misdeed but blamed God for Adam's evil heart.[50] Yet for all of the differences, Paul's interpretive strategy significantly overlapped that of Judaism. Both placed Adam at the head of a grand narrative that included Abraham, Moses, and David; both inferred some sort of solidarity between Adam and all humans.

Paul's writings affirm that he read Genesis 3 as the defining event structuring the human predicament. His juxtaposition of Adam and Christ in 1 Corinthians 15 justifies this conclusion. The Adam-Christ contrast consists of two points. First, Christ's resurrection represents the mirror image of Adam's act—"by a man came death, by a man has come also the resurrection of the dead" (1 Cor 15:21). The text assumes that both events are real events, not mythical or existential fictions.[51] The solidarity of Christ-followers with Christ in his resurrection corresponds to the solidarity of all humans in Adam's death. Second, Christ as the "life-giving spirit" represents the mirror image of Adam, the "living being" (15:45). Christ's resurrection becomes the cause of resurrection-life just as Adam's sin was the cause of death. Although the text does not mention guilt or moral corruption, its assumption of human solidarity in Adam—axiomatic for the doctrine of original sin—is present.

The old man/new man contrast in Paul also exhibits this solidarity. In Colossians 3 and Ephesians 4, the two are set beside each other. Christians are to "put off" the old man and "put on" the new after the analogy of cloth-

---

mSanh 4:5; *TargumPs-J* on Exodus 40:8; *FragmentTargumV* on Numbers 23:9. But note E. P. Sanders (*Paul and Palestinian Judaism*, 190–98), who argues (in my view unsuccessfully) against this thesis.

49. See the interpretation of Genesis 6 found in 1 Enoch 6–19. The idea that human moral corruption is partly explained by evil spirits and disobedient angels appears in the literature. But this does not detract from a real fall in Eden. For instance, in the *Manual of Discipline* (1QS 3.13–4.26) angelic influence on humans goes hand-in-hand with the recognition of humanity's real loss of the glory of Adam (4.23).

50. Fourth Ezra 3:6–7, 20–27; 4:30–32; 7:48, 116–18; 2 Baruch 23:4; 54:15. Similarly, see 1QS 3:17–18 along with the rabbinic doctrine of the two *yetzers* in *bQidd 30b*; *Sipre Deut* 45 to 11:18.

51. Recently, Peter Enns conceded that Paul assumed universal sin and death stem from what one primordial man did. But this is "Paul's *culturally assumed* explanation [italics original]" which "reflects his time and place"; *Evolution of Adam*, 124. By this circumlocution Enns appears to say that Paul's "culturally assumed" reading of Genesis 3 is wrong.

ing.[52] The "new man" is Christ/the Christian community in solidarity with Christ.[53] By implication, the "old man" is Adam/fallen humanity in solidarity with Adam.[54] The "new man" appears without the "old man" in Ephesians 2:15. Christ abolished the law separating Jew and Gentile so "that he might create in himself one new man in place of the two." We see the opposite in Romans 6:6; the "old man" appears without the "new man."[55] The Adam-Christ analogy in the preceding context (5:12–21) requires us to understand the "old man" as a reference to Christians' previous solidarity in Adam/the old humanity.[56]

Paul's defense of the goodness of the Mosaic Law in Romans 7 refers his readers back to Adam's temptation and sin in the Garden. This first-person story of the commandment producing sin and death brings Genesis 2–3 to mind.[57] Paul operated with a foundational premise from the Old Testament that Israel replaced Adam in God's purpose.[58] Consequently, the law's effect on Israel was comparable to the effect of God's command to Adam in Eden. By drawing this connection in chapter seven, Paul conveyed to his readers

---

52. In Colossians 3 the terms are ἀπεκδύομαι (*apekdyomai*, "put off"; 3:9) and ἐνδύω (*endyō*, "put on"; 3:10). In Ephesians 4, the former is replaced with a less explicit synonym, ἀπο-τίθημι (*apotíthēmi*, "put off"; 4:22) while the latter is retained (4:24). These verbs may reflect ancient practice of removing and replacing clothing during baptism. See Lohse, *Colossians and Philemon*, 141–42.

53. The parallels with Galatians 3:27 and Romans 13:14 ("put on [the Lord Jesus] Christ") point to a corporate solidarity in which the individual ("Christ") stands for the community united to the individual. As in Colossians 3:10 and Ephesians 4:24, the verb is ἐνδύω (*endyō*, "put on").

54. The term translated "man" (ἄνθρωπος, *anthrōpos*) is generic for a particular human or humanity in general (male or female). Because of this it translates well the Hebrew אָדָם ('*ādām*), except that the Hebrew is also the proper name of the first man. The LXX translators used both ἄνθρωπος (*anthrōpos*) and the Greek transliteration Αδαμ (*Adam*) to translate the Hebrew אָדָם ('*ādām*) in Gen 1–3. In addition, Paul explicitly alluded to Genesis 1:26 with the expression, "after the image" (κατ᾽ εἰκόνα, *kat eikona*) which exactly replicates the LXX.

55. Solidarity with Christ (the unmentioned "new man") is stated in the previous verse.

56. The reference is both corporate (life in Adam) and redemptive-historical (life in the age of Adam). See Käsemann, *Romans*, 169; Dunn, *Romans 1–8*, 318–19.

57. Romans 7:8–11 is particularly in view here. The "commandment" is singular, not plural. "I" was alive before the commandment came, but "I" died when sin came alive by way of the commandment. The commandment, which promised life, brought death. Sin, by the commandment, deceived and killed "me." All of these assertions apply directly to Adam. See Käsemann, *Romans*, 195–97.

58. "Israel is, or will become, God's true humanity. What God intended for Adam will be given to the seed of Abraham. They will inherit the second Eden, the restored primeval glory." Wright, *Climax of the Covenant*, 20–21.

that they were "implicated in the story of Adam."[59] Adam's disobedience to
God's command brought the consequences of death, moral enslavement to
sin, and the inability to obey God's command—all dimensions of Augustine's
delineation of original sin.

Romans 8:18–25 must also be considered in light of Paul's reading of
Genesis 3. The present distress (vv. 18, 22) prompted Paul to look toward future liberation, not just for believers (vv. 23–25) but also for all of creation (vv.
19, 21). But the present distress had a beginning—"the creation was subjected
to futility, not willingly, but because of him who subjected it, in hope" (v. 20).
So the passage looks forward to a reversal of what Adam wrought; creation
will be put right when Adam/humanity is put right.[60]

Romans 5:12–21 is the *crux interpretum* in the Pauline corpus. Paul introduced his Adam-Christ analogy in verse 12. He assumed that his hearers
were familiar with the Genesis narrative, that it depicted real events, and that
his hearers acknowledged corporate solidarity in Adam.[61] Verse 12 enunciates
Paul's starting point in four clauses. (1) Sin entered the world through Adam.[62]
(2) Death entered the world through sin. (3) Death passed to all in this way
(i.e., as in clauses 1–2).[63] (4) "Because all sinned." Most modern interpreters
translate the connective (ἐφ' ᾧ, *eph' hō*) beginning the fourth clause, "because," in light of its occurrences elsewhere.[64]

Interpretations of the fourth clause generally fall into three groups. The
first interprets the clause as asserting that death passed on all because all
sinned individually.[65] The verb "sin" (ἁμαρτάνω, *hamartanō*) almost always
refers to an individual act of disobedience. But if this is its reference, a ten-
sion is created with the first three clauses. Do all die through the one man or
do all die because of their personal sins? The second interpretation takes the

59. Käsemann, *Romans*, 196.
60. Wright, *Paul and the Faithfulness of God*, 1:487–88. So also Beale, *Temple and Church's Mission*, 120–21.
61. Though space precludes a defense of this statement here, I am aware of no second temple text that does not proceed on these assumptions. Even Philo, despite his Platonic tenden-cies, expounded the early chapters of Genesis with the presumption that Adam was a real man and that the human race of his day was marked by characteristics from the first man; *De opficio mundi*, 145–46.
62. The clause connectives at the beginning of v. 12 need not detain us except to note that Paul was making an argument ("therefore") and this argument was built on a comparison between clauses 1–2 and clause 3.
63. Greek: οὕτως, *houtos*; "thus," or "in this way."
64. Dunn, *Romans 1–8*, 273; Johnson, "Romans 5:12," 303–5.
65. Barrett, *Romans*, 111; Dunn, *Romans*, 272–73.

verb "sin" (ἁμαρτάνω, *hamartanō*) to assert that death passed on all because all acted on an inherited sinful nature from Adam.[66] But nothing in the passage suggests that the subject is the inheritance of a sinful nature from Adam. Certainly Paul can be seen to teach a universal moral corruption from other passages, but not in Romans 5:12–21. Finally, it is without precedent to construe the verb as acting on a received sinful nature.

The third interpretation argues that the expression "all sinned" means all participated in Adam's sin. This was Augustine's interpretation put forward partly on the basis of the Latin text, *in quo omnes peccaverunt* ("in whom all sinned," *Douay-Rheims Bible*).[67] Though Augustine was wrong about the significance of the connective, *in quo* ("in whom"), there are solid reasons to conclude that he was right about the basic significance of the text. First, the implications of corporate solidarity from the Old Testament and contemporary Jewish thinking undoubtedly influenced Paul. Second, an individualistic construal of the fourth clause runs counter to the first three clauses. Third, the prepositional phrase "through one man" in the first clause likely is implied, though unstated, in the last clause—"because all sinned [through one man]." Verses 13–14 may imply the same conclusion. All died between Adam and Moses despite the fact that sin was not reckoned and despite the absence of sin like Adam's.[68] Why? They sinned through Adam. Finally, the third interpretation is confirmed in Paul's statements in 5:15–19. The series of contrasts/comparisons focuses on the parallel between Christ's one act and Adam's one sin. Neither personal sins nor sinful nature enters the discussion. All that matters is the universal effect of Adam's one sin.

Human solidarity in the sin and death of Adam serves to substantiate the church's doctrine of original sin in its generic form. But is there support for the Augustinian position that humans inherit Adamic guilt? Paul's forensic language (5:16, 18) seems to provide that support. The one trespass brings God's condemnation just as Christ's one act brings justification.[69] Only by

---

66. Calvin, *Romans and Thessalonians*, 111–12; Cranfield, *Romans*, 1:279.

67. Augustine famously interpreted the Greek ἐφ᾽ ᾧ, *eph' hō* ("because"), as if it were the Latin relative phrase *in quo*, "in whom." In this he was following the Latin texts of Romans 5:12 of his day. However, it is not true that this was a simple mistranslation; the Latin *in quo* could mean "because" just like the Greek ἐφ᾽ ᾧ, *eph' hō*. Neither is it true that Augustine did not know or consult the Greek New Testament. See Beatrice, *Transmission of Sin*, 109–11, 236.

68. So Murray, *Romans*, 187–91.

69. Paul's forensic terminology is on both sides of the contrast. In verse 16, "judgment" (κρί-μα, *krima*) and "condemnation" (κατάκριμα, *katakrima*) are the result of Adam's sin;

separating the notions of guilt and condemnation could one evade Augustine's conclusion that all are guilty of Adam's sin.[70]

Paul's letters teach original sin. All humans, by virtue of their solidarity with Adam, are destined to die and possess a morally corrupted nature. That much is clear. In addition, the forensic language of Romans 5 offers substantive support for the Western form of the doctrine, which includes the transmission of Adam's guilt. Augustine's reading of Paul is possible and, in fact, highly probable.

THE PROPHETS AND THE WRITINGS ON GENESIS 3

One argument against the doctrine of original sin is that there is little imprint of the Fall in Genesis 3 on the Old Testament.[71] One possible exception is Hosea 6:7; however, the prophet's reference to Adam's violation of an Edenic covenant is unlikely.[72] If the Bible does teach a universal Fall, where is the evidence that it played a significant role in the theology of the Old Testament outside of the Pentateuch? In this section I argue that specific passages demonstrate that the Fall exercised formative influence on the rest of the Old Testament. But these passages draw their demonstrable force from several overarching characteristics of the Old Testament's message. We will therefore observe three of these characteristics before moving to specific passages.

First, the Old Testament lacks any identifiable "golden age" within the history of Israel. By "golden age" I mean a time of uniform prosperity, righteousness, and divine blessing. Eras when we would most expect such a presentation—the united monarchy under David or the conquest under Joshua—are mitigated by the persistent presence of human perverseness, covenantal disobedience, and divine judgment. Passages where the history of the covenant people is recounted (Judg 2; Ezek 16; Ps 106; Neh 9) mention no ideal era. Eden, then, is the only golden era in the Old Testament.

"justification" (δικαίωμα, *dikaioma*) is the result of Christ's act. In verse 18, the contrast is between "condemnation" (κατάκριμα, *katakrima*) and "justification" (δικαίωσις, *dikaiōsis*).

70. It is not my purpose here to address the issue of whether the solidarity between Adam's sin and all humanity is best understood in a federal, a seminal, or some other manner. The doctrine of original sin does not depend on any one of these views.

71. So Voltaire. Dubarle mentions no texts within the traditional Hebrew canon that exhibit the story of the Fall; *Biblical Doctrine*, 121.

72. "[L]ike Adam they transgressed the covenant." Cf. Wolff, *Hosea*, 121; Carroll, "Hosea," 8:259–60.

Second, the Old Testament uniformly depicts the present human predicament in terms of depravity, disobedience, and death.[73] Eden's uniqueness stands out against this uniformity. Only in the Garden is death not pervasive, is the human heart not bent toward sin, nor is the rejection of divine rule not the norm. The third overarching characteristic involves the role of Israel. Edenic blessings are partially realized within the chosen people; Israel's covenantal obedience becomes the means by which these blessings extend to the world.[74] The Prophets, for instance, show how Israel could bless the nations in fulfillment of the Abrahamic promise.[75] This blessing is presented as a restoration of original Creation (So Jer 3:16; Ezek 36:10–11; Isa 65:16–66:23).

Direct references to the Garden are rare outside of Genesis 2–3 and all use Eden as the obverse side of a contrast with destruction. Joel 2:3 compares locust swarms to an army that turns a land "like the garden of Eden" to "desolate wilderness." Two passages take Eden to symbolize the eschatological future. In Isaiah 51 those "who pursue righteousness" (v. 1) will be granted YHWH's salvation (vv. 5, 6, 8). YHWH's salvation fulfills his blessing to Abraham (vv. 1–2) and will mean the wilderness will be remade "like Eden," like "the garden of YHWH" (v. 3, my translation). Similarly, Ezekiel's prophecy of a renewed Israel (chs. 36–37) involves the restoration of the land to "become like the garden of Eden" (36:35). This restoration includes return from exile (36:24; 37:11–12) and moral renewal (36:26–27; 37:9–10, 23).[76] All of these texts portray Eden as a lost perfection made more pronounced by the desolate misery of the present.

---

73. Although many texts support this notion, Jeremiah's description of the incorrigible sinfulness of the chosen people is poignant; Jeremiah 2:22; 5:3, 23; 7:24; 9:26; 13:23; 17:1, 9; et. al.

74. The Pentateuch itself puts into parallel the Edenic, Noahic, and Abrahamic blessings (Gen 1:28; 9:1, 7; 12:1–3). The Mosaic covenant incorporates these elements into itself (Deut 7:12–14). Dumbrell, *Creation and Covenant*, 61–64, advances the thesis that Abram's call constitutes God's effort to accomplish the original mandate of Genesis 1.

75. See particularly Jeremiah 4:1–4. The prophet calls Israel to return to YHWH by submitting to the Mosaic call for heart circumcision (Deut 10:16; this text also includes an allusion to the Abrahamic blessing in v. 22) so that, in words reminiscent of Genesis 22:18, the nations will be blessed. This paradigm is present in some of the Isaianic prophecies, for example, 42:6; 48:18–19; cf. 49:6.

76. Israel's reentry into the land is comparable to a return to Eden. Furthermore, the moral restoration of Israel is described as a resurrection, which has a conceptual (not verbal) similarity with the account of Adam's creation in Genesis 2:7. The significant difference is that in Genesis 2:7 God infused Adam with "breath" (נְשָׁמָה, něšāmâ) while in Ezekiel it is God's Spirit (רוּחַ, rûaḥ; 37:5, 8–10; cf. 36:27; 37:14).

Ezekiel contains two extended passages pointing back to Eden. Ezekiel 28:11–19 portrays the king of Tyre in terms of a cherub of the Garden of Eden.[77] We cannot here treat the extensive interpretive and theological problems this passage contains.[78] What is pertinent for our purposes is that Ezekiel presents this "blameless" cherub within a primordial perfection—Eden (v. 13). But his created perfection is terminated by sin and a consequent exile from "the mountain of God" (v. 16). Three chapters later, Ezekiel 31 refers to Eden in an extended and rather convoluted metaphor.[79] Within this metaphor, Eden is depicted with a multitude of lush trees representing humans growing near a multitude of streams (vv. 4, 5, 7). As with Ezekiel 28:2–19, a tree's pride moves God to destroy it and consign it to the "pit." Since the trees represent humans, the leveling of the trees of Eden represents the universal destiny of "the children of man."[80] All are "given over to death, to the world below"; all "go down to the pit" (v. 14). For Ezekiel's readers, Assyria's consignment to death parallels the universal death experienced by all because of the Fall in Genesis 3. For both passages Eden represents a pristine state without sin and without death, utterly distinct from the present.

Other allusions to Eden corroborate the above observations. Three references to the "tree of life" in Proverbs (11:30; 13:12; 15:4) seem purely metaphorical, but indicate that the traditions of Eden were alive. More common is the adage that humans are from dust and will return to dust.[81] But the presence of this saying reveals the character of the Garden events. In Genesis 2:7 humans are created from dust; it is only in 3:19 that the second part of the maxim becomes true—humans return to dust.

Several Old Testament passages point directly to the events of Genesis 3. In Job 10:8–12, the poet alluded to God's creation of man in the complaint,

---

77. The difference, of course, is that the cherubim of Genesis 3:24 enforce Adam's exile from the tree of life. The cherub in Ezekiel begins blameless, but turns to sin and is destroyed.

78. Whether the sinning cherub represents a man exiled from paradise by sin or Satan exiled from paradise by sin, the primordial state depicted is comparable.

79. The expression "garden of God" appears three times in verses 8–9; "trees of Eden" appears four times in verses 9, 16, 18. The passage is a complex fabric of images comparing Assyria—recently conquered by the Babylonians—to a great tree felled by God. The "tree" Assyria is unrivaled by the trees of "Eden," the "garden of God." Pharaoh, the ally of Assyria, is another great "tree" that God will cut down. See Zimmerli, *Ezekiel, Chapters 25–48,* 141–53.

80. בְּנֵי אָדָם, *běnê ʾādām,* "children of men," could also be translated "sons of Adam."

81. For instance, to make someone dust is to kill the person (2 Kings 13:7; Isa 41:2; Ps 7:5; 30:9). Someone who lies in the dust is dead (Ps 22:15; Job 7:21; 21:26). Resurrection is to rise from the dust (Isa 26:19; Dan 12:2).

"You have made me like clay; and will you return me to the dust?" Life and death are unnatural. Humans are created by God and God has determined to return them to dust. In Job 34:14–15, an even more direct allusion to Genesis is made:[82]

> If he should set his heart to it
>> and gather to himself his spirit and his breath,
> all flesh would perish together,
>> and man would return to dust.

Near-parallels can be found in Psalm 104:29 and Ecclesiastes 3:20. All speak of humans as destined to "return to dust" in language mirroring Genesis 3:19.

The Old Testament outside the Pentateuch is quite aware of the traditions of Eden. Yet they know nothing of the present world but death, moral decay, and disobedience. The common recognition that all return to dust is not the norm—only the norm since Genesis 3. Israel's hope that the curse will be alleviated through covenantal obedience proves unrealized. Only the distant future holds any prospect of a return to the one golden age known to Israel—the Garden of Eden. All of this points to a recognition that what happened in the Garden brought about the disordered condition of Israel. In short, it is a rudimentary doctrine of original sin.

GENESIS 3 IN ITS PENTATEUCHAL CONTEXT

Up to this point I have argued that the doctrine of original sin pervades the Christian theological tradition and that Paul's letters justify Augustine's conclusion that moral corruption, death, and guilt have passed from Adam to his posterity. I have also noted that the writings and the prophets affirm this notion with how they allude to the event surrounding Genesis 3 as a golden age long past and the beginning of human death. I now turn to the preeminent question: Does the narrative of Genesis 3 itself support a doctrine of original sin? My affirmative answer is grounded in five key observations within the Pentateuch itself.

---

82. The allusion is both conceptual and verbal. The text in Job refers to man's breath (נְשָׁמָה, něšāmâ) and dust (עָפָר, 'āpār) as in Genesis 2:7. But the expression "return to dust" is nearly identical to the same expression in Genesis 3:19.

Adam's Transgression Disrupts the Created Order

The narrative of Genesis 3 presents Adam's transgression effecting far-reaching consequences on the created order. We see this by the narrator's explicit statements of universality in chapters two and three. The adage of Genesis 2:24, that a man "leave his father and his mother," applies not to Adam but to his descendants. The universal statement here prepares the readers to understand chapter three in similar categories. YHWH's address to the snake (3:14–15), despite the use of the singular, implies that the consequences of this snake's act are general. God did not curse this snake but all snakes.[83] The same is true of YHWH's address to the woman (3:16). Though her act did not bring an explicit curse, it did bring painful childbirth and a struggle with her husband.[84] But the text assumes that this penalty is universal, not particular.

YHWH's words to the man point in the same direction. Like his wife, the man is not cursed. In his stead, the ground is cursed so to resist his efforts. He will secure food from it only at the cost of painful toil. The presence of generic nouns (i.e., "man") in chapters two and three provides further evidence that the consequences of disobedience fall on humanity at large and not just the first couple.[85]

Two chapters later (5:29) Lamech's comment on the significance of his son Noah's name corroborates the enduring character of the divine judgment pronounced in chapter three. "[And Lamech] called his name Noah, saying, 'Out of the ground that the Lord has cursed, this one shall bring us relief from our work and from the painful toil [Hebrew: עִצָּבוֹן, 'iṣṣābôn] of our hands.'" Lamech's word testifies that the curse of Genesis 3 continued

---

83. Reyburn and Fry, *Genesis*, 91; Cassuto, *Genesis, Part I*, 160.

84. The last two stiches of 3:16, "Your desire (תְּשׁוּקָה, *těšûqāh*) shall be for your husband, and he shall rule over you," probably expresses YHWH's imposition of a form of talionic justice on the woman—she will long to rule her husband but he will (ruthlessly) rule her. The noun תְּשׁוּקָה, *těšûqāh*, appears only twice elsewhere in the Hebrew canon (Gen 4:7; Song of Sol 7:10). Genesis 4:7 is the most relevant parallel where the context seems to demand a translation, "sin's desire is to master you but you must rule it."

85. Arguably, the first time the proper name, "Adam," appears is in 4:25. The name "Adam" (אָדָם, 'ādām) is also the generic word translated, "humanity" or "mankind," without reference to gender. Hebrew generally distinguishes the personal name from the generic noun by the absence (name) or presence (generic noun) of the article. The first clearly anarthrous use of אָדָם ('ādām) in Genesis is at 4:25, although the presence of the article is disputed in three prior places (2:20; 3:17, 21). See Westermann, *Genesis 1–11*, 229, 64. Irrespective of the three disputed cases, the overwhelming use of generic nouns instead of personal nouns in Genesis 2–3 suggests the narrative's concern is not with this man and that woman, but with all women and men everywhere.

to lay on the men of his day—eight generations after Adam—the burden of this "painful toil."[86] This brief insertion into the genealogy from Adam to Noah presumes that YHWH's pronouncement of judgment on Adam in 3:17–19 continues to the Flood.

Adam's Transgression Brings Consequences on His Posterity

The disruption brought on Adam's posterity further demonstrates that the original transgression drastically altered the created order. The notion of corporate solidarity prevalent in Old Testament thought virtually demands that the disaster consequent on Adam's sin impact his descendants.[87] Corporate solidarity between descendants and ancestor(s) looms prominently in the Pentateuch. It is YHWH's basis for perpetual war against Amalek (Exod 17:16; cf.1 Sam 15:2–3); it justifies the rather bawdy tale of Lot's seduction by his daughters (Gen 19:30–38).[88] It provides the rationale for Noah's curse on Ham's son, Canaan, a curse embracing Canaan's posterity (Gen 9:25).

Does Genesis display evidence that corporate solidarity applies to Adam's transgression? There are several reasons, in my estimation, for an affirmative answer. First, the narrative logic of the early chapters of Genesis implies that this is so.[89] The blessing in chapter 1 presumes its validity for Adam's offspring (Gen 1:28–29):

> And God blessed them. And God said to them, "Be fruitful and multiply and fill the earth and subdue it, and have dominion…." And God said, "Behold, I have given you every plant yielding seed that is on the face of all the earth, and every tree with seed in its fruit. You shall have them for food.

---

86. The Hebrew term עִצָּבוֹן, *'iṣṣābôn*, translated "painful toil" in 5:29, is the same word used in YHWH's condemnation in 3:17, "in *pain* you shall eat of it all the days of your life," as well as his words to Eve in 3:16, "in *pain* you shall bring forth children" (italics added). In so doing the Pentateuch underlines YHWH's judgment on Adam as continuing and comprehensive.

87. Eichrodt opines that corporate solidarity in guilt needed no exposition in the Hebrew prophets because of their uniform "conviction that every member of the nation was involved in the mountainous corporate guilt"; *Theology of the Old Testament*, 2:435. See also Dubarle, *Biblical Doctrine*, 28–44; Robinson, *Corporate Personality*.

88. Allen Ross comments that the story justified the belief that the lewdness "fundamental to the character of" the Moabites and Ammonites "were inherited from their ancestors"; *Creation and Blessing*, 364.

89. Chapter 3 is only the first in a series of episodes in Genesis in which an ancestor's reprehensible conduct brings tragic consequences on his posterity; Dubarle, *Biblical Doctrine*, 82.

The parallel with two later divine blessings—the Noahic (Gen 9:1, 7) and the Abrahamic (Gen 12:1–3)—confirms the inclusion of the posterity.[90] The same is true in chapter 2. God permits eating from every tree of the garden, but prohibits eating from the tree of the knowledge of good and evil (2:16–17). The permission and prohibition extend to all humans, a fact the woman understood (3:2–3) despite her absence from 2:16–17.[91]

Second, posterity was involved when YHWH meted out punishment to the serpent, the woman, and the man (3:14–19). The collective noun "offspring" (3:15) directly states that the curse on the serpent impacts the posterity of both the serpent and the woman.[92] As explained above, the penalty YHWH pronounced on the woman and the man presumes application to their female and male posterity. Pain and return to dust is the destiny of all their descendants.

Third, the text also alludes to the inclusion of posterity in the damage wrought by sin by taking note of the couple's immediate reaction—their eyes were opened, they recognized their nakedness, and they "made themselves loincloths" (3:7).[93] The Old Testament uses the language of "nakedness" to speak of the uncovering of the human genitalia and, by metonymy, participation in proscribed sexual acts.[94] The contrast with chapters 1–2 is stark. Before transgression, the human capacity for procreation was an unmitigated blessing (1:28) and the procreative organs were uncovered without shame (2:25). After transgression, the couple experiences shame and their procreative organs are a threat.[95] By implication, their posterity—those who will come to

90. In both cases, the "offspring" (זֶרַע, zera') of the blessed one is included in the blessing; see 9:9 and 12:7.
91. YHWH's commands to the man in Genesis 2:16–17 are in the singular. But when the serpent and the woman discuss the command in 3:1–5, they use the plural exclusively. So the narrative logic presumes that the woman—and, I would add, the couple's posterity—are incorporated into YHWH's command to the man in 2:16–17. Cassuto notes that in the pronouncement against the serpent and the woman, "there is a blurring of the boundary-line between the prototype of the species as an individual and as a symbol of the succeeding generations." See Cassuto, Genesis, Part I, 164.
92. The noun, זֶרַע, zera' ("offspring") is a collective noun here and elsewhere in the OT. But this fact does not preclude a predictive Christological dimension of this text. See Collins, Linguistic, Literary and Theological Commentary, 155–59.
93. The term for "loincloth" (חֲגֹרָה, hăgôrâ) is usually translated "belt" in the OT. In contrast to כֻּתֹּנֶת, kuttōnet ("garment," "coat"), which appears in verse 21, חֲגֹרָה (hăgôrâ) is something that would cover only the pudenda.
94. See in particular the use of the related term, עֶרְוָה, 'erwâ ("nakedness") in Leviticus 18–20.
95. The Pentateuchal legislation is particularly concerned with the threat that human "nakedness" posed in the presence of God. See Exodus 20:26; 28:42.

exist by these organs—partakes of the couple's disobedience. Here, I would venture, Augustine's fundamental intuition that sin has radically deformed the originally good character of the procreative act is justified by the text.[96]

Adam's Transgression Inaugurates the Reign of Death

The narrative of Genesis highlights the fact that Adam's transgression makes death the norm for human existence. In this sense, the text is truly etiological. But to modern readers, the narrative poses an immediate question. In light of YHWH's threatened penalty, "in the day that you eat of it you shall surely die" (2:17; cf. 3:3–4), why did Adam and Eve continue to live?[97] But the text does not address this question. The narrative strategy emphasizes that in fact all do die. The initial command in 2:17 presumes that an obedient Adam would not die. Though the serpent denied this (3:4), the divine penalty imposed on the man ("to dust you shall return"; 3:19) and YHWH's barring of the way to the tree of life ("lest he … live forever"; 3:22) underline the notion that transgression has brought death to the human race. Here, as the structure of the Pentateuch itself intimates, disobedience and distrust of YHWH bring death and exile from the land of God's presence.[98]

Several observations corroborate this conclusion. First, YHWH's provision of coats of skins (3:21) and Abel's animal sacrifices (4:4) hint that one of the consequences of Adam's transgression is animal death. But the text is not explicit on this point.[99] Second, Abel's murder at the hands of his brother (4:8), Cain's fear that others will do to him likewise (4:14), and Lamech's boast about killing a man (4:23) emphasize the spread of violent death. This waxing of violence in the world comes to a climax in the conditions preceding the Flood (6:13): "And

---

96. That is not to say that Augustine got it entirely correct. He concluded that sexual desire itself was the result of the Fall. Had the first couple maintained their primal integrity, the human procreative act would have occurred without desire simply as an act of choice. See *De peccato originali*, 39–42; *De civitate dei*, 14:18–19, 22–24. OT texts that celebrate desire in marital intimacy (Prov 5:15–20; Song of Sol) militate against this aspect of Augustine's view.

97. The Hebrew expression, בְּיוֹם, *bĕyôm*, "in the day," may refer to a less immediate time and simply be translated, "when." But see Reyburn and Fry, *Genesis*, 70; von Rad, *Genesis*, 95.

98. As elsewhere in the Pentateuch, exile and death are closely connected (Lev 26:14–39; Deut 28:15–68). See the argument by Sailhamer, *The Pentateuch as Narrative*, 102–3, 110–11.

99. God's permissive command in Genesis 1:29–30 implies that humans and animals were herbivorous before Adam's transgression. Chapter 3 marks the beginning of animal death, though the *consumption* of animal flesh goes conspicuously unmentioned. Only in 9:2–3, after the Flood, does God give explicit permission to eat animal flesh, with the stipulation that the blood be drained. See Bauckham, "Humans, Animals, and the Environment in Genesis 1–3," 183–84.

God said to Noah, 'I have determined to make an end of all flesh, for the earth is filled with violence through them. Behold, I will destroy them with the earth.'"[100]

Finally, Genesis testifies to the inevitable tragedy of human death in its genealogy from Adam to Noah (5:1–32). The morbid refrain, "and he died," punctuates the mention of each one of Noah's ancestors, Enoch being the sole exception. The narrative logic is explicit. God's threat that disobedience would bring death has been carried out, not just to the original couple in the garden, but also to the whole of their posterity. In the words of Paul, "Because of one man's trespass, death reigned" (Rom 5:17).

Adam's Transgression Marks the Emergence of Sin as a Power within Human Nature

The Christian doctrine of original sin teaches that every human receives moral corruption from Adam, which is passed by natural generation. While such a teaching is far from explicit, the structural logic of Genesis and the Pentateuch compels us to infer something of the sort for several reasons.[101] First, the way Adam and Eve related to God is different than in chapter 2. In chapter 3, they recognized their nakedness to be a menace and acted to cover themselves.[102] Something had changed. They correctly perceived that their exposed sexuality constituted a threat.[103] YHWH's question, "Who told you that you were naked?" (3:11), emphasizes the internal source of their knowledge—as Paul said, "their conscience also bears witness" (Rom 2:15). YHWH's second question implicitly

---

100. Of course, the Flood itself is the best evidence that death rules human and animal life.
101. Sailhamer, *The Pentateuch as Narrative*, 102, 110–11, insists that there is an inherent parallelism between Adam in the Garden and Israel in the land within the Pentateuch. I believe the text supports such parallelism. But there are details in the text which demand that we recognize significant asymmetry as well, particularly with reference to Genesis 2. (1) God's command to Adam conditions a threat but contains no promise (in distinction from God's covenantal commands to Israel; Deut 6:1–3; 28:1–14). Why? Adam already possessed the blessed life. (2) God's command to Adam elicited no fear from him (in distinction from God's commands addressed to Israel at Sinai; Exod 19:16; 20:18–21). Why? Adam was sinless. (3) Adam's nakedness in the presence of God is completely benign (in contrast to the care taken that priests not expose their nakedness in the tabernacle; Exod 20:26). Why? Human procreation was an unmitigated good before Adam's transgression. This asymmetry points to the *sui generis* character of the events of Eden.
102. The attempt to cover their nakedness is itself praiseworthy as we see in YHWH's act to cover the couple more adequately (3:21) and the implicit approval Genesis gives to Shem and Japheth (in contrast to Ham) for covering their father's nakedness in 9:20–27.
103. There may be an almost counterintuitive parallel with the function of the tabernacle later in the Pentateuch. The couple's exposure to the menace of God's presence required that their bodies be hidden with animal skins in Genesis 3. In Exodus, Israel's exposure to the menace of God's presence required that his presence be hidden in a tent made of animal skins.

answered his first. They knew because they had eaten the fruit. Their stated fear of YHWH's "sound" (קוֹל, qôl; 3:8) also shows that something had changed.[104] Nothing in chapter 2 insinuates that the presence or voice of God is threatening in any way. Chapter three is different. God's "sound" incites the couple to flight. Their disobedience has fundamentally changed their relationship to God. Finally, their banishment from God's presence in the Garden (3:23–24) negatively impacted how they related to God, just as Israel's exile would.[105] Henceforth, God would deal with them from a distance.

Second, chapter four marks the beginning of the narrative account of exile from the Garden. Immediately there is alienation within the family of humanity. In this context the first occurrence of the word "sin" (חַטָּאת, ḥaṭṭāt) in the canon appears. Instead of a concrete act of disobedience (as it usually is), sin here is a power of domination and death rather like a fierce animal ready to strike (4:7). Where is this threatening power located? It appears not to be outside of Cain but within him.[106] As with chapter three, where there is something internal to Adam that prompted him to cover and hide, sin is an internal power moving Cain to murder his brother. But the level of arrogance has been raised. Adam and Eve cover and hide but Cain seems unapologetic. Lamech's tale (4:23–24) indicates a further elevation of sinful arrogance. In contrast to Cain's unapologetic stance, Lamech boasts in his act of murder. His reference to the protection YHWH afforded Cain (4:15) suggests that he believes he can kill with impunity.

Third, we see the crescendo of arrogance reaching its zenith in chapter six. The "sons of God" take as many women as they please (6:2) and violence fills the

---

104. The Hebrew word קוֹל, qôl is usually translated "voice" (in every instance in Genesis outside of chapter 3) and often in the context of God's command (so Gen 22:8; 26:5). The context precludes that translation here but the word may reflect the narrative's intention to compare the "sound" (קוֹל, qôl) here, which the couple feared, with the "sound" (קוֹל, qôl) Israel heard at the foot of Sinai (Exod 20:18).

105. Deuteronomy 4:15–31 warns Israel that covenantal disobedience—particularly idolatry— would precipitate exile and destruction; in Genesis 3, the couple's disobedience likewise results in banishment and death.

106. Westermann, Genesis 1–11, 299–300, considers the possibility that "sin" describes a demonic force threatening Cain from the outside, but ultimately discards it, and I think rightly. The previous mention of Cain's anger and despondency (4:5) suggests something internal. Some Targumim gloss the passage with a reference to the "evil inclination," as Tg Neofiti, Fragment Targum, and Tg Ps-Jon (but notably not Tg Onqelos) to Genesis 4:7. See also Maher, trans., Targum Pseudo-Jonathan: Genesis, 32, n. 16. Without embracing the Jewish notion of the two inclinations, the context does imply that "sin" refers to a power internal to Cain influencing him to do wrong.

earth (6:11).[107] The parallel between 6:1 and 6:5 indicates that as humanity increases in population, so does wickedness.[108] God's conclusion, "that every intention of the thoughts of his heart was only evil continually" (6:5b) provides the reason for the Flood.[109] To summarize my point in this section, Genesis 1–6 makes an argument that the transgression of Genesis 3 has brought moral corruption to all humans, a corruption whose progress was checked only by the Flood.

God's Response to Adam's Transgression Is Judgment with Imposed Penalties

The events of Genesis 3 portray a divinely imposed sanction on the disobedient couple. This observation seems obvious at first glance. As commentators have observed, YHWH's conversation with Adam and Eve bears the stamp of a legal process: (1) discovery, (2) interrogation and defense, and (3) sentence.[110] The three pronouncements against the snake, the woman, and the man are presented as penalties levied against guilty parties. I have argued above that the line of thinking within the narrative of Genesis 3 requires us to see that Adam's posterity participates in the real consequences of his transgression.

In light of the later development of the doctrine of original sin, however, we must ask a further question. Does the text imply that the *guilt* of Adam's sin has passed to his posterity? This question is difficult to answer because Hebrew did not possess the vocabulary to distinguish punishment either from the natural consequences of transgression or from guilt.[111]

---

107. For the purposes of this chapter, it is unnecessary to identify these "sons of God" and their actions except to note how this episode advances the Pentateuch's narrative strategy of portraying the progressive corruption of humanity.

108. The text implies a correlation between Genesis 6:1a and 6:5a—in the former "humanity" (אָדָם, 'ādām) "multiplies" (verb: רבב, rbb) while in the latter it is the wickedness of "humanity" (אָדָם, ādām), which has multiplied (adjective: רַבָּה, rabbâ). See Mathews, *Genesis 1–11:26*, 322, 340.

109. The ancient church, following 1 Peter 5:20–21, saw baptism as a saving ordinance after the pattern of the Flood. It may be that the Pentateuchal logic behind the narrative infers something similar. The Flood is a saving ordinance after the pattern of the ritual immersion for corpse uncleanness outlined in Numbers 19. The decadent wickedness of humanity and the ground on which they trod required an immersion to rid it of its uncleanness. So in that sense, the Flood "saved" the world by washing away its wickedness and preparing the world for a new start.

110. Westermann, *Genesis 1–11*, 252; Culley, "Action Sequences," 28–29. Cassuto, *Genesis, Part I*, 155, takes God's calling to Adam as a legal summons.

111. Eichrodt, *Theology of the Old Testament*, 2:413. See also Kellermann, s.v. "עָוֹן, 'āwōn" in *Theological Dictionary of the Old Testament*, 10 (1999): 546–62, and Koch, s.v. "אָשָׁם, 'āšām" in *Theological Dictionary of the Old Testament*, 1 (rev. ed., 1977): 429–37. Both articles attest to the ambiguity involved in trying to separate punishment from guilt on the basis of vocabulary. The clearest example of the distinction between guilt and punishment in the He-

Distinctive to the Western (Latin) construal of original sin, following Augustine, was that both the penalty (*poena*) and the guilt (*culpa*) of Adam's sin were passed to his posterity. As argued above, virtually all Christians in the ancient church agreed that the whole human race participated in Adam's primal sin and its consequences. But penalty and guilt can be distinguished.[112] Augustine's argument that all receive the guilt of Adam's sin was an argument from justice—God would not impose a penalty on those who were not guilty.[113]

Does the text support Augustine's argument? I find it difficult to conclude that the text of Genesis 3 *explicitly* supports the notion of guilt imputed to Adam's posterity. But the Hebrew Bible does *implicitly* link guilt with penalty.[114] If this premise is correct, that penalty implies guilt, Augustine's conclusion is sound—Adam's posterity partakes of the penalty and guilt of Adam's sin.

CONCLUSION

In the historical study within the first section, we considered the church's doctrine of original sin. Virtually all segments of the church affirmed that Adam's primal transgression brought as its consequence universal moral depravity and human death. Furthermore, the Western theological tradition prior to the modern era—both Catholic and Protestant—also maintained that all received legal guilt for Adam's violation of God's command. In the second section, we saw that this universal reception of depravity, death, and guilt from Adam's transgression is the most natural reading of key Pauline texts. This reading is supported by some notions prevalent in second temple Judaism. In the third section, Old Testament texts outside of the Pentateuch were seen to allude to the narrative of Genesis 3 supposing a primordial era without sin before the onset of death. In the final section, we observed elements within the narrative of Genesis 3 itself that implied a theology of original sin. The sin in the Garden brought detrimental consequences on all of creation, including

---

brew canon is found in 2 Samuel 12, the account of Nathan's rebuke of David. After David's confession, Nathan brings him the prophetic word (1) that YHWH had put David's sin away but (2) there would still be punitive consequences on David's house. But the distinction between guilt and punishment here rests on the logic of the narrative, not the vocabulary.

112. One can imagine a case in which a child, born of an incarcerated mother, can be said to suffer the penalty of the mother's crime without being imputed the guilt of that crime.

113. *De peccato originali*, 36.

114. Eichrodt, *Theology of the Old Testament*, 2:413–43.

Adam's posterity. It marked the beginning of the human experience of death. Sin became a corrupting moral power within human nature. Finally, it portrayed the sin of the first couple as a criminal act with penalties borne not just by the first couple, but also by their descendants. In sum, all of the elements of the broader Christian doctrine of original sin are displayed in Genesis 3 and the Augustinian notion of inherited guilt is strongly implied.

BIBLIOGRAPHY

Abelard, Peter. *Abailard's Ethics*. Translated by J. Ramsay McCallum. Oxford: Blackwell, 1935.

Althaus, Paul. *The Theology of Martin Luther*. Translated by Robert C. Schultz. Philadelphia: Fortress, 1966.

Anselm of Canterbury, "The Virgin Conception and Original Sin." In *A Scholastic Miscellany: Anselm to Ockham*, 184–200. Edited and translated by Eugene R. Fairweather. Library of Christian Classics. Philadelphia: Westminster, 1956.

The Anti-Nicene Fathers. Edited by Alexander Roberts and James Donaldson. 10 vols. N.p.; reprinted, Grand Rapids: Eerdmans Publishing, 1993.

Barrett, C. K. *Commentary on the Epistle to the Romans*. Harper's New Testament Commentaries. New York: Harper & Row, 1957.

Barth, Karl. *Church Dogmatics*. 4 vols. Edited by G. W. Bromiley and T. F. Torrance. London: T&T Clark, 1975–77.

———. *Protestant Theology in the Nineteenth Century: Its Background and History*. New ed. Translated by Brian Cozens and John Bowden. Grand Rapids: Eerdmans Publishing, 2002.

Bauckham, Richard. "Humans, Animals, and the Environment in Genesis 1–3." In *Genesis and Christian Theology*, edited by Nathan MacDonald, Mark W. Elliott, and Grant Macaskill, 175–89. Grand Rapids: Eerdmans Publishing, 2012.

Beale, G. K. *The Temple and the Church's Mission: A Biblical Theology of the Dwelling Place of God*. New Studies in Biblical Theology 17. Downers Grove, IL: InterVarsity, 2004.

Beatrice, Pier Franco. *The Transmission of Sin: Augustine and the Pre-Augustinian Sources*. Translated by Adam Kamesar. AAR Religions in Translation. Oxford: Oxford University Press, 2013.

Bushnell, Horace. *Christian Nurture*. New York: Scrivner, Armstrong, 1876. Electronic ed. Grand Rapids: Christian Classics Ethereal Library, http://www.ccel.org/ccel/bushnell/nurture.pdf (accessed 1/17/2014).

Calvin, John. *Calvin: Institutes of the Christian Religion*. 2 vols. Translated by Ford Lewis Battles. Library of Christian Classics, vols. 20–21. Philadelphia: Westminster, 1960.

Calvin, John. *The Epistles of Paul the Apostle to the Romans and to the Thessalonians*. Translated by Ross Mackenzie. Calvin's New Testament Commentaries, vol. 8. N.p.: Oliver and Boyd, 1969. Reprint, Grand Rapids: Eerdmans Publishing, 1973.

Carroll R., M. Daniel. "Hosea." In *The Expositor's Bible Commentary*, vol. 8: *Daniel–Malachi*, rev. ed., edited by Tremper Longman, III and David E. Garland, 215–305. Grand Rapids: Zondervan, 2008.

Cassuto, U. *A Commentary on the Book of Genesis, Part I: From Adam to Noah: Genesis I–VI 8*. Translated by Israel Abrahams. Jerusalem: Magnes, 1998.

Catechism of the Catholic Church. Mahwah, NJ: Paulist, 1994.

Charlesworth, James H., ed. *The Old Testament Pseudepigrapha*. 2 vols. Garden City, NY: Doubleday, 1983, 1985.

Clarke, William Newton. *An Outline of Christian Theology*. 20th ed. New York: Charles Scribner's, 1912.

Clendenin, Daniel B. *Eastern Orthodox Christianity: A Western Perspective.*
   2nd ed. Grand Rapids: Baker, 2003.

Collins, C. John. *A Linguistic, Literary and Theological Commentary.* Phillipsburg, NJ: P&R, 2006.

Cranfield, C. E. B. *A Critical and Exegetical Commentary on the Epistle to the
   Romans.* 2 vols. The International Critical Commentary. Edinburgh:
   T&T Clark, 1975.

Culley, Robert C. "Action Sequences in Genesis 2–3." *Semeia* 18 (1980): 28–29.

Dubarle, Andre-Marie. *The Biblical Doctrine of Original Sin.* Translated by
   E. M. Stewart. New York: Herder and Herder, 1964.

Dumbrell, William J. *Creation and Covenant: A Theology of the Old Testament Covenants.* Nashville: Nelson, 1984.

Dunn, James D. G. *Romans 1–8.* Word Biblical Commentary, vol. 38A.
   Dallas: Word, 1988.

Eichrodt, Walther. *Theology of the Old Testament.* 2 vols. Translated by J. A.
   Baker. The Old Testament Library. Philadelphia: Westminster, 1961,
   1967.

Ellis, Mark A. *Simon Episcopius' Doctrine of Original Sin.* American University Studies, series 7, vol. 240. New York: Peter Lang, 2008.

Enchiridion Symbolorum. Edited by Henry Denizinger. Translated by Roy J.
   Deferrari. Fitzwilliam, NH: Loreto, 1954.

Enns, Peter. *The Evolution of Adam: What the Bible Does and Doesn't Say
   about Human Origins.* Grand Rapids: Baker, 2012.

Fitzpatrick, Joseph. *The Fall and the Ascent of Man: How Genesis Supports
   Darwin.* Lanham, MD: University Press of America, 2012.

Hodge, Charles. *Systematic Theology*. 3 vols. N.p. Reprint, Grand Rapids: Eerdmans Publishing, 1981.

Hoekema, Anthony A. *Created in God's Image*. Grand Rapids: Eerdmans Publishing, 1986.

Johnson, S. Lewis, Jr. "Romans 5:12—An Exercise in Exegesis and Theology." In *New Dimensions in New Testament Study*, edited by Richard N. Longenecker and Merrill C. Tenney, 298–316. Grand Rapids: Zondervan, 1974.

Käsemann, Ernst. *Commentary on Romans*. Translated by Geoffrey W. Bromiley. Grand Rapids: Eerdmans Publishing, 1980.

Kelly, J. N. D. *Early Christian Doctrines*. Rev. ed. San Francisco: Harper & Row, 1978.

Klauber, Martin I. "The Helvetic Formula Consensus (1675): An Introduction and Translation." *Trinity Journal* n.s. 11 (1990): 103–23.

Lohfink, Norbert. "Genesis 2–3 as 'Historical Etiology': Thoughts on a New Hermeneutical Concept." In *Theology of the Pentateuch: Themes of the Priestly Narrative and Deuteronomy*, 18–34. Translated by Linda M. Maloney. Minneapolis: Fortress, 1994.

Lohse, Bernhard. *Martin Luther's Theology: Its Historical and Systematic Development*. Translated by Roy A. Harrisville. Minneapolis: Fortress, 1999.

Lohse, Eduard. *Colossians and Philemon*. Hermeneia. Translated by William R. Poehlmann and Robert J. Karris. Philadelphia: Fortress, 1971.

Maher, Michael, trans. *Targum Pseudo-Jonathan: Genesis*. The Aramaic Bible 1B. Collegeville, MN: Liturgical, 1987.

Mathews, K. A. *Genesis 1–11:26*. The New American Commentary, vol. 1A. Nashville: Broadman and Holman, 1996.

Melanchthon, Philip. "Loci communes theologici" In *Melanchthon and Bucer*, ed. Wilhelm Pauck, 18–152. Library of Christian Classics, vol. 19. Philadelphia: Westminster, 1969.

Moore, George Foot. *Judaism in the First Centuries of the Christian Era, the Age of the Tannaim*. 3 vols. Cambridge, MA: Harvard University Press, 1927–30.

Murray, John. *The Epistle to the Romans*. 2 vols. New International Commentary on the New Testament. Grand Rapids: Eerdmans Publishing, 1965.

Nicene and Post-Nicene Fathers of the Christian Church. Series 1, edited by Philip Schaff, 14 vols. Series 2, edited by Philip Schaff and Henry Wace, 15 vols. N.p.; reprinted, Grand Rapids: Eerdmans Publishing, 1993.

Norris, Richard A., Jr., trans. *The Christological Controversy*. Minneapolis: Fortress, 1980.

Oesterley, W. O. E. *The Jews and Judaism During the Greek Period: The Background of Christianity*. Port Washington, NY: Kennikat, 1941.

Pagels, Elaine. *Adam, Eve, and the Serpent*. New York: Random House, 1988.

Pagels, Elaine. "The Politics of Paradise: Augustine's Exegesis of Genesis 1–3 versus that of John Chrysostom." *Harvard Theological Review* 78, nos. 1–2 (1985): 67–99.

Pelikan, Jaroslav. *The Spirit of Eastern Christendom (600–1700)*. The Christian Tradition: A History of the Development of Doctrine, vol. 2. Chicago: University of Chicago Press, 1974.

Racovian Catechism with Notes and Illustrations. Translated by Thomas Rees. London: Longman, Husts, 1818.

Reyburn, William David, and Euan McGregor Fry. *A Handbook on Genesis*. UBS Handbook Series. New York: United Bible Societies, 1998. Electronic ed., Logos Research Systems, n.d.

Robinson, H. Wheeler. *Corporate Personality in Ancient Israel.* Rev. ed. Philadelphia: Fortress, 1980.

Ross, Allen P. *Creation and Blessing: A Guide to the Study and Exposition of Genesis.* Grand Rapids: Baker, 1988.

Sailhamer, John H. *The Pentateuch as Narrative: A Biblical-Theological Commentary.* Library of Biblical Interpretation. Grand Rapids: Zondervan, 1992.

Sanders, E. P. *Paul and Palestinian Judaism: A Comparison of Patterns of Religion.* Philadelphia: Fortress, 1977.

Sandmel, Samuel. *Judaism and Christian Beginnings.* New York: Oxford University Press, 1978.

Schleiermacher, Friedrich. *The Christian Faith.* Edited by H. R. Mackintosh and J. S. Stewart. Philadelphia: Fortress, 1928.

Schoof, T. M. *A Survey of Catholic Theology 1800–1970.* Translated by N. D. Smith. Glen Rock, NJ: Paulist/Newman, 1970.

Strong, Augustus Hopkins. *Systematic Theology.* 3 vols. Philadephia: American Baptist Publication Society, 1907. Electronic ed., Logos Research Systems, n.d.

Tennant, F. R. *The Sources of the Doctrines of the Fall and Original Sin.* N.p., 1903. Reprint, New York: Schocken, 1968.

Theological Dictionary of the Old Testament. Edited by G. Johannes Botterweck, Helmer Ringgren, and Heinz-Josef Fabry. 15 vols. (to date). Grand Rapids: Eerdmans Publishing, 1977–2006.

Voltaire. *A Philosophical Dictionary.* In *The Works of Voltaire: A Contemporary Version.* New York: DuMont, 1901; electronic ed., University of Adalaide, South Australia, http://ebooks.adelaide.edu.au/v/voltaire/dictionary (accessed 2/10/2014).

von Rad, Gerhard. *Genesis: A Commentary*. Rev. ed. Translated by John H. Marks. Old Testament Library. Philadelphia: Westminster, 1972.

Westermann, Claus. *A Continental Commentary: Genesis 1–11*. Minneapolis: Fortress, 1994. Electronic ed., Logos Research Systems, n.d.

Whitelaw, Thomas. "The Biblical Conception of Sin." In *The Fundamentals*. 4 vols. Edited by R. A. Torrey, A. C. Dixon, et al. Los Angeles: Bible Institute of Los Angeles, 1917. Reprint, Grand Rapids: Baker, 2000.

Wolff, Hans Walter. *Hosea*. Hermeneia. Translated by Gary Stansell. Philadelphia: Fortress, 1974.

Wright, N. T. *Paul and the Faithfulness of God*. 2 books. Christian Origins and the Question of God, vol. 4. Minneapolis: Fortress, 2013.

Wright, N. T. *The Climax of the Covenant: Christ and the Law in Pauline Theology*. Minneapolis: Fortress, 1991.

Zimmerli, Walther. *Ezekiel: A Commentary on the Book of the Prophet Ezekiel, Chapters 25–48*. Hermeneia. Philadelphia: Fortress, 1979. Electronic ed., Logos Research Systems, n.d.

Zwingli, Ulrich. "Of Baptism." In *Zwingli and Bullinger*. Edited by G. W. Bromiley, 119–75. Library of Christian Classics, vol. 24. Philadelphia: Westminster, 1953.

CHAPTER 6

THE SEED AND SCHAEFFER

William Varner

In 1968 Francis Schaeffer published a little book titled *Escape from Reason*, but its popularity and effect far outdistanced its short compass (125 pages).[1] Schaeffer accused modern thought, which he traced back to Aquinas, as being guilty of attempting to operate in a divided field of thought. He called this the upper and lower stories. These two divisions were originally called "nature" (lower story) and "grace" (upper story). These two "stories" would be called by other names throughout the following centuries. According to Schaefer, the dualism of history (lower) and faith (upper) has strongly influenced the discussion of religious thought and belief from pre-modern days into the current post-modern ideas.

As Schaeffer described the scene, religious existentialism recognized the lower sphere as one field, the realm of history and bald facts. The upper sphere, on the other hand, was the realm where faith was affirmed.[2] German neo-orthodoxy could use two different terms for "history." *Historie* could describe the lower story; *Geschichte* could describe the upper story of history. Theologians adopted a word coined in the nineteenth century, *Heilsgeschichte* (literally "holy history"), to describe the "salvation history" that could exist in

---

1. Schaefer, *Escape from Reason*.
2. See Schaeffer, *Complete Works*, Vol 1, 238–44.

the upper story, without necessitating that it described the space-time events of history in the lower story.[3]

The danger of all of this, however, was the idea of exercising faith when there was no possibility of any historical basis for such a faith. In any case, the upper sphere was that of faith and it mattered not, to the religious existentialist, if there were any verifiable facts in the lower sphere that formed the basis of that faith. In essence, such faith could be described as "faith in one's faith," not faith in some objectively verifiable events in space-time history.[4]

While Schaeffer's analysis of the complexity of modern philosophy and culture was often criticized as overly simplistic, it does offer a paradigm that can be useful in addressing some of the issues raised in this book. Did the events that are related in Genesis 3 really take place in space-time history (Schaeffer's lower sphere) or can we Christians be satisfied with affirming faith in the message that these stories convey (his upper sphere) without any concern that they actually took place?[5]

The purpose of this chapter is twofold: (1) to investigate whether the promise that is enunciated in Genesis 3:15 can really be called a prophecy that predicts a coming deliverer commonly called the Messiah; and (2) to investigate whether it is really that important to affirm the actual existence of Adam, Eve, and the serpent as the characters mentioned in that chapter who figure in that promise. In other words, is there a harmony or a disjunct between the history described in Genesis 3 and faith in the message conveyed by those events?

Genesis 3:15 as a Messianic Prophecy

In addressing the first issue—is Genesis 3:15 messianic?—we read the verse initially in the form of its most venerable expression, the King James Version, followed by the version which we will use in this chapter, the ESV.

And I will put enmity between thee and the woman, and be-

---

3. For a clarification of *Heilsgeschichte* ("salvation history"), both in its negative and positive effects, see Ferguson, Wright, and Packer, *New Dictionary of Theology*, 612–13.
4. Schaeffer developed his epistemology further in another work titled *The God Who Is There* (1968) and in *He Is There and He Is Not Silent* (1972). The three volumes were published together as a trilogy: *The Complete Works of Francis A. Schaeffer: A Christian Worldview*.
5. Schaeffer expounded Genesis 3 as describing actual historical events in *Genesis in Space and Time*, 103–8.

tween thy seed and her seed; it shall bruise thy head, and thou shalt bruise his heel.

I will put enmity between you and the woman, and between your offspring and her offspring; he shall bruise your head, and you shall bruise his heel.

Context of Genesis 3:15

It is important to note that this verse is part of a larger narrative involving a man, a woman, and a serpent. It is not an isolated statement but actually comes as part of the judgment that is pronounced by the Lord on the woman, the man, and the serpent because of their sin and the serpent's temptation toward that sin. The movement progresses from the conversation with the woman (3:1–5), to the committing of the sin (3:6), to the consciousness of the sin (3:7–8), to the confronting of the sinners (3:9–13), to finally the consequences of the sin (3:14–24). While our focus will be on 3:15, we will briefly trace this narrative of events that lead up to the promise. As we will see, the narrative reads like a historical account and involves profound theological realities. The context shows that Genesis 3 is not just a simple tale of a man, a snake, and a woman.

The Conversation with the Woman (3:1–5)

The conversation between a serpent and a woman in Genesis 3 is one of the most important and decisive of all the many conversations recorded in the Bible.[6] The man and the woman had been placed in an ideal environment with only one restriction: Do not eat from one tree (Gen 2:16–17). That command actually had been given to the man before the woman was created. It was his responsibility to communicate God's words correctly to his wife. This fact must be recognized to fully understand the woman's response to the serpent's question and statements.

Employing the instrument of a serpent, Satan launched a twofold attack on the "woman."[7] While the word *Satan* is not employed in the chapter, the text is obviously describing more than a creature. In the words of one writer,

---

6. Skeptics sometimes mock the account as obviously ahistorical because of the serpent's talking. It should be kept in mind that in this and in only one other occasion, Balaam's donkey in Numbers 22, do animals speak in the Bible. This is *not Aesop's Fables* or an ancient version of the *Chronicles of Narnia*!

7. There seems to be a deliberate play on words between the Hebrew word for "naked" in 2:25 (עָרוֹם, *'arom*), and the word describing the serpent as "crafty" (עָרוּם, *'arum*). Perhaps the connection between the two ideas is that whatever is naked is free from impediments

the serpent is "the mouthpiece of a Dark Power, whom later texts would call Satan."[8] Remember that the "woman" was not named "Eve" until after the fall (Gen 3:20). First, Satan attacked the *Word of God*: "He said to the woman, 'Did God actually say, "You shall not eat of any tree in the garden"?'" (Gen 3:1b). He sought to cast doubt in her mind about what God had actually said. The woman's response sounds good at first, but she adds something. "You shall not eat of the fruit of the tree that is in the midst of the garden, neither shall you touch it, lest you die" (3:3). Evidently the man had not communicated God's Word faithfully to his wife, since she added the matter about not touching the tree.

Satan's next thrust was to attack the *will and wisdom of God*:

> But the serpent said to the woman, "You will not surely die. For God knows that when you eat of it your eyes will be opened, and you will be like God, knowing good and evil" (3:4–5).

The enemy launched his frontal attack by calling God a liar as well as impugning God's motive. He accused God with not wanting any creatures to have the kind of knowledge that He possessed. The word translated as "God" earlier in the verse (אֱלֹהִים, *'elohim*) should be rendered "God" in its second occurrence as well. While not attempting to minimize the act of rebellion as a feature of their sin, it should be noted that what was driving the man and woman was not just rebellion but a desire for wisdom, but not from the right source.

The Committing of the Sin (3:6)

> So when the woman saw that the tree was good for food, and that it was a delight to the eyes, and that the tree was to be desired to make one wise, she took of its fruit and ate, and she also gave some to her husband who was with her, and he ate (3:6).

The fruit had a threefold appeal to the woman, corresponding to a later threefold appeal to Jesus (the second Adam) in the wilderness (Matt 4) and also to the three-fold attraction of the world in 1 John 2:16. The tree was (1)

---

and can act in a more effective manner than that which is encumbered by hindrance. In other words, unlike the woman, the serpent was not encumbered by "innocence."

8. Collins, *Genesis 1–4*, 156.

"good for food" (i.e., "desire of the flesh"); (2) "pleasant to the eyes" (i.e., "desire of the eyes"); and (3) "desired to make one wise" (i.e., "pride of life"). The tempter used the same threefold approach in tempting the Second "Adam," the Lord Jesus, in Matthew 4:1–11. In that decisive encounter, Satan asked Jesus to turn stones into bread (i.e., "desire of the flesh"); to cast Himself down from the Temple before a marveling crowd (i.e., "desire of the eyes"); and to receive the world's kingdoms through worshipping the "prince of this world" (i.e., "the pride of life").[9] Had the woman responded as Jesus had, by citing the Word of God, she would have been able to thwart the tempter. However, she and her husband succumbed and satisfied their desires.

The Consciousness of the Sin (3:7–8)

Whereas previously they each had enjoyed a harmonious personality free from guilt, the man and woman now attempted to cover their shame with fig leaves. Rabbinic commentators have suggested that the unnamed "fruit," so often referred to mistakenly as an "apple" in popular thought, was most likely a fig since its leaves were later used to cover their nakedness.[10] No matter the kind of fruit they ate, fig leaves were inadequate to remove their guilt. Later in the chapter, the Lord covered the humbled pair with skins from slain animals, possibly prefiguring the truth that sinners are restored by blood and not by their own meritorious actions.

The couple's consciousness of sin extended not only to themselves but also to their relationship to God. Whereas previously they had enjoyed close fellowship with the Lord, their new attitude was different.

> And they heard the sound of the LORD God walking in the garden in the cool of the day, and the man and his wife hid themselves from the presence of the LORD God among the trees of the garden (3:8).

---

9. Rather than viewing the temptations of Jesus as linked back either to Israel's wilderness wanderings (the quotations from Deuteronomy) *or* back to the Garden (the three desires), it is best to see a set of intertextual links from the Temptation *through* Deuteronomy/Israel in the wilderness back to the Garden. As the son of God, Adam (Luke 3:38) and God's son, Israel (Hos 11:1; Matt 2:15), both failed their tests, the Son of God passed His. Note the words of the tempter, "If you are the Son of God…" (Matt 4:6).

10. Rashi and other Talmudic commentators suggested that the fig was also the forbidden fruit on the tree of life. In other words, the means of their Fall became the means of their restoration (Cohen, *The Soncino Chumash*, 13).

One cannot practice sin and at the same time enjoy that sweet fellowship of unbroken communion with God. Again there is nothing in this simple and straightforward narrative to make us think that anything other than space-time events are being related. There is, however, an overall message with intertextual links to later events that clearly communicates that this "story" is more than a nice little tale about a man, a woman, and a snake.

The Confronting of the Sinners (3:9–13)

The Lord God first questioned the man concerning his whereabouts and asked if he had eaten of the forbidden tree. God did not ask these questions to gain knowledge, but wished to elicit a response from Adam. The man, however, responded with the oft-quoted excuse, "The woman whom you gave to be with me, she gave me fruit of the tree, and I ate" (3:12). Thus began the long history of one of the favorite pastimes of fallen humanity—the evil practice of blame-shifting.

The response of the woman was to blame her behavior on the serpent who had beguiled or tricked her (3:13).[11] Instead of assuming responsibility for her action, she also was guilty of blame-shifting. Of course the serpent had no one else to blame.

The Consequences of the Sin (3:14–24)

The rest of the narrative can be summarized in three sections: (1) The Pronouncements of Judgment (3:14–19); (2) The Provision of Covering (3:20–21); and (3) The Precaution against Eating (3:22–24). What will concern us in this chapter, however, is the series of sentences pronounced on the three guilty parties. The man must toil in physical labor (3:17–19), while the woman must toil in maternal labor (3:16). Before these pronouncements, however, the Lord promises judgment on the serpent:

> The LORD God said to the serpent, "Because you have done
> this, cursed are you above all livestock and above all beasts of
> the field; on your belly you shall go, and dust you shall eat all
> the days of your life. I will put enmity between you and the

---

11. Paul makes use of the Greek word used by the LXX (ἀπατάω) in his treatment of the woman's transgression in 1 Timothy 2:14. Note another possible allusion to the Fall and the subsequent promise in his expression "saved through childbearing" in 2:15.

woman, and between your offspring and her offspring; he shall
bruise your head, and you shall bruise his heel" (3:14–15).

Notice that the order of the Divine judgments of the three characters
is reversed from the order of the Divine confrontations in a sort of chiastic
structure (A B C C' B' A'). The man was confronted (3:9–12); then the woman
was confronted (3:13); and then the serpent was confronted (3:14). The serpent was then judged (3:14–15); then the woman was judged (3:16); and then
the man was judged (3:17–19). Thus the word of hope about the woman's seed
actually is part of the judgment on the serpent.

Having set Genesis 3:15 within its narrative flow, we must conclude that the
author's intention in this chapter was to present these events as if they actually
happened. This is a straightforward account, structured as a narrative and not as
poetry. What now can be said about the nature and significance of this promise?
For those who interpret 3:15 as a messianic promise, the words embedded within
these ominous words of doom portray an individual who will be mankind's only
hope—the seed of the woman, called by such names as the Deliverer, the Savior,
and most famously, the Messiah. That *coming one* will not arrive, however, before
a fierce conflict develops. Here is a promise not only of hope but also of warfare:
a battle between followers of the Lord and of Satan. Ultimately, the conflict will
focus on two individuals. The word "seed" in Hebrew (זֶרַע, *zera '*) has both a collective and an individual meaning, just like its English equivalent as well as its
equivalent in Greek (σπέρμα, *sperma*), which is used in the Septuagint (LXX)
translation of this verse. The masculine singular pronoun used in the promise,
"*he* (KJV: *it*) shall bruise your head," indicates that a male member of the human
race will deliver a fatal and final blow to the serpent. This crushing blow will not
come, however, without the woman's seed also receiving a wound, although not
as serious, on His heel. Thus in Christian interpretation this promise is the *prote-
vangelium*, a Latin word for the "first mention of the gospel."

Can this messianic interpretation be sustained, or have we been guilty of
reading too much into the admittedly cryptic language of this verse? We will
need to look at more details of this verse and also to interact with others (especially Jewish writers) who deny any messianic role in Genesis 3:15 or think
that Christians have too zealously seen a promise of the Messiah here.

To defend a messianic interpretation of Genesis 3:15, we must first look
even closer at its context and some of its details. In 3:14 the Lord addresses the
serpent with the following words.

The Lord God said to the serpent,
 "Because you have done this,
 cursed are you above all livestock
 and above all beasts of the field;
 on your belly you shall go,
 and dust you shall eat
 all the days of your life."

The punishment of the serpent is that it would be perpetually a crawler on the earth. The medieval rabbi, Shlomo Yitzaki, also known by his acronym, *Rashi*, suggested that the serpent was previously an upright and glorious creature with legs.[12] This interpretation, however, is not needed since nothing in the context states that he had been upright. The judgment is that he would continue to be that way and "eat dust." This judgment implies defeat and the expression is used that way in later scriptures (Ps 72:9; Isa 49:23). In other words, "You may have been victorious today, but it will not always be so." There is also some biting irony here, in that the serpent tried to get the woman to eat, but he also will end up eating—namely, dust! Eschatological prophetic passages teach that even when the curse is lifted, this aspect of it will remain as the lot of the serpent (Isa 65:25).

So, is this really just a story about snakes and women? Even from the fact that the serpent spoke and indicated a high intellectual power to seduce, it is evident that there was a supernatural power behind serpent. Thus, the Lord primarily addresses the serpent in 3:14, and then primarily addresses the power behind the serpent in 3:15.[13]

Traditional Interpretation of Genesis 3:15

So what does Genesis 3:15 say? To answer this question, let us approach the text more closely. For those who read Hebrew, here is the text of Genesis 3:15:

---

12. Cohen, *The Soncino Chumash*, 15. Occasionally, one may read a popular commentator or hear a preacher who mentions this interpretation (Boice, *Genesis*, 159).

13. A recent scholar who defends the Messianic interpretation of Gen 3:15 writes: "Although in Gen 3:14 the Lord addresses the actual serpent, in the following verse (3:15), He appears to address the dark power animating it. I believe this is similar to the way the king of Tyre is addressed in Ezek 28:1–10 followed by an oracle against Lucifer, the anointed cherub, as the power behind the throne (cf. Ezek 28:11–19), yet with no textual indication of a change of addressee" (Rydelnik, *The Messianic Hope*, 136–37).

וְאֵיבָה וֹ אָשִׁית בָּינְךָ וּבֵין הָאִשָּׁה וּבֵין זַרְעֲךָ וּבֵין זַרְעָה הוּא יְשׁוּפְךָ רֹאשׁ וְאַתָּה תְּשׁוּפֶנּוּ עָקֵב:

Here is the English translation of the ESV:

> I will put enmity between you and the woman,
> and between your offspring and her offspring;
> he shall bruise your head,
> and you shall bruise his heel.

First, we should notice that it is the Lord God Himself who will insti-
gate the hostility between the characters mentioned in the verse. The word
for "enmity," the Hebrew אֵיבָה (*'eyvah*) occurs outside this verse only three
other times in the Hebrew Bible. In each of these other appearances, the word
always describes a hostility or enmity or even hatred that exists between persons: Numbers 35:21–22 (a murderer); Ezekiel 25:15 (Philistines); and Ezekiel 35:5 (Edomites). These usages point out that the hostility described in
3:15 is more than the dislike that a woman has for a snake.

Second, we may observe that the fulfillment of the future statements of this
verse actually moves on three levels. First, there will be hostility between the woman and the serpent (15a). Eve will detest him for what he has done in tricking her.
He will detest her because he has lost an ally and gained an enemy. Second, there
will be hostility between the followers of the one who is the power behind the serpent and the followers of the woman (15b). The serpent's seed will be the people
who follow the serpent's deceptive ways of offering wisdom apart from its divine
source. John 8:44 comes into definite play at this point: "You are of your father
the devil." The woman's seed must be understood as followers of the Lord because
the woman is the object of the Lord's redemption in this account. Thus on this
second level, it is proper to see predicted a clash depicted between the godly and
the ungodly in the future history of redemption. Finally, on a third level, the verse
foresees the ultimate hostility and clash between the individual descendant of the
woman and the individual power behind the serpent, which later history will call
"the devil and Satan" (Rev 12:9). It is that individual or messianic interpretation
that we have attempted to explain. So how have others read this promise?

Objections to the Messianic Interpretation of Genesis 3:15

It hardly needs to be mentioned that theologically liberal commentators,
who deny the possibility of any accurate human knowledge of the future, uni-

formly deny the messianic interpretation of Genesis 3:15.[14] What may be surprising, however, is the increasing number of professedly evangelical commentators who deny that this verse should be used as a prophecy of Jesus the Messiah.

There have been three primary differing interpretations of this important verse.[15] These could be called the "natural interpretation," the "spiritual/symbolic interpretation," and the "individual/Messianic interpretation." The natural view sees the language of this verse as describing a very long conflict between mankind and snakes. Many Jewish commentators, but not all, adopt this view.[16] We will see later that while this is the general modern Jewish view, a number of ancient and medieval Jewish rabbis saw more than snakes and women in this verse. The spiritual/symbolic view sees this verse as describing a serious spiritual struggle between good and evil people throughout history.[17] Such passages as Jesus' charge against the religious leaders are mentioned as evidence of this approach. See, for example, John 8:44: "You are of your father the devil, and your will is to do your father's desires. He was a murderer from the beginning, and does not stand in the truth, because there is no truth in him. When he lies, he speaks out of his own character, for he is a liar and the father of lies." Finally, the individual/Messianic view sees Genesis 3:15 as a prediction of the Messiah's ultimate victory over Satan, while not totally discounting but incorporating the other views.[18]

Thus not all interpreters have seen the Messiah in these promises in Genesis 3:15. It is expected that Jews and Protestant liberals would be part of this opposition. It may be surprising, however, to learn that there are evangelicals who doubt and even strongly object to seeing Jesus anticipated here.[19]

---

14. Driver, *The Book of Genesis*, 49; Skinner, *Critical and Exegetical Commentary on Genesis*, 79–81.
15. For a concise history of the interpretation of Genesis 3:15, see Lewis, "The Woman's Seed (Gen 3:15)," 299–319.
16. Lewis, 304–5. See also Newman, *Commentary of Nahmanides*, 78.
17. Keil, *Biblical Commentary on the Old Testament*, 100–2.
18. The following is a sampling of authors writing in English from the nineteenth through twenty-first centuries who have espoused this messianic view: Baron, Briggs, Brown, Cooper, Delitzsch, Fruchtenbaum, Gloag, Hengstenberg, Kaiser, Lindsey, Meldau, Rosen, Rydelnik, Sailhamer, Alexander (in Satterthwaite), Smith, Van Groningen, Varner, and Wright.
19. Because there is enough of a polemical tone in the following paragraphs, this writer is hesitant to list the names of evangelical scholars known to him who object to the messianic interpretation of Genesis 3:15. Suffice it to say here that the evangelical-sponsored NET Bible is representative of these writers when it criticizes what it calls this "allegorical" interpretation. This approach falters in many ways, as will be shown in the following discussion. It also faces the stark reality that an intertextual reading of both Old and New Testaments reveals that later writers of Scripture interpreted Genesis 3:15 in a messianic manner. Appeals to a so-called historical-grammatical hermeneutic that leads away from the Messiah in this verse are simply

One of the most often mentioned objections to the messianic interpretation of Genesis 3:15 is the appeal to the collective, not individual, meaning of the Hebrew word for "seed" (זֶרַע, zera).[20] Two of the standard Jewish translations of the Hebrew Bible into English reflect this collective and thus non-individual sense. "And I will put enmity between thee and the woman, and between thy seed and her seed; *they* shall bruise thy head, and thou shalt bruise their heel."[21] Sometimes, these Jewish writers appeal to the ancient *Jerusalem Targum* that paraphrases the Hebrew into the Aramaic as follows: "When the sons of the women keep the commandments *they* shall smite you on the head" (italicized words in these two quotations are provided by the author).

The analysis above already shows that we can have both. The enmity between "her seed" and "your seed" denotes that. However, the next line ("He shall bruise your head") seems to refer to an individual. In support of this, further examination of the term "seed" reveals some overlooked factors in the search for its meaning. The word *seed* is used in Bible in both a collective *and* in an individual sense and we do not have to look far beyond Genesis 3:15 to see that taking place! See for example, Genesis 4:25: "And Adam knew his wife again, and she bore a son and called his name Seth, for she said, 'God has appointed for me another offspring (*zera'*) instead of Abel, for Cain killed him.'" Here Adam reflects the joy over the birth of the individual Seth that Eve had earlier expressed over the birth of the individual Cain (Gen 4:1). See also the use of *zera* in Hannah's prayer for a child in 1 Samuel 1:11.[22]

That a singular meaning of *zera'* is intended is further confirmed by the fact that all pronouns and accompanying verbs in the verse are singular. Note the use of "he" (הוּא, *hu*) and "his" (masculine singular suffix וֹ, *nu*).[23] Translations that render the pronouns as "they" and "their" read into the text ideas that simply are not there. When singular pronouns are used with "seed" the singularity of the

---

wrong-headed and neglect the apostolic hermeneutic that pays attention to the broader canonical and theological context of a passage in addition to its immediate "historical" context.

20. Sigal, *The Jew and the Christian Missionary*, 3.
21. *The Holy Scriptures*, 6; *The Tanakh*, 6–7.
22. The reference to her "seed" is often obscured by translations that render the word as "son" (for example, the ESV).
23. Roman Catholic art depicting Mary crushing the head of a serpent arises from Jerome's mistranslation of the masculine pronoun as *ipsa*, a Latin feminine pronoun rather than the masculine pronoun *ipse*. The Douay English version, based on the Vulgate, translates the expression as "she will crush." Jerome did mention that the pronoun referred to the Lord in his commentary on Genesis, but the translation was done and was not corrected! Hayward, *Jerome's "Hebrew Questions on Genesis,"* 33.

seed is emphasized.[24] Furthermore, it appears that Eve may even have considered
the birth of her first child Cain (wrongly) to be the fulfillment of this promise
(Gen 4:1b). Lastly, although not believing that the promise was messianic, there
are even Jewish translations that render the pronouns and verbs in a singular
fashion. "And I will put enmity between thee and the woman, and between thy
seed and her seed; he shall bruise thy head, and thou shalt wound his heel."[25]
"And I will put enmity between thee and the woman, and between thy seed and
her seed; he shall bruise thy head, and thou shalt bruise his heel."[26]

Another objection, often arising from Jewish writers, is that it is simply unwarranted to see the Messiah in this verse. Some critics argue that a messianic
rather than a natural or collective interpretation involves a huge dose of *eisegesis*,
i.e., wrongly reading the Messiah *into* the verse rather than legitimately reading
Him *out of* the verse (*exegesis*).[27] Our response is that if this is a valid charge, why
did so many ancient exegetes adopt the messianic interpretation? For example, the
earliest Jewish reading of Messiah was probably in the LXX.[28] The translator used
the masculine pronoun αὐτός as the subject of the verb "bruise" and the masculine pronoun αὐτοῦ for "his" seed. Other early Jewish interpreters continued the
messianic interpretation in the Aramaic paraphrases called the "Targums." These
declare clearly that the fulfillment of this promise will take place "in the days of
King Messiah."[29] An early rabbinic commentary on Genesis says, "Eve had respect
to that seed which is coming from another place. And who is this? This is Messiah
the King."[30] A respected medieval rabbinic commentator, David Kimchi, wrote
on Genesis 3:15, "As thou went forth for the salvation of thy people by the hand of
the Messiah, the son of David, who shall wound Satan, the head . . . of the house
of the wicked."[31] Early Christian interpreters such as Justin Martyr, Theophilus of
Antioch, Irenaeus, Origen, Tertullian, and Augustine are just a sampling of the

---

24. Collins, "A Syntactical Note (Genesis 3:15)," 148. For further syntactical evidence of this singu-
    lar use of "seed," see Alexander, "Further Observations on the Term 'Seed' in Genesis," 363–67.
25. Leeser, *Torah nevi'im u-ketuvim: Twenty Four Books of the Holy Scriptures*, 4.
26. Harkavy, *The Holy Scriptures: English Version*, 4.
27. Sigal, *The Jew and the Christian Missionary*, 4.
28. Martin, "Earliest Messianic Interpretation of Genesis 3:15," 425–27.
29. Levey, *The Messiah: An Aramaic Interpretation*, 2.
30. *Bereishit Rabba*, 23.
31. Edersheim mentions Kimchi and other rabbinic commentators on Genesis 3:15 in Ap-
    pendix 9 of *Life and Times of Jesus the Messiah*, vol. 2, 710–11. See also the discussion in
    Williams, *Christian Evidences for Jewish People*, 112–18. Note also the reference to Kimchi
    in Cooper, *Messiah: His Names and Person*, 28.

Patristic writers who saw the Messiah, and specifically Jesus, in the verse.[32] Now of course it is possible that all these ancient writers could be wrong, but it should never be charged that the messianic interpretation of the verse did not commend itself strongly to respectable Jewish and Christian minds.

Another objection to the messianic interpretation of our text may have more validity. Many have remarked that to see a virgin birth predicted is simply unwarranted. Some Christians have seen a hint at a virgin birth by the reference to a *woman's* seed when we know that the *man* provides the seed and the woman the egg. However, Scripture does not demand such a modern understanding and can speak of a woman like Hagar having a *seed* when it is obviously only meant to describe her offspring (Gen 16:10). While an unusual birth may be implied, we probably are going too far to squeeze a virgin birth out of Genesis 3:15. But it is not necessary to see a virgin birth predicted in the verse to legitimately maintain its messianic character.

Fulfillment of Genesis 3:15

When it is recognized that the enemy behind the serpent must be supernatural, it follows that this demands a supernatural deliverer, although His human descent must come through the woman. But what is meant by the crushing of the head and the crushing of the heel? And why are they in this chronologically reversed order (head then heel) if they refer to Jesus and Satan?

The word for "crush" ("bruise" in the KJV) is the Hebrew verb שׁוּף (*shup*). The word appears only four times in the Hebrew Bible, twice of which are in this verse. The other references are Psalm 139:11 and Job 9:17, the first is clearly metaphorical but Job's reference is physical, referring to his own condition, and could be rendered as "battered."[33] The word is a strong one, but the target of the crushing for the serpent's seed and the woman's is different—a head and a heel. Since the Messiah is the ultimate seed of the woman, this crushing could be viewed as the initial indication that He will suffer in some way. While we should not forget that this reference is still in "seed" form (to mix a metaphor), this prepares the reader for what will be other references

---

32. See Lewis, "The Woman's Seed (Genesis 3:15)," 305–14, for documentation of these and other Fathers who interpreted the verse as messianic.
33. The LXX translation of שׁוּף by τηρήσει ("he will keep or watch") has always been a bit perplexing. A standard LXX lexicon suggests that the word is a corruption in transmission of a classical verb τειρήσει which can mean "rub hard" or "bruise" (Lust, Eynikel, and Hauspie, *Greek-English Lexicon of the Septuagint*, II, 475).

to the suffering of the Messiah. For example, the Servant in Isaiah 53 will be "pierced" and "crushed" (53:5) and will be "cut off" and "die" (53:8–9).

As serious as this crushing of the heel is, it is not as severe as the "head-crushing" that will be experienced by Satan. His crushing will not only be *fatal* (Messiah's will be also) but it will also be *final*.[34] While the New Testament writers of course viewed the Messiah's death as a past action, the final destruction of Satan is still future to Paul and John. Romans 16:20 states: "The God of peace will soon crush Satan under your feet." This verse expresses the truth of corporate solidarity, the idea that what is spoken about the Messiah (Son, Serpent, and Seed) can also refer to His followers who are corporately "in" Him.[35] The apocalypse describes Satan's war with Jesus' people (Rev 12:9, 17) as well as his *final* crushing by Jesus in the lake of fire (Rev 20:7–10). There is a sense that Satan was initially crushed by the cross work of Jesus and in reality defeated, yet he continues fighting as a defeated foe until his "military" activity hinted at in Genesis 3:15 is ended forever before the launch of the new heaven and earth.[36] The writer of Hebrews provides his own commentary on Genesis 3:15 with these words: "Since therefore the children share in flesh and blood, he himself likewise partook of the same things, that through death he might destroy the one who has the power of death, that is, the devil, and deliver all those who through fear of death were subject to lifelong slavery" (Heb 2:14–15).

Regarding the unexpected order in the verse (head then heel), an appeal to the progressive history of redemption is the best answer. Beginning with this verse, the crushing of the head of Satan begins. While the messianic work of crushing Satan is progressing, Satan will crush the Messiah's heel. It is actually the crushing of Messiah's heel that ironically leads to the final crushing of Satan's skull.[37]

---

34. An overlooked eschatological reference to this crushing is found in Psalm 110:6, where it is foretold that the Messiah will "smash the head (רֹאשׁ מָחַץ, *mahats roš*) over many nations." Most English translations render the noun as plural ("heads"), thus obscuring what is another intentional intertextual reference to Genesis 3:15. The apocalypse sees this fulfilled in the satanic beast who will be a ruler over many nations (Rev 13:7–8) and finally be destroyed by the victorious Messiah (Rev 19:19–21).

35. Space does not allow a further development of this hermeneutical move called *corporate solidarity*, but it can be witnessed in how prophecies about the Messiah are also applied to His people by Paul (Acts 13:47) and Jesus (Rev 2:26–27, citing Ps 2:8–9). This last text is applied to believers but is also applied to Jesus later in the book (Rev 19:15). See also an allusion to Genesis 3:15 in the statement about the victorious king: "his enemies lick the dust" (Ps 72:9).

36. For an insightful treatment of this aspect of Genesis 3:15, see Hamilton, "The Skull Crushing Seed of the Woman," 30–54.

37. John Sailhamer stresses that the Pentateuch is one book, and creatively traces the effect of Genesis 3:15 in the rest of the Pentateuch. There are three major collections of "poems" in

Summary of Genesis 3:15

As important as it is to not make a text say more than what it says, it is also important to not limit what it says and miss out on its clearly expressed declarations as well as its clearly expressed implications. So what is a fair summary of what can be deduced from Genesis 3:15 about the Messiah? I will offer my own four theses and then a summary by a recognized Old Testament scholar.

1. The Messiah will be a male from the human race.
2. The Messiah will also be supernatural.
3. The Messiah will suffer while accomplishing His messianic role.
4. The Messiah will defeat Satan completely.

Van Groningen sums up the message of this prophecy with these well-chosen words: "The messianic task will be executed; there will be an agent. There will be a time when the crushing of the tempter and its consequences will take place. The fact that there is to be a conflict, there is to be an eventual crushing of the tempter, and that there is to be the possibility of a reversal on the part of the royal couple are essential ingredients. More information is required for a fuller understanding of the plan of God which is to be unfolded in the future."[38]

As Van Groningen has warned, it must be kept in mind that this messianic prophecy is only the first of a long series of messianic prophecies. As revelation unfolds, more information will be unveiled and Messiah's credentials will progressively narrow the focus on one who is not only a descendant of the woman but also a descendant of Shem (Gen 9:26), of Abraham (Gen 12:3), of Isaac (Gen 26:3), of Jacob (Gen 35:11–12), of Judah (Gen 49:10), of David (2 Sam 7:12–16), of Zerubbabel (Hag 2:23), and who will be born in

---

the Pentateuch (Gen 48–49; Num 23–24; and Deut 32–33). The focal point of these major poems is a coming king. The poems have an almost identical introduction in Genesis 49:1; Numbers 24:14, and Deuteronomy 31:29. In each a leader (Jacob, Balaam, Moses) calls their audience together to tell them what will happen "the days to come." What is said about the king in Numbers 24:9a is an almost verbatim statement of Genesis 49:9b (lion crouching, etc.). *Central to this inner textuality of the Pentateuch is the connection of that future "warrior" of Genesis 3:15 ("crusher of the head") with the messianic king of the later poems.* In Numbers 24:7–9, for example, Jacob's seed/king is higher than "Gog," a reading that is found in the LXX, Samaritan Pentateuch and ancient versions. Furthermore, Deuteronomy 33 expects a future king who with God's help (33:26–29) will unite the tribes (33:4–7) and bring peace (33:28a), abundance (33:28b), salvation (33:29) and blessing (33:29). Sailhamer expounds this in a number of his works, but it is clearly explained in his seminal article titled "The Messiah and the Hebrew Bible."

38. Van Groningen, *Messianic Revelation*, 114–15.

Bethlehem (Mic 5:2) before the Temple is destroyed (Dan 9:24–26; 70 AD). Like an inverted pyramid, this portrait of the Messiah rests on the only One who could fit these and the many other prophecies concerning Him—Jesus of Nazareth, the One who was born of a woman (Gal 4:4) and who vanquished Satan and sets free those who are in satanic bondage (Heb 2:14–15).

ADAM, EVE, GENESIS 3:15, AND ISSUES OF HISTORICITY

We return to the opening words of this chapter and to Francis Schaeffer's paradigm of the upper story and lower story of human thinking about epistemology (i.e., how we know what we know). If we view Adam and Eve as simply characters in a wonderful *myth* (that operates only in the upper story) about good and evil but do not affirm that they were real people in space-time history (that actually happens in the lower story), then we run the dangerous risk of also placing the coming of the Messiah and His eventual triumph over Satan in that same upper story of "faith." When we do this we not only remove the account of their Creation and Fall from space-time history, we also "gut" the very heart of our hope for redemption in this fallen world. Redemption must take place *in* this world if it is going to offer any lasting help to people who live *in* this world. This is a hope that centers in a real descendant of a real woman who died and rose again in history and defeated a real foe in history. His victory, as it is prophesied in Genesis 3:15, assures us of our own victory in this very real world of history in which we live.

I do not believe that such a solidly grounded hope is worth sacrificing for some imaginary upper story "faith." Do you?

BIBLIOGRAPHY

Alexander, T. D. "Further Observations on the Term 'Seed' in Genesis." *Tyndale Bulletin* 48 (1997): 363–67.

Baron, David. *Rays of Messiah's Glory: Christ in the Old Testament*. Grand Rapids: Zondervan, 1886.

Bateman, H. W., D. L. Bock, and G. H. Johnston. *Jesus the Messiah: Tracing the Promises, Expectations, and Coming of Israel's King*. Grand Rapids: Kregel, 2012.

Beecher, Willis. *The Prophets and the Promise*. Grand Rapids: Baker, 1975.

Beshore, F. K. *The Messiah of the Tanach, Targums and Talmuds*. Costa Mesa, CA: World Bible Society, 1971.

Boice, James Montgomery. *Genesis*. Vol 1. Grand Rapids: Zondervan, 1982.

Boyarin, Daniel. *The Jewish Gospels: The Story of the Jewish Christ*. New York: The New Press, 2012.

Briggs, Charles A. *Messianic Prophecy*. Peabody, MA: Hendrickson Publishers, 1988.

Brown, Michael. *Answering Jewish Objections to Jesus*. 5 vols. Grand Rapids: Baker, 2000–10.

Cohen, A., ed. *The Soncino Chumash*. London: Soncino Press, 1956.

Collins, C. J. *Genesis 1–4: A Linguistic, Literary, and Theological Commentary*. Phillipsburg, NJ: P&R, 2006.

Collins, Jack. "A Syntactical Note (Genesis 3:15): Is the Woman's Seed Singular or Plural?" *Tyndale Bulletin* 48 (1997): 139–48.

Cooper, David L. *The Messianic Series*. 7 vols. Los Angeles: Biblical Research Society, 1933–62.

_____ . *Messiah: His Names and Person*. Los Angeles: Biblical Research Society, 1933.

Delitzsch, Franz. *The Messianic Prophecies in Historical Succession*. Edinburgh: T&T Clark, 1891.

Driver, S. R. *The Book of Genesis*. London: Methuen, 1909.

Edersheim, Alfred. *Life and Times of Jesus the Messiah*. 2 vols. Grand Rapids: Eerdmans Publishing, 1967.

Ferguson, Sinclair, David Wright, and J. I. Packer. *New Dictionary of Theology*. Downers Grove, IL: InterVarsity Press Academic, 1988.

Fruchtenbaum, Arnold. *Messianic Christology*. Tustin, CA: Ariel Ministries, 1998.

Frydland, Rachmiel. *What Rabbis Know about the Messiah*. Worthington, OH: Messianic Literature Outreach, 1991.

Gloag, Paton J. *The Messianic Prophecies*. Edinburgh: T&T Clark, 1879.

Hamilton, James. "The Skull Crushing Seed of the Woman: Inner-Biblical Interpretation of Genesis 3:15." *Southern Baptist Journal of Theology* 10/2 (Summer 2006): 30–54.

Harkavy, Alexander. *The Holy Scriptures: English Version*. New York: Hebrew Publishing Co., 1936.

Hayward, C. T. *Jerome's "Hebrew Questions on Genesis."* Oxford: Clarendon Press, 1995.

Hengstenberg, E. W. *The Christology of the Old Testament*. Grand Rapids: Kregel, 1970.

The Holy Scriptures. Philadelphia: Jewish Publication Society, 1917.

Kaiser, Walter C. *The Messiah in the Old Testament*. Grand Rapids: Zondervan, 1995.

Keil, C. F. *Biblical Commentary on the Old Testament*. Vol 1. The Pentateuch. Grand Rapids: Eerdmans Publishing, 1949.

Klausner, Joseph. *The Messianic Idea in Israel*. New York: Macmillan, 1955 (tr.).

Leeser, Isaac. *Torah nevi'im u-ketuvim: Twenty Four Books of the Holy Scriptures*. New York: Hebrew Publishing Co., 1915.

Levey, Samson. *The Messiah: An Aramaic Interpretation: The Messianic Exegesis of the Targum.* New York: KTAV Publishing, 1974.

Lewis, Jack. "The Woman's Seed (Gen 3:15)." *Journal of the Evangelical Theological Society* 34 (1991): 299–319.

Lindsey, Hal. *The Promise.* Eugene, OR: Harvest House, 1974.

Lust, J., E. Eynikel, and K. Hauspie. *Greek-English Lexicon of the Septuagint.* Parts I and II. Stuttgart: Deutsche Bibelgesellschaft, 1992, 1996.

Martin, R. A. "Earliest Messianic Interpretation of Genesis 3:15." *Journal of Biblical Literature* 84 (1965): 425–27.

Meldau, Fred John. *The Prophets Still Speak.* Bellmawr, NJ: Friends of Israel, 1988.

Newman, Jacob. *Commentary of Nahmanides.* Leiden: E. J. Brill, 1960.

Patai, Raphael. *The Messiah Texts.* Avon Books, 1979.

Riggans, Walter. *Yeshua Ben David.* Crowborough, U.K.: MARC, 1995.

Rosen, Moishe. *Y'SHUA.* Chicago: Moody Press, 1982.

Rydelnik, Michael. *The Messianic Hope: Is the Hebrew Bible Really Messianic?* Nashville: Broadman and Holman, 2010.

Sailhamer, John. "The Messiah and the Hebrew Bible." *Journal of the Evangelical Theological Society* 44 (2001): 5–23.

Satterthwaite, Philip E., Richard S. Hess, and Gordon J. Wenham. *The Lord's Anointed: The Interpretation of Old Testament Messianic Texts.* Grand Rapids: Baker, 1995.

Schaeffer, Francis. *The Complete Works of Francis A. Schaeffer: A Christian Worldview.* Chicago, IL: Crossway, 1982.

_____. *Escape from Reason*. London: InterVarsity Press, 1968.

_____. *Genesis in Space and Time*. Downers Grove, IL: InterVarsity Press, 1972.

_____. *The God Who Is There*. Downers Grove, IL: InterVarsity Press, 1968.

_____. *He Is There and He Is Not Silent*. Wheaton, IL: Tyndale House Publishers, 1972.

Sigal, Gerald. *The Jew and the Christian Missionary: A Jewish Response to Missionary Christianity*. New York: KTAV Publishing Co., 1981.

Skinner, John. *A Critical and Exegetical Commentary on Genesis*. 2nd ed. Edinburgh: T&T Clark, 1930.

Smith, James. *The Promised Messiah*. Nashville: Thomas Nelson Publishers, 1993.

Tanakh: The Holy Scriptures. Philadelphia: Jewish Publication Society, 1985.

Van Groningen, Gerard. *Messianic Revelation in the O.T.* Grand Rapids: Eerdmans Publishing, 1990.

Varner, William. *The Messiah: Revealed, Rejected, Received*. Indianapolis: AuthorHouse, 2004.

Williams, A. Lukyn. *Christian Evidences for Jewish People*. 2 Vols. Eugene, OR: Wipf and Stock Publishers, 1998.

Wright, Christopher. *Knowing Jesus through the Old Testament*, Downers Grove, IL: InterVarsity Press, 1992.

PART 3:

WORLDVIEW RAMIFICATIONS OF THE CREATION AND FALL

CHAPTER 7

AFTER THE FALL—THREE EFFECTS ON HUMAN ENTERPRISE

R. W. Mackey II

INTRODUCTION

When my colleagues and I began our collaboration on this book, I imme-diately felt like my contribution would be the easiest. After all, they were tasked with the "heavy lifting": biblical exegesis, historical analysis, and scientific exploration. All of these pursuits require a great deal of academic preparation coupled with hard work and a keen mind. My chapter, on the other hand, seems to be a statement of the obvious: The introduction of sin into the world (the Fall), as described in Genesis 3, has marred the (business) world. If this proposition is true, an objective look at creation should convince the observer. This chapter ex-plores three effects of the Fall on human enterprise—the efforts made to subdue and harness the environment—effects which remain apparent and lasting.

To say the world is "marred" by sin is not to say that creation is completely bad or totally devoid of any value. God pronounced His creation "good," and the inherent goodness remains. Sin, however, infected that goodness in a way that adds toil, frustration, misery, pain, weariness, and (eventually) death to what would have otherwise been perfectly good (as pronounced by God) and subsequently life-giving.

This marring caused what Francis Schaeffer called the "abnormal universe." He explains:

> It is interesting that almost all of the results of God's judgment because of man's rebellion relate in some way to the external world. They are not just bound up in man's thought life; they are not merely psychological. Profound changes make the external, objective world abnormal.[1]

I often tell my students that anyone who believes in the inherent goodness of this world never raised a garden or a child. In a "good world" we would expect good things to happen if the environment was left to itself. One step "below" a good world would be a dualistic world (containing a balance between good things and bad things). In a dualistic world, we would expect both good and bad things to happen simultaneously and with equal frequency. Gardens and children, however, do not unfold wonderfully or dualistically. If the garden is left to itself, it becomes worse (i.e., the "bad" plants take over). The child's first words are not "yes" and "yours" (i.e., "no" and "mine" seem to monopolize the little one's vocabulary). Both the garden and the child require the relentless application of intelligent effort to overcome the effects of the Fall.

These prosaic observations, introduce the oft-cited question, "What would we expect?" framing the rationale for the remainder of this chapter. In other words, if every part of the world was marred by sin, what would human enterprise look like in that place and among its inhabitants? This *a priori* approach is akin to the reasoning adopted by C. S. Lewis when he wrote, "I believe in Christianity as I believe that the sun has risen. Not only because I see it, but because by it I see everything else."[2] As applied to the study at hand, if the biblical account of creation's Fall into sin is real, then our understanding of the world should be accurate and, therefore, helped by accepting this reality.

Looking for the results of the Fall is not hard because every corner of our lives overflows with these. Offering examples, then, will be an exercise in selective perception. At least three "macro" results of the Fall, as it affected (and affects) human enterprise, are: communicative distortion, economic scarcity, and managerial control.

---

1.   Schaeffer, *Genesis in Space and Time*, 95.
2.   Lewis, "Is Theology Poetry?," 140.

THE FIRST EFFECT: COMMUNICATIVE DISTORTION

When contextualizing the first effect of the Fall *on* human enterprise, it is interesting to note that the introduction of sin into God's creation occurred as mankind was engaged *in* enterprise. Adam worked in the enterprise given to him by God: keeping the Garden (Gen 2:15). The original temptation (and sin) happened in the work world.

Much of economic theory explains the conditions of human enterprise as a result of cost/benefit analysis. Simply stated, if the benefit of option A outweighs the cost of option A, then option A becomes a viable (attractive) alternative. If the cost exceeds the benefit, the option is undesirable. This basic theorem explains a great deal about human activity. Even the essence of following Jesus is inextricably bound up in the cost of discipleship compared with its reward (Luke 9:57–62).

In the Garden, God established the cost and the benefit derived by eating from the tree of the knowledge of good and evil using clear, direct communication (Gen 2:16–17). Life would be forfeited for a taste. The serpent's "rationality" eroded the straightforward statement from God. His distortion of God's command began by discounting the cost—"you will not surely die"—and then proceeded to enhance the benefit: "you will be like God." By the time the dialogue ended, Eve had been tricked by crafty verbiage, which was followed by Adam deliberately transgressing God's command (1 Tim 2:14).

Interestingly, since the moment sin entered the world, straightforwardness was lost in communication. Barrier-free communication left creation. Some barriers are intended: The serpent intended to demonstrate guile toward Eve, and Adam showed guile toward his Creator (Gen 3:12, 15). Clear, logical analyses and responses were supplanted by rationalized, crafty statements. One cannot help but think of the stark contrast to Jesus teaching that the agreements made by God's people should "be simply 'Yes' or 'No'" (Matt 5:37). Now, a massive legal industry has evolved largely due to semantics. The original loophole introduced by the serpent has resulted in a world full of loopholes. The old saying, "The big print giveth and the small print taketh away," is a sad commentary on the guile imbedded in semantics (prototyped in the Garden).

Some barriers to clear communication, however, are unintended. Yet, even if people are attempting to communicate without guile, their chances of being understood are only fair. Every person stumbles in her or his communication (Jas 3:2). The sender is not perfect in choosing the right words, the correct channel, or the clearest nonverbal accompaniment. The receiver may have the message distorted through ignorance, bias, background noise, or disability. Both the sender and the receiver are inherently marred and are operatives in a marred environment. Even accomplished speakers and writers struggle with their messages, never believing the things spoken or penned are completely adequate. (This chapter certainly falls into that category.)

Generally, when transgression materialized in the Garden, the nature of enterprise (effort) changed because of God's curse: toil for the serpent (crawling on his stomach), toil for the woman (pain and danger in childbirth), and toil for the worker (a working environment which now required relentless, strategic, frustrating effort). An environment in which work was entirely a pleasure changed into a mixture of satisfying accomplishment, with newly introduced discomfort and anxiety. As we have seen, one component necessary for successful enterprise—cooperative effort rooted in effective communication—became a struggle. The strategic nature of communication in enterprise is evidenced in a colossal communicative distortion, caused by God, which did not just cause human enterprise (the tower of Babel) to be hampered, but to be stopped in its tracks (Gen 11).

If communicative distortions characterize human enterprise, we would expect a myriad of communication lessons, ranging from successful teamwork helps to cross-cultural enhancements. One book, aimed at helping professionals communicate in the workplace, went so far as to warn its readers to assume that the next message sent by the reader will be misunderstood.[3] This assumption unwittingly flows logically from the Fall and will only find its correction when there is no longer any curse and all communication is faithful and true (Rev 22:1–6).

THE SECOND EFFECT: ECONOMIC SCARCITY

When did the formalization of the concept of "economic scarcity" begin? Some say the start of modern economic thought originated in a short book penned by Thomas Robert Malthus (1766–1864), a British clergyman. His work, *An Essay on the Principle of Population as It Affects the Future Improvement of Society* (1798), predicted human population growth would be approximately three percent annually, which would double the earth's inhabitants

---

3.   Deep and Sussman, *Smart Moves*, 3.

roughly every twenty-five years.[4] Based on these numbers, he believed that the earth's agricultural resources would be unable to sustain the population growth, eventually resulting in hungry people killing each other for food. The Malthusian scenario was gloomy indeed, causing economics to be dubbed "the dismal science," a nickname that has persisted.

When examining these issues, Malthus identified the very foundation of economics: scarcity. He knew that food was a scarce commodity, existing in finite amounts. Furthermore, an item becomes significantly scarce when it exists in less-than-desired amounts.

The account of Creation is initially a description of abundance: An ample amount was made available by God for the earth's human inhabitants. God told Adam and Eve, "Behold, I have given you every plant yielding seed that is on the face of all the earth and every tree with seed in its fruit. You shall have them for food"(Gen 1:29).

This statement occurred after God made the earth inhabitable for plant, animal, and human life through introducing life-sustaining components such as land, water, atmosphere, light, heat, and seasons. These conditions not only sustained human life directly, but also maintained the conditions necessary for the food that humans would need. The result: All that Adam and Eve needed to live was available for the gathering. Abundance may best be seen in the command to eat freely (Gen 2:16).

Not only did abundance characterize initial Creation, but cooperation was present as well. Initially, Adam was created to complement his Creator—to subdue, multiply, and cultivate the created realm. The scriptural commentary on the second human's (woman's) creation is: "Then the Lord God said, 'It is not good that the man should be alone; I will make a helper fit for him'" (Gen 2:18).

Eve's God-given role was not to compete with Adam, but rather to complement him in the cultivation of the Garden (Gen 2:18). As Adam's complement, Eve accepted his household leadership and worked to help him accomplish the mandates spoken by God. She was designed for this role by God and assumed this role for a time. This complementary activity was true cooperation, not in an egalitarian context, but in fulfillment of God-ordained roles within creation.[5] Competition was not an issue at this point, for at least two reasons:

---

4.   Malthus, *An Essay on the Principle of Population.*
5.   Boice, *Genesis: Volume I—Creation and Fall,* 223.

1. Since the earth's resources were abundant, plenty existed for everyone
    and there was no reason to compete.
2. Since Adam's and Eve's motives were pure, they cooperated perfectly.
    Each performed within the roles that God had designed for them and
    experienced homeostasis (efficiency).

One outcome of sin was the advent of scarcity. God said to Adam, "Because you have listened to the voice of your wife and have eaten of the tree of
which I commanded you, 'You shall not eat of it,' cursed is the ground because
of you; in pain you shall eat of it all the days of your life; thorns and thistles it
shall bring forth for you; and you shall eat the plants of the field. By the sweat
of your face you shall eat bread, till you return to the ground"(Gen 3:17–19).

Abundance became scarcity due to the introduction of "thorns and thistles." Good things became difficult to cultivate while potentially productive
things, left alone, deteriorated. Human enterprise, initially focusing on existence, became a struggle with the circumstances that were set in motion
by sin. Scarcity partnered with sweat. Getting enough and keeping enough
devolved into an anxious endeavor.

Scarcity resulted from and was accompanied by competition. Adam
would now compete with the earth's marred conditions—thorns and thistles.
These "curses" did not create equilibrium between crops and weeds, but initiated the domination of harm in the creation without constant, intelligent human effort. Equilibrium left the household as well. Adam would now compete
with his wife for domestic leadership, since God had pronounced that her desire would be for her husband (Gen 3:16; 4:7); Eve would attempt to dominate
Adam.[6] Later, the competition became more pronounced between people and
devolved into abject corruption as recorded in Genesis 6. Those who possessed superior attributes dominated less-endowed people for evil purposes
(i.e., a raw "survival of the fittest" scenario). The source of this corruption
was genetic imbalances (i.e., the lack of parity or balance in innate abilities),
coupled with depravity, producing a deplorable culture—so deplorable that
God removed it through a worldwide flood.

The world is still characterized by scarcity and competition. Economists
could even offer this thumbnail definition of economics: "studying the allocation of scarce resources among competing ends." How this allocation should/

---

6. Ibid.

would occur fueled the theories of Adam Smith and Karl Marx. Millions of lives have been lost as nations have imposed their economic viewpoints on populations (e.g., the spread of Communism). Current political debates revolve around this issue. It's somewhat discouraging to think that progress can be made, but that a fallen world will always suffer from scarcity. Jesus, aware of all truth, stated, "For you always have the poor with you" (Matt 26:11). The news, however, is ultimately heartening: The eternal existence in the new heaven and earth will restore the abundance and the cooperation found only in humanity's proper relationship to God. Christians would expect this to be so, since the Father is totally sufficient; everlasting life with Him, therefore, will be free from want. It is little wonder that, historically, believers who have undergone great persecution thought often of heaven and saw death as a joyous release. Sometimes, affluent believers focus more on this life and see death as a more dreaded event. God can even use a result of the Fall to craft a good result: scarcity can cause a longing for redemption.

The Third Effect: Managerial Control

My wife and I had just arrived home from church on Sunday, August 31, 1986. Almost immediately the telephone rang. Our neighbor, watching for us to get home, asked if we had heard "the news." An Aeromexico DC-9 jetliner had crashed over the city of Cerritos on its approach to Los Angeles International Airport. Although I was shocked and saddened by the tragedy, I failed to understand why my neighbor had made a point of watching for me and then immediately telephoning me. He then told me that another neighbor's wife and two young daughters were on the jetliner. I accompanied my neighbor to the airport to find a man grief-stricken beyond any measure I had ever witnessed. As I stayed with that man through those initial hours, the age-old question *why?* was posed. I told him I didn't have *the* answer, but I did tell him what I was thinking:

> We live in a marred world. In this marred world, things do not always go as planned; mistakes are made. Some of the mistakes seem to have little or no harmful consequence. Some mistakes, however, have tragic consequences.

My response probably raised more questions than it answered. Nevertheless, the response was valid because it highlighted the tragic way the Fall impacts our lives.

As I thought about that air disaster, logic told me that the crash occurred either because of overt failure (sinful intent) or covert failure (unintended error). As it turned out, an analysis of the crash attributed the disaster to the latter, which was shared by the pilot of the small plane that hit the jetliner and a "busy" air traffic controller.[7] The crash may have been averted if the controller had been controlling.

Managing human enterprise is classically divided into four functions: planning, organizing, leading, and controlling. Planning is beginning with the end in mind. Objectives are established; an outcome is envisioned. To accomplish the plan, resources are acquired and properly arranged (i.e., organized). Keeping the enterprise focused and motivated is the leadership function. Eventually, the question "Are the goals being achieved?" requires an answer. Seeking that answer is the act of controlling.

More specifically, controlling is an attempt at discovering if accepted standards are being met and then taking some type of action if the discovered outcomes are not ideal. This activity introduces accountability into a situation. Sometimes control is summarized as "whatever is expected must be inspected." If the world were perfect, the outcomes would be perfect; control would be unnecessary. However, the world is not perfect. Bad things happen due to intentional behaviors (transgressions) or due to unintentional circumstances (falling short of perfection). Controls are intended to recognize these bad outcomes and to keep them from happening again. If our understanding of the Fall is correct, we can minimize bad outcomes, but never eradicate them.

Although every managerial function is affected by the Fall, the control function flows directly from (i.e., finds its beginning in) this sad event. Everything God created was declared "good" by this all-knowing Creator. Every event had gone as intended and would progress as originally intended if God's commands were obeyed. When sin entered the world, however, the Creator's original design was replaced by a grossly inferior substitute and the outcomes suddenly changed. Attempting to bring outcomes back into that original state of being "good" introduced the heretofore unnecessary function of control into human enterprise. In a very real sense, the control function becomes a counterbalance to the sinfulness flowing from the Fall. In a sinful world, "protection" from sin must be afforded. Attempts at protection constitute control.

---

7.   Woodhouse, "1986 Aeromexico Crash Rained Horror from the Sky."

The introduction of the control function occurred as an addition to the process of delegation. Delegation, getting work done through others, is fundamental to organization. It is normally viewed as a three-step process: assigning responsibility, allocating resources, and implementing accountability (control). Before sin entered creation, the first two functions were present. God assigned responsibility when He gave the agricultural mandate (i.e., dominion; Gen 1:28) and then provided the necessary resources (Gen 1:29). No initial mention is made of accountability. However, after Adam and Eve sinned and hid, God asked, "Where are you?" (Gen 3:9) This question was not posed by an omniscient God for information's sake; rather, it was designed to convict Adam and Eve of their failure and, therefore, implies the advent of accountability (control). Sin was exposed, its effects identified, and remedies initiated.

The original sin and its curse had introduced the first curse on the human race: broken fellowship with God with its eternal consequences. People are now spiritually fallen—separated from God (Rom 3:23; 5:12). God identified the problem and, in His mercy and grace, took action to correct the deathly deviation (Gen 3:15, 21; Rom 8:1). The other curses, placed upon the serpent, the woman and the man, were temporal in scope; conditioning earthly existence (Gen 3:14–19). These curses were not remediated by God, but remain part of creation's environment until the establishment of a new heaven and a new earth (Rev 21, 22). Human enterprise occurs within a problem-laden context, which necessitates ongoing control.

It is worth noting that human enterprise is not completely thwarted by problems because "image-bearers" live in the fallen world. The Bible says people are created in the "image" and "likeness" of God (Gen 1:26–27). One likeness to God is creative problem-solving; for example, woman was created by God to solve a problem (Gen 2:18–25). As such, people are capable of arranging various components of their environments in creative ways (only God can create something out of nothing) to solve problems. This image-bearing has resulted in some spectacular achievements! My generation has witnessed atomic energy, space travel, medical breakthroughs, telecommunications, digital information storage and transfer, and an amazing array of life-enhancing products and services! Yet the need for quality control remains constant. Things still go wrong. People plow the fields; weeds grow. Will there ever be a dryer that does not eat socks?

Because the world is marred, good managers are sometimes described as people who are looking for something to fix. Formally, this is called "management by exception." (If Murphy's Law is axiomatic, the exception may be the rule.) The bad news is, things rarely go as planned this side of heaven. The Apostle Paul states, "the whole creation has been groaning together in the pains of childbirth until now" (Rom 8:22). The good news: Job security rewards the effective manager—control will always be indispensable!

The effects of the Fall extend beyond enterprise to all of the God-ordained entities (which certainly affect enterprise): individuals, families, churches, and government. Each of these entities should exercise internal controls (to minimize weaknesses) and external controls (to neutralize threats). These entities not only are interrelated within a general environment, but also have some measure of influence in exercising control on each other. Notably, the Bible is not silent on the responsibilities of each entity.

God will eventually create a new heaven and a new earth, which will make perfect that which was marred by the Fall (Rev 21–22). In the meantime, however, He has resourced earth's current inhabitants to measure up to His expectations.

Summary

If the world we inhabit is marred by sin, what would we expect? We would expect to see the effects of the Fall touching every part of human existence, including human enterprise. This chapter identified three effects of the Fall on enterprise.

Offering a somewhat exhaustive list of specific examples of the three effects examined in this chapter would take millions of pages. Those pages would describe everything from business communication literature to economic policies; from laws passed and interpreted to quality control manuals; from military war theories to parenting classes; from background checks to standardized testing; from audits to guardrails...all of these being the tip of the tip of the effects iceberg. Some examples would even include all three effects occurring in tandem: such as a panel of experts attempting to garner and comprehend enough information to determine the next human organ transplant recipient. In fact, fewer examples exist of supposed perfections in these affected areas than of imperfections. All this to say that the goal of this chapter was not to offer an exhaustive list of the triple realities of communicative distortion, economic scarcity, and managerial control, but to show that if the narrative of the Fall in Genesis 3 is historically factual, the expected result would match present realities. Furthermore, if the effects and their attendant conditions are predictable, based upon the assumed cause, a measure of truth has been identified.

In this life, each person will ultimately decide the cause of the effects in a temporal environment with eternal implications in the balance.

BIBLIOGRAPHY

Boice, James Montgomery. *Genesis: Volume I—Creation and Fall.* Grand Rapids: Baker, 1998.

Deep, Sam, and Lyle Sussman. *Smart Moves.* New York: Addison-Wesley, 1990.

Lewis, C. S. "Is Theology Poetry?" *The Weight of Glory and Other Addresses.* New York: HarperCollins Publishers, 1980.

Malthus, Thomas R. *An Essay on the Principle of Population.* London: J. Johnson, 1798.

Schaeffer, Francis A. *Genesis in Space and Time: The Flow of Biblical History.* Downers Grove, IL: InterVarsity Press, 1972.

Woodhouse, Andrea. "1986 Aeromexico Crash Rained Horror from the Sky." *Los Angeles Daily News*, November 14, 2007.

CHAPTER 8

THERMODYNAMICS AND THE FALL—HOW THE CURSE CHANGED OUR WORLD

Taylor B. Jones

INTRODUCTION

The Fall of Adam and Eve in the Garden of Eden is usually discussed from the standpoint of either the rebellion itself or the effects of that act. The spiritual dimension is largely the focus. Life would be substantially different for us if the impact of the couple's actions stopped at this point. However, physical death and the spiritual penalty of separation from God were far from the only consequences. There were other physical consequences as well. In our haste to observe the spiritual dimension, we may miss the details of Genesis 3 and what they entail: the physical environment was radically changed, down to the very core of its being.

The impact of the curse on our surroundings is felt by each and every one of us on a daily basis. We are all engaged each day in pushing back the effects of the Fall. We could list the things done in this regard, but we will speak to this in a more scientific way. A useful approach is to observe how energy flows through the universe and how it has changed as a result of the Fall.

188 Taylor B. Jones

The study of the flow of energy through the universe is called "thermodynamics."[1] A consideration of the individual components of the curse pronounced upon the earth indicates how that flow of energy changed from the pre-Fall to the post-Fall world. The laws of thermodynamics provide a structured approach to consider the change in energy flow as a result of the Fall.

The approach taken in this examination of the effects of the Fall involves an effort to harmonize the biblical record of Genesis 1–3 with thermodynamics. The results of such a study will not have the scientific reliability of a repeatable, reproducible study like physics. Neither will it exhibit the reliability of studies involving multiple trials followed by statistical analysis like medicine. The former involves deductive reasoning;[2] the latter, inductive reasoning.[3]

Analyses of this type fall into the category of abductive reasoning, where one makes the best explanation of all the data together.[4] All of these approaches are scientific in that they lead to further results that must be harmonized with the preceding data. However, abduction cannot and should not be treated as if it were as reliable as approaches involving deductive or inductive reasoning. Nevertheless, the conclusions herein serve as a useful way to understand how the Fall of Adam and Eve forever, irreversibly subjected the world and all mankind to a burden of monumental, unforeseen conditions.

METHODOLOGY

Before dealing with how thermodynamics and the Fall relate, we need to understand certain realities about science, the Bible, and how science relates to the Bible. For purposes of a meaningful discussion, this groundwork is most vital. The presuppositions that lead to the conclusions come from this analysis. We cannot afford to gloss over these issues. The validity and utility of our conclusions depend on a rigorous, accurate understanding of the nature of our sources.

---

1. *Merriam-Webster Dictionary*, s.v. "thermodynamics." *Dynamics* means "motion"; *thermo* means "heat," the energy associated with molecular motion.
2. Copi, *Symbolic Logic*, 4–6.
3. Skryms, *Choice and Chance: An Introduction to Inductive Logic*, 28–51.
4. Lipton, *Inference to the Best Explanation*, 1.

Science

Before we think through the issues of thermodynamics and Scripture, we need to make some observations on the general nature of science. The underlying basis for all of science is the assumption that the universe is characterized by cause and effect relationships. It is poor grammar, but "Nothing ever happens for no reason" is a succinct, accurate summary of cause and effect. From how rockets are launched to how fetal development occurs, this presuppositional perspective frames how we understand what we observe. No effect occurs without a corresponding cause.

Cause and effect is the foundation of the scientific method. If certain causes did not produce certain effects, then a rational study of the universe would be impossible. The systematic study of cause and effect relationships is carried out by employing the scientific method.[5] In this method, results obtained either by experiments or other data-gathering techniques have to be non-contradictory.

Properly carried out, this approach to science allows arrival at a logically, self-consistent understanding. This means that we can explain a cause and effect relationship by taking into account all the known data. This does not constitute a proof that the cause and effect relationship is true. It is merely a working model or a theory.[6]

The value of theories is that they allow scientists to predict outcomes of situations. Theories, such as the theory of relativity, result from numerous observations.[7] Scientists test these theories continually for necessary refinements or revisions. Any theory must account for all the existing data from studies that employ that theory.

Future data could arise that would demand a change in the theory or a complete jettisoning of theory. For example, proteins were thought to be have been biosynthesized in the sequence DNA → RNA → proteins. The discovery of reverse transcriptase enzymes demonstrated that DNA could be synthesized from RNA.[8] The previously accepted dogma that the above sequence was the only one possible had to be abandoned. Books had to be changed.

Unlike a theory, laws in science are summaries of behavior that have no exceptions. Examples are the law of gravity and laws of electromagnetism. We

---

5. Jones, "A Scriptural View of Science," 221–38.
6. Ibid., 226.
7. Gardner, *Relativity Simply Explained*; Einstein, *Relativity*.
8. Lodish, et al., *Molecular Cell Biology*, 158–60.

can be confident that studies in these disciplines will not produce any results that call the validity of the law into question. An additional benefit is such reliability allows one to describe such sciences mathematically. The resultant equations allow prediction of outcomes without the necessity of testing each and every one.

The summaries of virtually all of the observable cause and effect behaviors studied in the context of the scientific method are theories. Theories are logically self-consistent summaries of the existing data. And as noted above we often have to change, revise, and, on occasion, discard theories. We always have to be open to conflicting data and willing to address a flawed theory that does not account for all the cause and effect data. This is particularly true when we deal with science and the Bible.

Science and the Bible

People approach harmonizing theories of science with the biblical record in several ways.[9] The main point of contention is how to treat science. The idea that "all truth is God's truth," while well meaning, has brought confusion to the discussion that continues to this day.[10] Attempts to harmonize science and the Bible must be treated carefully, *since even widely accepted scientific theories have been later proven false*. Certainly, God's truth is without error. The problem in reconciling any apparent conflict between science and the Bible is rooted in a failure to grasp the difference between the two sources. The nature of the Bible is fundamentally different from the nature of science. This has an enormous impact on how we are to understand each area and relate one area to the other.

Science is part of human epistemology; it is a branch of knowledge.[11] The discovery of information by man has to be understood in the light of its susceptibility to error, misinterpretation, and even abuse. We may have to completely alter our theory in light of new information. Science is necessarily fluid. Scripture, on the other hand, is revelation. This special revelation is without error in the original autographs.[12] The Bible claims verbal, plenary inspiration for itself.[13]

---

9. Carlson, *Science and Christianity: Four Views*.
10. Gaebelein, *The Pattern of God's Truth*, 20.
11. Jones, "A Scriptural View of Science," 221.
12. Grudem, *Systematic Theology*, 90–104.
13. Hodge, *Systematic Theology*, 1:164–65.

The Bible claims to be the Word of God (Heb 1:1–2).[14] The Scripture is inspired; it is God-breathed (2 Tim 3:16–17).[15] And God oversaw the writing of Scripture in which the Holy Spirit superintended the human authors (2 Pet 1:21).[16] The Bible clearly affirms divine authorship for itself.[17]

Consequently, the text of the Bible must conform to the character of its Author. It is true in every sense of the word, and always will be true (John 17:17).[18] This is demanded by the immutability of the divine author (Mal 3:6).[19] Science can make no such lofty claim for itself. Being more reliable and accurate by nature, Scripture must be taken as the standard by which science must be understood at those places where Scripture comments on science.

However, if one assumes that the understanding of the universe we have from science is just as accurate, reliable, and trustworthy as Scripture, then a conflict between the two becomes a clash of informational titans. The unstoppable force meets the immovable object. This is the so-called "two book" approach.[20] This does a disservice to both science and Scripture, because it raises science to the same level of reliability as Scripture. This is to ascribe to man the same qualities as God. The approach inevitably denigrates God and His Word, because conflict tends to be dealt with by forcing the meaning of Scripture to change until it agrees with the current state of scientific knowledge, which, as previously noted, is fluid.

Instead, the correct approach is the so-called "one book" approach.[21] In this approach, at those places where science and the Bible intersect, science has to be understood in light of the biblical account. This is the priority that must be used (and what I will use in this chapter), since the revelation of God is always superior to and more accurate than the knowledge of men.

Basic Thermodynamics

Before we state and discuss the laws of thermodynamics, we should note that treating the laws of thermodynamics quantitatively involves some

---

14. Grudem, *Systematic Theology*, 73–77.
15. Warfield, *The Inspiration and Authority of Scripture*, 132–33.
16. Thiessen, *Introductory Lectures in Systematic Theology*, 107.
17. Warfield, *The Inspiration and Authority of Scripture*, 299–348.
18. Grudem, *Systematic Theology*, 90–104.
19. Ewell, *Evangelical Dictionary of Theology*, 453–54; Grudem, *Systematic Theology*, 163–68.
20. Jones, "A Scriptural View of Science," 234.
21. Ibid., 236.

foreboding mathematics.[22] For our purposes we can treat these concepts qualitatively without having to resort to complex mathematical treatments. Consequently, these concepts can be rather simply stated, even though at the molecular level the processes can be enormously complicated. The basic properties of a system can be discussed and changes understood without requiring the use of mathematical terminology and symbology.

As a starting point, we should note that thermodynamics is ubiquitous. Energy flow and transformation is constantly occurring throughout the universe. The increase in temperature that accompanies sunrise, the winds blowing across the surface of the globe, and the observation of color that is caused by differential absorption of light of different energies are examples of thermodynamics. The reality largely goes unnoticed by the vast majority of earth's inhabitants as they live each day.

Before beginning a study in thermodynamics one must decide which portion of the universe one wants to study. The portion of the universe being subjected to thermodynamic study is called the "system." The remainder of the universe is called the "surroundings." The first law refers to an isolated system, one that is not exchanging energy or mass[23] with the surroundings. The size of the system is chosen for convenience. For example, to discuss plant growth on the earth, one would have to take into account at least the portion of the solar system that includes the portion of the sun's energy impinging on the earth and the portion of the earth under consideration.

The flow of energy today through the universe, thermodynamics, is summarized in three laws.[24] The first law is relatively straightforward and follows from a consideration of what is going on around us. It says that the total energy of the universe is constant.[25] This law perfectly reflects the Creation account in Genesis 1 and 2. At the end of this period, all the energy that would ever be available for all the requirements of the universe

---

22. A working knowledge of ordinary and partial differential equations and calculus based physics is necessary for a full understanding of a quantitative approach to thermodynamics.
23. Mass is a measure of the amount of matter of a given amount of a substance.
24. Only the portion of thermodynamics necessary for an understanding of the issues raised will be addressed in this chapter. Vocabulary, mathematical variables, etc., not directly pertinent to the discussion at hand have been omitted for the sake of brevity and clarity.
25. The mathematical expression for the first law of thermodynamics is $\Delta U = U_f - U_i = 0$, where U is the internal energy, U_f is the final state of the system, and U_i is the initial state. As energy changes from one state—defined to be a set of chemical and physical conditions—to another state, no change in internal energy occurs. The symbol ΔU is read as "delta U." U_f and U_i are read as "U sub f" and "U sub i", respectively.

for all time had come into being. No more energy is being made anywhere in the universe.

In other words, the first law states that energy can neither be created nor destroyed; it can only be converted from one form to another. The chemical energy of the breakfast you ate this morning was converted to usable energy by your body and made available for your daily activities. The energy required by your brain to read and understand this sentence came from the food you ate earlier. The kinetic energy, the energy of motion, of your car comes from the chemical energy liberated by the combustion of gasoline in the cylinders. The resultant expanding gases produce the force that moves the vehicle. Numerous other examples could be cited.

The other two laws of thermodynamics involve the concept of *spontaneity*. Spontaneity in a thermodynamic sense means the natural direction in which change occurs. An opened perfume bottle results in a room filled with fragrance. The longer people live, the older they get; nobody ever gets younger with age. Soiled clothing in soapy water leads to cleaner clothes and dirtier water. Again, spontaneity in thermodynamics deals with the way change naturally occurs.

However, a spontaneous process can be reversed, but only with the input of energy. A messy room can be cleaned. A set of randomly handed-in exams can be alphabetized. Clean clothes can be folded and put away. We all understand intuitively how such processes occur and what is required to accomplish them. It is very important to note that random energy cannot accomplish any of these tasks. One cannot buy modestly charged hand grenades for cleaning up a room, à la Mary Poppins. In addition to the energy input, one must also have a plan. It requires directed, controlled energy to reverse a spontaneous process.

Spontaneity, in turn, is related to a concept called "entropy." It can be discussed several ways, but it is best if we consider it to be disorder or randomness.[26] Randomness is a measure of relative molecular disorder; e.g., there is more entropy or randomness in gaseous water than liquid water.[27] Larger distances between molecules in the gas phase as opposed to a liquid correspond to increased randomness.

In a spontaneous process, there generally is an increase in the randomness

---

26. Entropy is given the symbol S; its algebraic meaning is $S = q_{rev}/T$. T is the Kelvin temperature and q_{rev} is the heat gained or lost under reversible conditions. Reversibility refers to changes in infinitesimally small increments.
27. Tro, *Principles of Chemistry*, 672–73.

of the system.[28] Burning a gallon of gasoline in our cars produces gaseous water and carbon dioxide. The volume of the gaseous products far exceeds the volume of the gasoline. So the products are more "random" than the reactants. Like gasoline, the end products of the metabolism of table sugar are carbon dioxide and water. These products, too, are more random. The fact that everything wears out is another example of the randomness associated with spontaneous processes. Whether it is clothing, appliances, furniture, or even human life, everything eventually is overcome with the effects of entropic increase in the world.

Having defined and described entropy, we can state the second law of thermodynamics. The entropy change of an isolated system (one that cannot exchange energy or mass with its surroundings) can never be negative.[29] And like entropy, the second law can also be expressed in another way: *energy cannot be completely converted into work*.[30] If the first law states that the best one can do is break even when energy is converted into another form, the second law states that you cannot break even. Any attempt to convert energy into work will always result in an accompanying loss of some of that energy. And that energy will normally be lost as *waste heat*. Waste heat is thermal energy that is irrecoverably lost.[31]

---

28. More exactly, spontaneous processes are characterized by the loss of Gibbs free energy, $\Delta G < O$. This means that that the total amount of usable energy in the universe is continually decreasing. Delta G can be defined in terms of entropy and another variable, enthalpy. Enthalpy is given the symbol H and means heat content. The complete expression is $\Delta G = \Delta H - T\Delta S$, where T is the Kelvin temperature. When ΔH is negative (< 0), heat is lost to the surroundings; it is exothermic. Conversely, when ΔH is positive (> 0), heat is gained by the system (lost from the surroundings); it is endothermic. It is possible for a spontaneous process to lead to a decrease in entropy, a more ordered system, if it is accompanied by a heat loss to the surroundings that is greater than the product, $T\Delta S$.

    Entropy can also be expressed in terms of microstates, the number of ways in which the molecules of a system can be arranged. In this approach, $S = k \ln W$, where k is a constant, ln is the natural logarithm, and W is the number of microstates (Dill and Bromberg, *Molecular Driving Forces*, 81–82, 90).

    It is possible for spontaneous processes to produce a decrease in entropy in some part of the system. The growth of a human embryo clearly leads to something more ordered, less random, as development occurs. This means that elsewhere a larger increase in entropy is occurring or that the heat lost is greater than the product, $T\Delta S$.

29. A perfectly insulated, closed thermos bottle from which no liquid could escape and in which its liquid contents never changed temperature would be an isolated system.

30. In physics, work is the product of force moving through a distance: $W = F \times d$. The standard unit of work is the Joule (J), a kg x m^2/sec^2. The unit of forces is a Newton (N), a kg x m/sec^2.

31. The third law of thermodynamics will not have an impact on this discussion. For the sake of completeness, the third law of thermodynamics states that the entropy of a perfect crystal at absolute zero is zero. A perfect crystal is one with complete regularity and no defects.

We are now in a position to consider energy as it appears in the opening chapters of Genesis, and to observe these chapters through the lens of thermodynamics. Entropy will receive the particular focus in Genesis 3.

Biblical Backdrop

Creation and Thermodynamics

The principles of thermodynamics that govern energy flow through the universe today are in some ways substantially different from the principles that were operative immediately prior to the events of Genesis 3 or during the Creation week. Since all the energy in the form of matter, including man, had not been created until the end of the Creation week, the first law of thermodynamics did not apply. During the Creation week the total energy of the universe was not constant, because God was still creating.

The opening verse of the Bible describes the first recorded creative act of God. Such an effort necessarily involved God's power (Ps 68:34; Isa 40:26; Jer 51:15).[32] The energy of God became visibly manifest in the form of the created heavens and the earth.[33] From the very beginning of the history of the universe, energy has been part of the equation. The power put on display during the Creation week will never be equaled in human history until the destruction of the present universe and the creation of the new heavens and the new earth (2 Pet 3:10).

The first creative act of God was to initiate a display of thermodynamics. In Genesis 1:3, God said, "Let there be light." From this point on visible energy was a part of God's created order.[34] There is no power in the universe apart from the power of God, since everything that is came into existence through His power. That He would first demonstrate His power in the form of visible, radiant energy is a logical and reasonable starting point for the beginning of Creation.[35]

Absolute zero, 0 K, is -273ºC; it is the complete absence of heat and the temperature at which all molecular motion ceases.

32. These verses speak of the power (energy) of God in the Creation of the universe.

33. In physics, power is energy per unit time (Freedman, et al., *College Physics*, 784). In the Bible, energy and power would be synonymous, although the word "energy" is not found in the English Standard Version in the Old Testament.

34. Normally, only radiation in the form of heat, light, etc., is considered to be energy.

35. Matthew 17:2: "And he was transfigured before them, and his face shone like the sun, and his clothes became white as light." On the Mount of Transfiguration, the Lord Jesus Christ

On the same day, God separated the light from the darkness. This resulted in a partitioning of energy that gave rise to evening and morning.[36] Thus, the movement of energy through the universe had been sectioned off for the first time: there is light and its absence. God has limited where energy can and cannot exist. Boundaries in thermodynamics have been established.

The manifestations of energy in the form of light were set into motion during the Creation week. The energy that sustains our world from the sun was created in its entirety. The sun today is the same sun that existed at end of the third day of Creation. The light of the moon is merely the reflected light of the sun.[37] Light is streaming into creation. The flow of energy in the universe has begun.

For all of the remaining creative acts of Genesis 1 and 2, God called matter into existence. In each case God was creating matter, introducing energy into His universe. The first law of thermodynamics was still being compiled. At the conclusion of all God's creative activity, the universe would then be subject to this fundamental relationship. The first law of thermodynamics would be forever in place.

Natural law, the consistent, predictable behavior of the world, including thermodynamics, has always been part of creation as we currently know it. The changes in season, the ebb and flow of tides, and the force of gravity are always functioning. The world operates with a functional consistency that allows one to predict the activity of substantial portions of the world. The phase of the moon on Valentine's Day, the time the sun will set on Christmas, as well as how much the temperature of a given volume of water will rise when a known mass of iron metal at a temperature of 100°C is added to it—each one of these can be calculated. Man can do nothing to change these laws, whether they are in the realm of astronomy or thermodynamics.

God, however, has no such limitations. Even though God is the Creator of thermodynamics, He is not subject to His system of laws. The Creation of the universe was a supernatural event. The Creation was brought into existence *ex nihilo*, meaning "out of nothing."[38] There was no previously existing matter

---

revealed a physical manifestation of His deity. The only heretofore unseen characteristic was light. Light is the most-fitting first proclamation of the Author of Creation.

36. Since the sun and moon were not created until verse 14 of chapter 1, the night and day could not have arisen from the rotation of the earth with respect to the sun. This does not preclude rotation of the earth prior to creation of the sun; neither does it necessarily demand it.

37. Frova and Marenzana, *Thus Spoke Galileo*, 183–207.

38. *Merriam-Webster Dictionary*, s.v. "ex nihilo." This term was first used in 1656. In Gen-

that was transformed into different matter in the universe. The universe was spoken into existence in a series of creative acts.

The creative miracles in the gospel accounts of the feeding of the multitudes provide additional examples of where God brought matter into existence, temporarily suspending the first law of thermodynamics (John 6:1–13; Matt 15:32–38).[39] God as a supernatural Creator is not restricted to natural law, particularly with regard to energy. We may be familiar with the formula $E = mc^2$. Based upon this, we could calculate all the energy to create the universe if we knew of all the mass in the universe. However, God's creative work is not constrained within this equation. After all, His act of Creation of matter did not lessen His energy or power contrary to what the formula states.[40] But God is not constrained to such relationships, nor would such an investment have diminished the energy of the omnipotent God by any measurable amount.[41]

God's Assessment of Creation

Seven times in the Creation account it is recorded that God's assessment of His Creation was that it was good (Gen 1:4, 10, 12, 18, 21, 25, 31). The Hebrew word translated "good" is טוֹב (ṭôb) and has a wide range of meanings.[42] It can mean, among other things, pleasing or beautiful, in order or usable, qualitatively good or efficient, or appropriate for that which something was designed. All of Creation was a reflection of the Creator when the universe came into existence.

At the conclusion of the six days of creation, God "saw everything that he had made, and behold, it was very good" (Gen 1:31). The expression here is טוֹב מְאֹד (ṭôb m'ōd). The point here is that the Creation, taken in its totality, was exceedingly good.[43] Currid rightly observes, "Describing God's judgment of His

---

esis 1:3, 6, 14 the phrase "let there be" refers to the coming into existence of matter where formerly it did not exist.

39. When the Lord turned the water into wine in John 2:1–11, it is possible that the water molecules were transformed into the molecules that comprise wine apart from its water base. If this is what happened, then strictly speaking, this creative act would not have been an *ex nihilo* act of creation.

40. Matter and energy are now known to be energy in different forms and are related by $E = mc^2$, where E is energy, m is mass, and c is the speed of light.

41. Subtracting any finite amount from infinity equals infinity.

42. Koehler and Baumgartner, *The Hebrew and Aramaic Lexicon of the Old Testatment*, 2:370–72; Harris, Archer, and Waltke, *Theological Wordbook of the Old Testament*, 1:345–46; Brown, Driver, and Briggs, *Hebrew and English Lexicon of the Old Testament*, 373–75.

43. Harris, Archer, and Waltke, *Theological Wordbook of the Old Testament*, 1:487.

own creation with great emphasis, it is perfect in every detail, even down to the very intricacies of its being."[44]

It was not good merely in the sense of being lovely and functional. It was also usable and efficient with respect to function. Every chemical and physical process that happened in the Garden of Eden and in the world was completely efficient.[45] Nothing was wasted; nothing was designed to be wasteful. The botanical and zoological creation was functioning exactly as it was designed.

One might allege that such observations are speculations that cannot be justified or substantiated. When the individual consequences of the Fall are considered from the standpoint of thermodynamics, the assessment given above is tenable. Additionally, the meaning of טוֹב מְאֹד (ṭôb m 'ōd) and the character of the assessor make this characterization of Eden all the more reasonable.

THE FALL AND ITS IMPLICATIONS

How are we to understand the effects of the Fall changed from the perspective of thermodynamics? Since this cannot be studied directly, we will have to infer abductively from the biblical text and our understanding of post-Fall thermodynamics. We can consider the specific details of the curse and how they introduce new aspects of energy movement in the world. By making these observations, we will also be in a position to consider the thermodynamics in the pre-Fall Garden of Eden.

Before we relate the effects of the Fall with thermodynamics, we need to make a broader observation. The Fall did change the universe. The perfection that existed in the pre-Fall world was shattered. New characteristics were set into motion that initiated events completely foreign to Adam and Eve. In a real sense, the Fall resulted in a universe whose thermodynamics are best characterized as controlled chaos. Because we live in that chaos daily and have never known anything else, it seems normal.

For example, childbirth was forever changed as a result of the Fall (Gen 3:16). The pronouncement that pain would be multiplied in childbirth has to be understood in light of a hypothetical, pre-Fall birth. Before the Fall, there would

---

44. Currid, *A Study Commentary on Genesis*, 1:89.
45. A chemical process is one that occurs when a substance is converted to another substance, e.g., burning wood. A physical process is one in which the material is in a different state, but its chemical composition is unchanged, e.g., ice melting.

have been no pain in childbirth. The characteristics of the new heavens and new earth (Rev 21:4) support this view. The absence of pain, death, and tears speak of a situation that arguably reproduces the characteristics of pre-Fall Eden. Since there is no pain in the new heavens and the new earth, there was no pain before the Fall. To every woman in history who would give birth, especially before the advent of anesthesia, the pain of childbirth is a declaration of the penalty of rebellion in the Garden, even if it is not understood or acknowledged.

Moreover, the change for the inhabitants of the Garden of Eden extended to the edge of creation. In Romans 8:21, it says "that the creation itself will be set free from its bondage to corruption and obtain the freedom of the glory of the children of God." The expression "bondage to corruption" describes the changes that were part of God's curse upon the universe. For Adam's rebellion, there would be perpetual and expansive consequences as a result of this sin. All of this shows the Fall had consequences on the physical universe. Let us now proceed to see how this impacts the laws of thermodynamics.

The first part of the curse was placed on the ground (Gen 3:17). Adam would now be forced to work the ground to support life. There would be no more free lunches in the Garden. Work would not be a casual effort; it would be toil. It would be a painful exercise, and it would never end. Adam's entire life would have to be devoted to this ongoing, agrarian effort.

But it got worse. There would be complications of incomprehensible magnitude (Gen 3:18). The earth that formerly was an ally took on an adversarial posture. The agrarian exercise would be complicated by thorns and thistles that would pose a continual impediment to growing the food Adam and Eve would need. At the curse, germination and the spread of pesky plants were "turned on." Landscaping woes became the norm. We now have to invest time and effort to continually fight against the out-of-control growth of thorns and thistles. The randomness of man's environment would now be continually expanding, and man would either have to curtail that expansion by his own efforts or be left to live with the results of that unchecked expansion.

What did all these outcomes of the curse mean in terms of thermodynamics? What was intrinsically different about the universe now that was not in operation before sin entered the world? *This increase in entropy has a destructive component.* Seeds from plants would now blow all over the earth, an increase in entropy. Plant growth was more random. This explains how we are always growing weeds in our lawns and grass in our flower beds. It is one of the countless destructive results of Adam's sin. This increase in randomness associated with the curse can be called "dissipative entropy." A scientist might put it this way: This is the destructive increase in randomness associated with spontaneous processes that is over and above functional entropy.[46] In lay terms, the randomness occurring in natural process now has a destructive nature. This did not occur prior to the Fall where "randomness" actually was beneficial or functional to Creation.

The woes associated with the rebellion continued. We can see this destructive randomness as we continue to look at the consequences of Genesis 3. The next consequence of original sin was that work would become even more difficult (Gen 3:19). Exertion would now be accompanied by perspiration. Man would now have his efforts complicated by having to sweat to accomplish his goals. This means that more effort would have to be expended than formerly to accomplish any task. For the first time in human history, man would have to work to the point of sweating to accomplish his goals.

Consequently, the Fall meant the second law of thermodynamics had come into play. Energy could not be completely converted to work. Part of the energy would be lost as waste heat. This explains why a car has to have a radiator to rid the engine of the otherwise destructive waste heat that would destroy the engine. In mechanical devices friction between moving surfaces creates heat, so that all the energy driving the mechanical device cannot be completely converted to useful work. This waste heat is responsible for all mechanical failure. Electrical motor burnout, light bulbs burning out, appliances dying—all these happen because of the second law. Mold on bread, rusting cars, houses needing constant cleaning are additional examples of the randomness that is ongoing and incessant.

After the Fall, every newly encountered difficulty and challenge would likely bring to Adam's mind his pre-Fall world and would remind him of what he had thrown away through his disobedience. Being unable to exactly envision what a pre-Fall world was like, we cannot know the magnitude of Adam's guilt, remorse, and regret. Surely it was great. Not only his mind would confront him with his transgression, his body would also.

And too, for the first time, hygiene would become part of man's daily regime. The mess, odor, and general unpleasantness associated with perspiration entered man's daily existence. And time and effort would have to be set

---

46. A more complete statement of post-Fall thermodynamics is that the total available energy in the universe is continually decreasing. For every spontaneous process that occurs, more Gibbs Free Energy is irreversibly lost. Cf. footnote 28. Gibbs free energy is like money; you can only spend it once. And, in general, these losses contain dissipative entropy increases.

aside to deal with these consequences. The implications were much broader than water seeping through man's pores.

"Uncleanness" in general would now be part of daily life. Dissipative entropy would appear in the form of dirt and grime moving through the environment. The water of perspiration would collect the dirt in the air. Adam and Eve would have dirt cling to their bodies, and their hair would become dirty. Food particles would stick to their teeth.

From such a reasoned position, tooth decay, and later crooked teeth—in short, anything that now requires either a dental procedure to correct—ultimately can be traced to the randomness that was introduced at the Fall. Similarly, cancer falls into the category of uncontrolled growth of cells. Hormonal imbalance, graying hair, loss of muscle tone, weight gain, and all the other effects of aging became part of life.

The final and most important result of the Fall is the introduction of death into creation (Gen 3:19b). Prior to the Fall there was no death at any level. No organism or any cell was subject to death before the decision to rebel. God's warning in Genesis 2:17, "in the day that you eat of it you shall surely die," contained the spiritual death of separation from God on the one hand and incipient physical death on the other. Without this sin, death would have never entered the world and spread to all mankind (Rom 5:12). What is death in terms of thermodynamics? At some point our bodies lose the ability to sustain life. Susceptibility to contagious disease because our immune system becomes impaired, the uncontrolled randomness of a malignant tumor, heart attack—each of these things could cause our death. And they all have one thing in common: the second law of thermodynamics is operative in each case. But how did this occur at the cellular level?

Before the Fall, no cell died. A perfectly functioning cell in a perfectly functioning world would never wear out. No new cells would have to be synthesized. It was only with the Fall that the death of cells and cellular reproduction would have been necessary. At this point dissipative entropy, destructive randomness, is part of the process. How would it manifest itself? It would show up as inexact replication of cells. This destructive randomness that accompanies all processes is the origin of mutation. This explains why we get gray hair, skin spots, arthritis—in short, all the complications of aging. Ultimately, it is this inexact replication of cells that kills everyone, although it can be complicated by external agents, such as disease. Since mutation is a post-Fall phenomenon and is destructive in nature, it could not be the source of new, useful genetic material that could lead to new species. Without mutation as a constructive tool to be the source of new, more complex species, evolution becomes a molecular impossibility. This means evolution cannot account for the origin of new species.

Before the Fall

First Law of Thermodynamics

Since no one has ever seen Eden, we are left to construct a picture based on abduction. The starting point for the discussion is the biblical record and what we can infer from that about Edenic conditions. The creative action of God ceased at the end of the six days of the Creation week. All of the matter and energy that would ever be were created during this period. Everything today that is visible or detectable by means of instrumental analysis has been in existence in one form or another since the end of the Creation week.

Since all the energy in the universe had already been created, the first law of thermodynamics can be applied without contradicting the biblical record. Energy transformation was occurring since the chemical energy of the sun and the stars was being converted into light. From the biblical text, the sun was functioning according to its designed processes of nuclear fusion, streaming both light and heat into the solar system and beyond (Ps 19:1–6). The loss of energy by the sun has to be found someplace else in the universe.

Second Law of Thermodynamics

By considering what was lost and introduced at the Fall, we can construct a picture of how Eden likely was with respect to the second law. In a seminal work, Whitcomb and Morris contended the second law was inoperative in the pre-Fall world.[47] We will argue against this view. Recently, how the second law of thermodynamics may have worked the in the pre-Fall world has been reconsidered.[48]

Everything suggested in this section is merely an inference, so we can hardly be dogmatic. Nevertheless, some interesting observations can be made. A consideration of Eden from a thermodynamic perspective also affords insight into the validity of a plain reading of the biblical record of origins. At this point, we can make some observations:

---

47.   Whitcomb and Morris, *The Genesis Flood*, 224–25.
48.   Anderson, "Thoughts on the Goodness of Creation"; Faulkner, "The Second Law of Thermodynamics and the Curse."

The Nature of Eating in the Garden

As we know, the biblical account describes the pre-Fall world as very good (Gen 1:31). Arguably, a way that it was "very good" was it was fully functional. Eden functioned exactly the way it was designed. The conversion of the chemical energy of food to useful energy for work would have likewise been a functionally complete process. There would not have been any loss of the energy of the food Adam and Eve ate. All of the complex carbohydrates of a piece of fruit would have been completely converted to carbon dioxide and water. It would have been completely converted into energy. This perfectly efficient conversion ratio would have allowed Adam and Eve to eat less, since metabolism would have not led to any energy that could not be utilized.

However, such a process would still have been accompanied by an increase in entropy. The gas volumes of the exhaled gases, occupying a greater volume than the carbohydrate they came from, technically is an increase in entropy. However, this entropy is different from that which we see post-Fall. It did not harm Adam and Eve. This is entropy associated with how the world was supposed to be. We call this "functional entropy."[49] The second law of thermodynamics was operative before the Fall. However, it operated as part of a perfectly functioning creation.

The Nature of Work in the Garden

It is clear that Adam had pre-Fall responsibilities in the Garden to work and keep the Garden (Gen 2:15). The words "work" and "keep" refer to the investiture of responsibility rather than cultivation *per se*, although it is possible that cultivation of the Garden in the traditional sense of the word was involved. In Genesis 2:5, the term "work" refers to manipulation of the ground. This was probably some sort of cultivation to facilitate plant growth.

The Nature of Waste in the Garden

The physiological capability of ridding the human body of waste from incomplete, post-Fall metabolism was a necessary, built in capability. The fact that the Fall was ordained was also taken into account, since the ability to

---

49. This term was coined to describe the increase in entropy that occurred prior to the Fall, but was in keeping with God's design for a correctly functioning thermodynamic system. For example, ripples in water in a stream moving over an uneven streambed would have more entropy than water running over a flat surface, but each would function for the effect desired by the Creator.

deal with all the consequences of the Fall would have to have been necessarily present in Adam and Eve, albeit in abeyance.[50] There would have been no reason for these post-Fall abilities to have been operative at this time, since the conditions that would have necessitated their utilization did not exist in the pre-Fall environment.

Since the Fall was ordained, God designed human physiology with additional capabilities, even though they too would not be needed until after the Fall. Even though there was no cellular death before the Fall, the ability to biosynthesize and replace dying cells of human tissue was likewise built into human physiology.

Again these are just speculative inferences. In any case, we can say that creation was fully functioning prior to the Fall and that after the Fall, things changed. We may not know exactly what they changed *from* but we do know what they changed *to*. As discussed above, the destructive nature of entropy we now face was not present prior to the Fall. Now, though, we daily encounter and fight against the increase in entropy as it complicates our environment and, ultimately, our own lives.

CONCLUSION

Being able to observe the Fall using the unique lens of thermodynamics to focus on the effects of Adam's sin and our participation in it affords insights that are otherwise unavailable. Thermodynamics reveals aspects of the attributes of God that are truly remarkable. To design a universe that will always have all the energy it needs for its lifetime vividly displays God's omniscience and omnipotence. The rebellion of Adam can be more fully understood in light of the severity and pervasive presence of dissipative entropy. One can only marvel at God's justice and, yet, His mercy. The pain and agony of the randomness of the second law is surely something that is calling us back to Him—for relief in this age and deliverance in the age to come. And that deliverance is rooted in the comforting thought that the Lord Jesus Christ will come back and restore the creation to its original function to the praise of the glory of God (Rev 22:20).

---

50. Both Isaiah 46:10 and Ephesians 1:11 speak to the sovereignty of God over all aspects of His creation. If God were not omnipotent, omniscient, and omnipresent, He could not declare the end from the beginning, nor could He work all things according to the counsel of His will.

Bibliography

Anderson, Lee. "Thoughts on the Goodness of Creation: In What Sense Was Creation 'Perfect'?" *Answers Research Journal* 6 (2013): 391–97.

Brown, Francis, S. R. Driver, and C. A. Briggs. *Hebrew and English Lexicon of the Old Testament*. Oxford: Clarendon Press, 1966.

Carlson, Richard F., ed. *Science and Christianity: Four Views*. Downers Grove, IL: InterVarsity Press, 2000.

Copi, Irving M. *Symbolic Logic*. New York: Macmillian Company, 1965.

Currid, John D. *A Study Commentary on Genesis*, Vol. 1. Webster, NY: Evangelical Press, 2003.

Dill, K. A., and S. Bromberg. *Molecular Driving Forces*. New York: Garland Science, 2011.

Einstein, Albert. *Relativity*. New York: Crown Publishers, 1961.

Ewell, Walter A., ed. *Evangelical Dictionary of Theology*. Grand Rapids: Baker, 1984.

Faulkner, Danny. "The Second Law of Thermodynamics and the Curse." *Answers Research Journal* 6 (2013): 399–407.

Freedman, Roger A., et al. *College Physics*. New York: W. H. Freeman and Company, 2014.

Frova, A., and M. Marenzana. *Thus Spoke Galileo*. Oxford: Oxford University Press, 2006.

Gaebelein, Frank. *The Pattern of God's Truth*. Winona Lake, IN: BMH Books, 1968.

Gardner, Martin. *Relativity Simply Explained*. Mineola, NY: Dover Publications, 1997.

Grudem, Wayne. *Systematic Theology*. Grand Rapids: Zondervan, 1994.

Harris, R. Laird, Gleason L. Archer, Jr., and Bruce K. Waltke. *Theological Wordbook of the Old Testament*, 2 Vols. Chicago, IL: Moody Press, 1980.

Hodge, Charles. *Systematic Theology*, Vol. 1. Grand Rapids: Eerdmans Publishing, 1979.

Jones, Taylor B. "A Scriptural View of Science." In *Think Biblically!* Wheaton, IL: Crossway, 2003.

Koehler, Ludwig, and Walter Baumgartner. *The Hebrew and Aramaic Lexicon of the Old Testament*, Vol. 2. New York: E. J. Brill, 1995.

Lipton, Peter. *Inference to the Best Explanation*. New York: Routledge, 1991.

Lodish, Harvey, et al. *Molecular Cell Biology*. New York: W. H. Freeman, 2008.

Skryms, Brian. *Choice and Chance: An Introduction to Inductive Logic*. Belmont, CA: Dickensen Publishing Company, 1966.

Thiessen, Henry C. *Introductory Lectures in Systematic Theology*. Grand Rapids: Eerdmans Publishing, 1963.

Tro, Nivaldo J. *Principles of Chemistry*. Boston: Pearson, 2013.

Warfield, B. B. *The Inspiration and Authority of Scripture*. Phillipsburg, NJ: Presbyterian and Reformed Publishing Company, 1948.

Whitcomb, J. C., and H. M. Morris. *The Genesis Flood*. Phillipsburg: P&R Publishing, 1961.

CHAPTER 9

IN RE ADAM AND EVE:
REFLECTIONS ON THE CREATION AND FALL OF MAN—A LEGAL PERSPECTIVE

George A. Crawford

INTRODUCTION

From start to finish, the biblical account of the Fall of man in Genesis 3 has great legal significance. The text describes a scenario familiar to anyone trained or experienced in the law. A law existed—and was violated. Investigation follows. Exercising His proper role as a completely just judge, God extracts a confession and determines the factual record, following the questioning of Adam and Eve. He then applies the law to the facts and reaches a decision. An appropriate and commensurate sentence is pronounced. Thus, the first humans are judged guilty of violating the law and expelled from the Garden, that they may not live eternally by eating of the tree of life. God demonstrates His grace, however, in the midst of man's just guilt. He provides bodily covering (v. 21) and thereby foreshadows what we know today as the Atonement.

Not fully grasped, by and large, the just punishment imposed by God also has monumental legal significance. If the Fall did not occur, the entire legal profession would probably not exist. Due to the Fall and as illustrated by biblical text and example, we see the development of law, both in general and in specific areas. We also see the development of the state, the judicial process, and the nature of adjudication (i.e., the process of hearing and deciding cases). These are "exhibits" of the shadows of the Fall as well as the tarnishing of man's special Creation. They thereby provide at least indirect support to the veracity of the biblical account. In addition, they also demonstrate a biblically valid role for believers serving in the areas of law and government. Because of the Fall, law and government continue to be areas of legitimate service for committed Christians.

Exhibit 1: The Nature of Law in General

The impact of the Fall, as described in Scripture, was as pervasive as it was cataclysmic. One thing we may overlook due to that pervasiveness is that Scripture indicates that the Fall created the need for codified law, both in general and for specific issues. The continuing realities of the legal challenges and conflicts described in Genesis immediately following the Fall both imply and ultimately depend on the historicity of the Fall.

The Reformation theologian John Calvin is one of the best writers in helping us understand the repercussions of the Fall as described in Genesis 3 and as clarified in other passages of Scripture. And, at least arguably, no other writer has a better grasp of the proper relationship between the Christian, law, and government.

How does the existence and development of law, as we know it today, indirectly argue for the veracity of the biblical account of the Fall? We'll begin with Scripture: Romans 2:14–16 tells us that the law of God is written on the hearts of men. The text observes that Gentiles, who do not have the law, actually do by nature what the law requires. This shows that a sort of law is written on their hearts and conscience. Thus, they stand guilty before God.

That sense of right and wrong feeds the conscience and has been referred to as "natural law." Calvin makes the connection clear:

> Now, as it is evident that the law of God which we call moral,
> is nothing else than the testimony of natural law, and of that
> conscience which God has engraven on the minds of men,
> the whole of this equity of which we now speak is prescribed

in it. Hence it alone ought to be the aim, the rule, and the end of all laws.[1]

However, the Fall also explains another important factor about natural law. While natural law exists empirically, we see that our grasp of its content is fragmented at best.

Thus, man's cognitive ability of that natural law has been obscured. This too is a reality that was caused by the Fall. Romans 8:7 tells us that the mind of man in the wake of the Fall "does not submit to God's law" and "indeed, it cannot." First Corinthians 2:14 also tells us that man, after the Fall, will find God's law to be both incomprehensible and "folly." Calvin tells us that, by comparison with man prior to the Fall, our grasp of natural law has been reduced to a "shapeless ruin." Calvin rightly argues that natural law or the knowledge of good and evil is not totally destroyed in man. Nevertheless, our grasp of it is corrupted by the Fall.[2]

This corruption gives rise to the need for codified laws. Natural law would have provided an adequate regulation of human conduct. However, since our sense of right and wrong (natural law) has been obscured, we need a known and articulated law to govern our conduct. We see this in the Scripture itself. A major portion of the Scripture is that which we know as the law. Much of the books of Exodus and Numbers, as well as the books of Leviticus and Deuteronomy, provide normative statements of that which God has prohibited and allowed. In turn, God has also allowed for the creation of local government and civil law (Rom 13:1–7).

In modern terminology, we would understand that law to be statutory or codified law, appellate or case law, and regulation. Comparable to the Ten Commandments, statutory or codified law (corresponding roughly to the Hebrew *ḥuqqîm*) tells us that certain conduct is expressly prohibited or mandated, as evil or good. Since no body of statutory law can anticipate all questions that will develop as to its meaning or application, appellate or case law will develop. This too illustrates man's darkened understanding of right and wrong after the Fall. This confusion demands that duly authorized tribunals make authoritative and precedential decisions. At least some of those decisions inevitably will also be considered as law (case law corresponding, again

---

1. Calvin, *Institutes of the Christian Religion* 2.2.12, 664.
2. Ibid., 233–34.

roughly, to the Hebrew *mišpāṭîm*). As the codified law and case law will need to be implemented and enforced, a "living law," the government, will inevitably develop.[3] That branch of the government will also inevitably issue statements of coercive or binding policy, known in modern law as "regulations" (corresponding, again roughly, to the Hebrew *piqqûdîm).*[4]

The Fall explains how there can be both an innate sense that certain conduct is inherently right or inherently wrong while concurrently having voluminous law addressing that same matter. For example, we can see this in modern statutes, which use great detail to define concepts innately understood as intrinsically evil, or *malum in se*; California's Penal Code, for example, uses nearly eight thousand words and eighteen sections to develop the concept of "murder" and its appropriate punishment.

We should reiterate that if man's grasp of natural law was not distorted, the legal profession would almost certainly not exist. If all still had the same accurate knowledge of that natural law, there would be no compulsion or need for any individuals to develop an expertise in the written law. However, we learn in Genesis 3 that man learned about good and evil through disobedience. He, now, inherently does not understand right and wrong correctly. The above discussion illustrates that reality. Thus, after the Fall, we differ in our ability to study, comprehend, and apply both the Scripture and civil law. If it comes to a point where questions are raised as to the meaning or applicability of a particular law, we want to consult with someone who knows that law and who knows it very well. The biblical epitome is illustrated by Ezra, who Scripture records had "set his heart" to study, practice, and teach the law of God (Ezra 7:10).[5]

Exhibit 2: The Development of Both the State and Specific Areas of Law

In addition to creating the need for law, in the broad general sense, a careful review of the text also indicates that the Fall set in motion the need for specific areas of law. We can observe this in Genesis 3 itself as well as in the texts that

---

3. Ibid., 663.
4. The rough nature of the "correspondence" is demonstrated in 1 Samuel 30:24–25 where a pronouncement by David, following a dispute concerning the relative "shares" in plunder of those in the military, is referred to as both a "statute" and a "rule" for Israel.
5. Significantly, the position and role of the judge was recognized no later than the time of Abraham, Lot, and Job (Gen 18:25; 19:9; cf. Job 12:17; 31:11, 28).

come immediately after it. The narrative implies that the consequences of the Fall give rise to sins and the need for specific laws that we have even today. This too supports the historical veracity of Genesis 3.

The Law of Succession

Probably the most immediately recognized impact of the Fall was the introduction of death as a reality of human existence. In Genesis 2:16–17, God told Adam:

> And the Lord God commanded the man, saying, "You may surely eat of every tree of the garden, but of the tree of the knowledge of good and evil you shall not eat, for in the day that you eat of it you shall surely die."

The woman, then Adam, ate and facilitated death entering the world.

The inevitable result was that there would need to be some standard concerning the proper and improper disposition of belongings. This we know, today, as the law of succession. Demonstrating both the need for a law of succession, and the development of appellate or case law, the daughters of Zelophehad, and the leaders of their tribe, the tribe of Manasseh, obtain what we would know today as "declaratory relief" concerning the relative rights of the descendants and relatives of a decedent and the corresponding responsibilities they would have to the tribe (Num 27:1–11; 36:1–12).

The Law of Property

Of crucial significance, Scripture indicates that the Fall created what we know today as the problem of scarcity. Contrary to life in the paradise of Eden before the Fall, we now only have limited resources and those resources require great effort to access and use. As God told Adam after the Fall, weeds can choke out crops and people would have to work by the sweat of their brow (Gen 3:17–18). Moreover, the physical environment itself was intrinsically cursed. Romans 8:20–21 tells us that the entirety of creation was "subjected to futility" and placed in "bondage to corruption".

Consequently, and in contrast with the Garden, man had to learn to deal with times of severe shortage. With the problem aggravated by the impact of the Flood, and within ten generations of Noah, man had to learn to cope with periods of severe agricultural shortage, or famine (Gen 12:10).

It should not escape notice that the familiar account of Joseph and the seven years of plenty followed by seven years of famine also tells of government taking action to provide the necessities of life and doing so by the appointment of a regulatory administrator. Joseph was given the authority to issue regulations necessary to implement policy approved by a monarch (Gen 41; 47:13–26). As acknowledged by Calvin, the purposes of government therefore necessarily include providing for necessities of life, as well as the protection of property.[6]

Family Law

In the wake of the Fall, the institutions of marriage and the family, part of God's common grace, were subject to a curse. Genesis 3:17 tells us:

> To the woman he said, "I will surely multiply your pain in childbearing; in pain you shall bring forth children. Your desire shall be for your husband, and he shall rule over you."

As pointed out by Dr. John MacArthur, wives will tend to want to control their husbands, while husbands will tend to oppress their wives.[7] That curse on marriage eventually leads to the need for law to govern family relationships and particularly the dissolution of marriage (Deut 24:1–4; Matt 5:31–32).

Surrogacy Law

In keeping with the subjection of creation to futility at the time of the Fall (cf. Rom 8:20), men and women began to experience a lack of fertility. That leads to the development of a form of surrogacy law in which the child

---

6. Calvin, *Institutes of the Christian Religion*, 4.20.3, 652–53. In Calvin's own words: "But we shall have a fitter opportunity of speaking of the use of civil government. All we wish to be understood at present is, that it is perfect barbarism to think of exterminating it, its use among men being not less than that of bread and water, light and air, while its dignity is much more excellent. Its object is not merely, like those things, to enable men to breathe, eat, drink, and be warmed (though it certainly includes all these, while it enables them to live together); this, I say, is not its only object, but it is, that no idolatry, no blasphemy against the name of God, no calumnies against his truth, nor other offences to religion, break out and be disseminated among the people; that the public quiet be not disturbed, that every man's property be kept secure, that men may carry on innocent commerce with each other, that honesty and modesty be cultivated; in short, that a public form of religion may exist among Christians, and humanity among men."

7. MacArthur, *MacArthur Study Bible*, note to, Genesis 3:17; Mathews, *Genesis 1–11:26*, 251.

born to a woman, whom we would now consider a surrogate, was considered the child of the woman otherwise unable to conceive. Genesis 16, 17, and 21 describe Sarah's inability to conceive without the divine intervention leading to the birth of Isaac. In the interim, she provides her maidservant, Hagar, to Abraham with the express understanding that she, Sarah, would obtain children by her (Gen 16:2). Similarly, both Rachel and Leah, the wives of Jacob, understood that the children born to him by their maidservants, Bilhah and Zilpah, were their own (Gen 30:3–13).

Criminal Law

Within the generation immediately following the Fall, the first murder occurs, with the killing of Abel by his brother Cain, after Cain invited him to an isolated location. "And when they were in the field, Cain rose up against his brother Abel and killed him" (Gen 4:8). Within five generations, Cain's descendant, Lamech, boasts of having killed *at least one* other man (Gen 4:23–24).

Those events illustrate the need for law and government to restrain evil.[8] Acknowledging the horror of the crime of murder, recognizing it as an attack on the "image of God" in created man, Genesis 9:5–6 recognizes the principle of *lex talionis*, and tells us that God will require comparable punishment for the perpetrator:

> And for your lifeblood I will require a reckoning: from every beast I will require it and from man. From his fellow man I will require a reckoning for the life of man.
>
> Whoever sheds the blood of man, by man shall his blood be shed, for God made man in his own image.

Scripture contains numerous instances of laws prohibiting specific conduct and prescribed punishments for violating those commands, many of which are comparable to modern criminal law (e.g., Exod 21–23; Num 35). Scripture thus provides necessary guidance as to the implementation of what we know today as criminal law. Scripture recognizes the serious nature of criminal punishment and the imperfection of human reasoning post-Fall. Accordingly, it contains procedural requirements for determining guilt and

---

8. Calvin, *Institutes of the Christian Religion*, 2.7.10, 307–8.

imposing a sentence, with an admonition that the deterrent impact can be lost if there is undue delay in punishment (Eccl 8:11). We can see the procedural requirements in Deuteronomy 19:15–19, which discusses the need for witnesses to testify and for the trier of fact to diligently inquire into their credibility. We can also see the seriousness of not following this in the execution of Naboth and his sons when these procedures were not followed (1 Kgs 21:1–19; 2 Kgs 9:26).

The Fall, therefore, created the need for government to develop, articulate, and publicize law and to then administer and enforce that law for public protection, to maintain public order, and to promote a certain public and common morality.[9] Doing so, the Fall created the need for law to confront fallen man with his own imperfections, sinfulness, and his need for a Savior (Gen 3:7–19; Gal 3:19–24).[10]

Intellectual Property

Within the sixth generation from the Fall, specialized skills and knowledge develop within the descendants of Adam because of the scarcity discussed above. Jabal is recognized as the "father" of those who "dwell in tents and have livestock" (Gen 4:20). His brother, Jubal, is similarly recognized as "the father" of those who "play the lyre and pipe" (Gen 4:21). Finally, their half-brother, Tubal-cain, is referred to as the "forger" of all instruments of bronze and iron (Gen 4:22). The strategic importance of limiting access to such knowledge was recognized in antiquity and became a crucial factor in the conflict between Israel and the Philistines (1 Sam 13:19–22). The existence of that specialized knowledge and ability, against a backdrop of scarcity, leads directly to the development of what we know today as copyright and patent law.

The Development of the State

Within two generations from the Fall, the stage was set for the development of the first city-state recorded in Scripture. Genesis 4:17 tells us that Cain built a city, which he named Enoch, after his son. The first major city-state recorded in Scripture occurs within thirteen generations of the Fall. Known to history as Babel, its collapse leads to the linguistic dispersion of people

---

9. Ibid., 652–53.
10. Ibid., 304–7.

groups, and subsequently, the development of a multiplicity of nation-states (Gen 11). Charged with the responsibility of curbing fallen man's bent to evil, the state is given the responsibility of exercising adjudication, approved coercion, and the punishment of evil (Rom 13:1–7; 1 Pet 2:13–17).

The Development of International Relations

Continuing from the development of a multiplicity of nation-states begun in Genesis 11, the Fall sets the stage for the resulting need for government to protect against the violent aggression of external city/nation-states and for the evaluation of how and when that is properly, or justly, done. Genesis 14 describes the development of two rival coalitions of city-states and the successful attack, by a coalition of four city-states, on Sodom and Gomorrah and three city-states affiliated with them. Lot is captured and taken as a slave until rescued by an armed force led by his uncle, Abraham. The nature of potential conflict between states will inevitably lead to the development of international standards and law concerning both the conduct of warfare (The Geneva Conventions)[11] and internationally recognized protections of human rights (The Universal Declaration of Human Rights). Overall, we observe that Genesis 3 sets in motion realities that give rise to the laws we have today. The consequences of the Fall are real and arguably confirm that it is historical as well.

EXHIBIT 3: THE NATURE OF THE JUDICIAL PROCESS

What we know today as the judicial process broadly and essentially involves the following component parts, all of which point more or less directly to the special Creation of man and the Fall. In general, the process begins with an allegation that there has been a violation or breach of some legally protected interest generating a conflict of some sort. Indicative of the Fall and scarcity, that breach or violation has caused a measurable loss to one or more of the individuals or groups involved. There will be a governing standard (pertinent law), a court (or other authorized body), and a duly scheduled and noticed hearing (cf. John 7:51). During that hearing, there will be the development of an appropriate, or relevant, factual record. The trier of fact, whether judge or jury, will carry out the application of the law pertinent to that record. A synthesis of the applicable law and the pertinent facts will be made to an au-

---

11. Ibid., 631–32.

thoritative statement of decision. Finally, there will be a process by which appeal can be made of error(s) in the development of the factual record, the identification of pertinent law, or the application of law to the factual record.

The judicial process, outlined above, is designed to right wrongs. This presumes a standard of right and wrong, which is what we observed in Genesis 2–3. The judicial process also attempts to balance fairness, accurately determine the facts in a particular matter and provide a process to apply the law. This too supports the details of Genesis 3. We noted that the Fall resulted in man having a deficient knowledge of good and evil, having violated God's explicit command. Because of this, man struggles to correctly implement what is right. Hence, the judicial process comes into being as a corrective to man's sinful biases. The existence of the judicial process supports what we see ensue from the Fall.

Exhibit 4: The Nature of Adjudication

God's first reported action after He rested on the Sabbath was this very activity. He confronts the wrongdoer and determines the facts of the case (Gen 3:10–13). He then determines guilt and makes a sentencing (Gen 3:14–17). He does not merely do this in Genesis 3. Other scriptural passages attest to the same activity (cf. Gen 4:10; 1 Sam 13:11–14; 2 Sam 12:7–12). Similarly, and in a matter reflecting the *imago Dei*, human judges handle matters brought to their attention. They are given the responsibility of determining the relevant facts and law. They are charged with evaluating the perceptual accuracy or bias of witnesses. Finally, they have the responsibility of making an authoritative decision, applying the pertinent law to the factual record. Thus, from a scriptural perspective, adjudication comes from God in Genesis 3.

For this reason, God through Scripture discusses the process of adjudication. He gives guidance and standards as to the implementation of the normative requirements of law. He also calls for the assignment of that task to men—and women—who are uniquely qualified for that role (cf. Exod 18:21–26; Deut 1:9–17; Judg 4:4–5).

However, unlike God, man distorts natural law and can only grope for the right application and implementation of that law. Accordingly, the Scripture provides written direction as to appropriate procedures for adjudication (see, e.g., Deut 19:15–20). Judges are admonished to "hear the cases between your brothers, and judge righteously between a man and his brother or the alien who is with him. You shall not be partial in judgment. You shall hear the small and the great alike. You shall not be intimidated by anyone, for the judgment is God's" (Deut 1:16–17). Similarly, Jehoshaphat admonished the judges, "Consider what you do, for you judge not for man but for the Lord. He is with you in giving judgment. Now then, let the fear of the Lord be upon you. Be careful what you do, for there is no injustice with the Lord our God, or partiality or taking bribes" (2 Chron 19:6–7).

Engaged in an inherently stressful and emotionally draining process,[12] judges are not to indulge in mind-numbing substance abuse or to pervert justice but are to "judge righteously" and are to defend the rights of the poor and the weak (Prov 31:5, 8–9). Judges are to avoid partiality in adjudication (Prov 24:23; 28:21). The admonition literally refers to adjudication based on outward appearance (i.e., "knowing faces"). This effectively prohibits adjudication in which social status and economic wealth (or lack thereof) would be controlling. Put another way, and borrowing a familiar cliché, the justice implemented by the judge is to be "blind."

Recognizing that some would attempt to subvert the process—again bearing witness to the depravity of man after the Fall—judges are to inquire diligently to determine the credibility of witnesses. They are to impose appropriate punishment upon a perjurer and must determine that the evidence is sufficient before finding guilt or imposing a punishment. Even in imposing a punishment, they are to ensure that the punishment fits the crime (cf. Deut 19:15–21). Echoing this requirement, Nicodemus reminds the chief priests and the Pharisees that their law would not "judge a man without first giving him a hearing and learning what he does" (John 7:51).[13]

Thus, appropriate notice and scheduling are required. Facts would be determined using pertinent evidentiary standards. Then they are evaluated in light of appropriate law. Judges have both the responsibility of determining facts and the responsibility of applying the law to the facts. Subsequently, opportunities for appeal would be provided (Exod 18:21–27; Deut 1:9–17).[14]

---

12. Parenthetically, the familiar commendation of the "excellent wife" in Proverbs 31 tacitly demonstrates that stress and its impact. As I have experienced in my own life—and for which I am extremely grateful—it is the excellent wife's diligent service at home that allows her husband to carry out adjudication as he sits "at the gate" (Prov 31:23).

13. Implicitly requiring the giving of adequate notice and expressly requiring a fair hearing for the accused, Nicodemus' rhetorical question raises the essence of what we know as "due process of law."

14. It should not escape notice that in applying the law to the facts, judges deal with nuances of fact not dealt with in previous statutory law; thus, judges will inevitably move

Bearing evidence that man has been created in the image of God, a judge is given the responsibility by God to issue judgment on His behalf; bearing evidence of the impact of the Fall, an appeal process also guards against bias or imperfect or inaccurate determination of fact or law on the part of the judge.

In summary, adjudication is consistent with a literal reading of Genesis 3. It supports that God was the first judge who perfectly adjudicates. It supports the need for adjudication from that point onward due to the entrance of sin. The scriptural articulations of adjudication account for man's skewed nature as a result of the Fall. Those same texts acknowledge that man is made in God's image and thus able at the same time to carry out judgments like He has done. That too is consistent with what we observe in Genesis 1:26–28.[15]

CONCLUSION

We see the seedbed or the source of law in Genesis 3. This is not only in demonstration of its general need (in light of a Fall from perfect Creation) but also in that Genesis 3 and the following narrative present the need for very specific types of laws that persist to this day. Even more, the need for and nature of adjudication as well as the judicial process all are consistent with what we observe took place in the Fall. All of this indirectly supports a conclusion that the details of Genesis 3 are true and that the Fall is real. Put another way, the realities of life in the legal world and the legal profession are consistent with what we expect if the Fall was historical.

Having said all of that, it is interesting that in Acts 1:3, Luke tells us that the bodily resurrection of Christ was demonstrated and confirmed by many "infallible" or legally decisive "proofs" (*en pollois tekmeriois*); at least a portion of that evidence is succinctly stated in 1 Corinthians 15:5–8. Regardless, the Scripture also indicates that unless God transforms the heart, such evidence will be rejected, again ultimately due to the impact of the Fall (John 6:36, 40, 45, 66; 1 Cor 2:11–15).

---

toward developing new law in appellate levels. This tendency is very biblical and practical (though subject to abuse), because if the facts do not fit the law there are but two options: to do nothing and leave the status quo, or to create new law.

15.   Commenting extensively on the role of magistrates or judges and in recognition of the responsibility of the position in a post-Fall world, Calvin states: "Their functions were expressly approved by the Lord. Wherefore no man can doubt that civil authority is, in the sight of God, not only sacred and lawful, but the most sacred, and by far the most honourable, of all stations in mortal life" (Calvin, *Institutes of the Christian Religion*, 4.20. 4–9, 654).

In the same manner, the evidence of the Fall provided in Scripture will also have no impact but for the will of the Father and the work of the Holy Spirit. That being the case, the appropriate conclusion of this chapter is not an impassioned plea to accept the veracity of the biblical account of the Fall. Rather, those led by the Spirit accept the reality of the Fall and must ask what we should do with our conviction that the Fall is an actual historical event. I would respond that part of a proper response is a conviction that law and government are, and continue to be, legitimate areas for Christian service.

Addressing the relationship of the Christian to the state while writing the *Institutes*, Calvin had to respond to those who taught absolute and total submission to the government and to those, largely from the Anabaptist community, who taught that the Christian should have no involvement in government. The error of the former was to, ultimately, compromise the lordship of Christ. While we would agree with the Anabaptists on the importance of "believer's baptism," the error of the latter view was, ultimately, to ignore the impact of the Fall.[16] Because of the reality of the Fall, law and government are legitimate concerns of the Christian.[17] While we will not create the Kingdom of God on earth or

---

16. Calvin, *Institutes of the Christian Religion*, 4.20.1–7, 655–56.
17. In the *Institutes of the Christian Religion*, Calvin writes: "Still the distinction does not go so far as to justify us in supposing that the whole scheme of civil government is matter of pollution, with which Christian men have nothing to do. Fanatics, indeed, delighting in unbridled license, insist and vociferate that, after we are dead by Christ to the elements of this world, and being translated into the kingdom of God sit among the celestials, it is unworthy of us, and far beneath our dignity, to be occupied with those profane and impure cares which relate to matters alien from a Christian man. To what end, they say, are laws without courts and tribunals? But what has a Christian man to do with courts? Nay, if it is unlawful to kill, what have we to do with laws and courts? But as we lately taught that that kind of government is distinct from the spiritual and internal kingdom of Christ, so we ought to know that they are not adverse to each other. The former, in some measure, begins the heavenly kingdom in us, even now upon earth, and in this mortal and evanescent life commences immortal and incorruptible blessedness, while to the latter it is assigned, so long as we live among men, to foster and maintain the external worship of God, to defend sound doctrine and the condition of the Church, to adapt our conduct to human society, to form our manners to civil justice, to conciliate us to each other, to cherish common peace and tranquility. All these I confess to be superfluous, if the kingdom of God, as it now exists within us, extinguishes the present life. But if it is the will of God that while we aspire to true piety we are pilgrims upon the earth, and if such pilgrimage stands in need of such aids, those who take them away from man rob him of his humanity. As to their allegation that there ought to be such perfection in the Church of God that her guidance should suffice for law, they stupidly imagine her to be such as she never can be found in the community of men" (652).
After commenting at length on the role of the magistrate in a fallen world, he goes on to state: "In regard to those who are not debarred by all these passages of Scripture from pre-

reverse the inevitable turn of evil men from bad to worse (2 Tim 3:13), Calvin reminds us that due to the lasting impact of the Fall, Christians can have a legitimate ministry in law and government both in curbing the evil in men and in helping men to understand their need for the Savior. Confined under the proper administration of justice and the law, men will understand the need for the atonement and, realizing their own helplessness and futility, may turn to Christ (Gal 3:21–24). The reality of Genesis 3 means that involvement in law and government, for the Christian, is not wrong but, rather, is appropriate in dealing with the real impact of a historical event.

BIBLIOGRAPHY

Calvin, John. *Institutes of the Christian Religion.* Translated by Henry Beveridge. Grand Rapids: Eerdmans Publishing, 1989.

MacArthur, John. *MacArthur Study Bible.* Nashville: Word Publishing, 1997.

Mathews, Kenneth A. *Genesis 1–11:26.* The New American Commentary. Nashville: Broadman and Holman, 1996.

---

suming to inveigh against this sacred ministry, as if it were a thing abhorrent from religion and Christian piety, what else do they than assail God himself, who cannot but be insulted when his servants are disgraced?" (655–56).

CHAPTER 10

THE SIGNIFICANCE OF SIN
FOR THE PSYCHOLOGIES

Ernie Baker

Karen and her husband came to discuss the possibility of marriage mediation after being married only for a little over a year. These were second marriages for both, and now their new relationship was in deep trouble. She believed that she had been lied to about his financial situation and she let him know it. Her tongue got her in trouble regularly as she lashed out and "told him the truth," whether he liked it or not. Nothing he could do would satisfy her. To top it off, anger and extreme anxiety, leading to health issues and lack of sleep, were a regular part of her life. Karen and, as you can imagine, her husband were both miserable. How do we make sense of her troubles? It is obvious that Karen has problems, but why is she like this?

When someone is ill, obtaining a proper diagnosis is essential. If not diagnosed precisely, a lot of time, energy, emotion, and money go into treating the symptoms inaccurately. This principle is also true of counseling issues. The counseling psychologies deal with the personal problems of humans and endeavor to understand what the problem is in order to then give a treatment plan.[1] If we are going to properly diagnose personal problems

---

1. I am using the term "psychologies" instead of psychology since there are many proposed

we must include a biblical view of what is truly wrong. This view of what is wrong is clearly portrayed in Genesis 3 and these details directly apply to the social sciences. In fact, the implications of both the cause (vv. 1–6) and effects (vv. 7–24) portrayed in this crucial chapter of Scripture lead to a robust model to explain the myriad of human issues.

For example, why are there mass shootings? Every time there is another mass shooting there is an onslaught of analysis over why someone would do something so horrible. Terms like "mental illness" are used and some decry that we are not putting enough into research of the brain to try to understand. Others might say it is the shooter's environmental pressures that caused him to pull the trigger. Yet others might say it is a combination of both a brain issue and environmental issues.[2] It is frustrating to many that we cannot figure this out. Out of love for people we desperately need the correct diagnosis so the treatment can address the true problem.

In the midst of this confusion and pain, as our cultures desperately try to understand why humans do what they do, I want to pose the same question as Dr. Karl Menninger, "Whatever happened to sin?" As a well-known psychiatrist he wrote, "It was a word once in everyone's mind, but now rarely if ever heard. Is it only that someone may be stupid or sick or criminal, or asleep?" He then added, "Is nothing now a sin?"[3] He was concerned about the moral direction of our culture. I have the same questions. Are we now so sophisticated that there is no soul sickness but only mental illness? Have we moved beyond the supposedly primitive idea of sin?

How does the doctrine of sin influence the way we understand the term "mental health"? Let me be the first to acknowledge that talking about sin related to the mental state of others is hard. It sounds calloused. But that is not

---

paradigms to explain what is wrong with humans and how to help them deal with their problems.

2. Typical thinking is described in this definition. "A mental disorder is a syndrome characterized by clinically significant disturbances in an individual's cognition, emotion regulation, or behavior that reflects a dysfunction in the psychological, biological, or developmental processes underlying mental functioning. Mental disorders are usually associated with significant distress or disability in social, occupational, or other important activities." American Psychiatric Association, *Diagnostic and Statistical Manual of Mental Disorders*, 20.

3. Menninger, *Whatever Became of Sin?*, 13–14. In quoting Dr. Menninger, it is not to be assumed that he believes in the biblical doctrine of total depravity. He is just trying to make the point that there is right and wrong and people are responsible for their behavior. He is also decrying that American culture had gotten to the point, even at the time of his writing, of not believing in right and wrong.

my demeanor. My desire is to have compassion (Col 3:5) and bear with others in love (Eph 4:2) as I help them truly get to the root of their problems. But a proper treatment plan demands a proper diagnosis. Therefore, my intent is to demonstrate how crucial a literal understanding of sin is to the social sciences. In other words, a biblical view of counseling must include the doctrine of sin and what it has done to humanity. Even if a psychological theory is making accurate observations, and even if there is a strong physical component to the issue, the diagnosis cannot be accurate if it does not include the immaterial part of our being and how it has been infected by sin.[4] Our culture is scrambling for answers and there is not unity on etiology (the source of the problem) partially because we are not operating from a biblical framework.[5]

COUNSELING THEORIES ARE DIAGNOSTIC FRAMEWORKS

Defining Psychology

Before studying the account of the Fall, let us look at some secular viewpoints on the source of problems and their solutions. To do that we must understand what a psychology is. Most psychology texts define their field in a way similar to the following: "Psychology is the scientific study of behavior and mental processes…consequently, the phrase "behavior and mental processes" in the definition of psychology must be understood to mean many things: it encompasses not just people's actions, but also their thoughts, emotions, perceptions, reasoning processes, memories, and even the biological activities that maintain bodily functioning."[6]

While most agree on this definition, there are many different theories of why we have the behavior and mental processes we do and a vast array of approaches for helping (various therapies). In other words, you could say that each psychology offers its own view of the problem and solution. Each solution has its own set of methodologies, consisting of types of questions, homework, and tests that are used to carry out the approach to people's problems.[7]

---

4. This immaterial part of our being is called "soul," "spirit," "mind," and "heart" throughout Scripture. I will seek to demonstrate that the term "heart" is the leading word, and is directly impacted by what happened in the Garden.
5. "1: cause, origin *specifically*: the cause of a disease or abnormal condition, 2: a branch of knowledge concerned with causes *specifically*: a branch of medical science concerned with the causes and origins of diseases." *Merriam-Webster's Collegiate Dictionary*, 11th edition, s.v. "etiology."
6. Feldman, *Understanding Psychology*, 5.
7. To test my understanding of this, we did a simple experiment. My assistant called five

Viewing this theologically, each psychology has a view of sin. Here they are answering the question, What is the source of the problem? Each then has a view of salvation[8] and sanctification,[9] answering the questions, What is the solution to the problem and the methodology for carrying it out?[10]

Examples of Various Diagnostic Frameworks

Volumes of books have been devoted to explaining all the various approaches to counseling, but here are some of the most common: cognitive behavioral therapy, the biomedical model, and Maslow's needs theory.[11]

Cognitive Behavioral Therapy (CBT)

A leading therapist in the counseling psychologies is Aaron Beck, who developed an innovative approach called cognitive behavioral therapy, or CBT. "The basic idea behind CBT is that thinking controls or largely affects behavior. If you change thinking, you have a good chance of changing behavior. As Alfred Adler, a psychotherapist who developed a precursor to CBT, stated, 'I am con-

---

different counseling offices and asked the director or head therapist what they believe is the source of anger. In other words, why do people struggle with anger, and then how do we help them deal with it? Guess what? We got five different answers as to the source and solution to the problem! The answers were the typical range of brain chemistry, unmet needs, and family upbringing (environment). The treatment plans then matched what the therapists perceived the problem to be.

8. Even some secular psychologies use this terminology. Psychologist Paul Vitz quotes Jungian practitioner Jolande Jacobi as describing Carl Jung's psychology as "a way of salvation." Vitz, *Psychology as Religion*, 3.

9. "That gracious and continuous operation of the Holy Spirit, by which He delivers the justified sinner from the pollution of sin, renews his whole nature in the image of God, and enables him to perform good works." Berkhof, *Systematic Theology*, 532. I will explain in more detail how this fits into a biblical counseling methodology toward the end of the chapter.

10. You can actually breakdown the psychologies as individual belief systems by using more S's. Every psychology has a "source of authority" (epistemology). Each has a view of the problem to be solved, that is, "sin" (etiology). They then propose a "salvation" (the solution to the problem) and a methodology or "sanctification." The psychologies also have "support systems" like mental hospitals and universities to teach their viewpoint. Finally, each psychology does apologetics or "sparring" to defend their understanding of people's problems. This sparring takes place in various journals and research studies as articles are written to demonstrate why this approach to counseling is superior to others. I am thankful for Dr. David Powlison introducing me to this type of thinking; he is the director of The Christian Counseling and Educational Foundation (CCEF). He is also the editor of *The Journal of Biblical Counseling*. If you are interested in gaining more insight into how Biblical Counseling views people and problems, this journal and David's writings in particular would be a great resource.

11. There are many therapies, e.g., Family Systems Therapy, and other psychodynamic approaches.

vinced that a person's behavior springs from his ideas.'"[12] Thus, the main focus would be the belief that if thinking changes, behavior changes as well.

Biomedical

Others are not convinced of CBT but believe that the source is biological, specifically the brain. Brett Deacon puts it very succinctly, "The biomedical model posits that mental disorders are brain diseases and emphasizes pharmacological treatment to target presumed biological abnormalities."[13] At this moment, at least at the media level, culture accepts this as the explanatory lens to understand human problems.[14]

Many psychologists, though, would not buy into a strictly biological model but instead say we are bio/psycho/social beings and that all three of these elements are interacting to create issues. In other words, our biology, our mental state, and our social relations all interact with one another to create our responses to the world.

Maslow's Needs Theory

Another common theory is that basic needs are not being met. When Maslow presented this view of the source of human problems he also consciously rejected the idea of a sinful nature. "As far as I know we just don't have any intrinsic instincts for evil. If you think in terms of basic needs, instincts, at least at the outset, are all 'good' or perhaps we should be technical about it and call them 'pre-moral,' neither good nor evil."[15]

His solution was to learn to be a "self-actualized" person like Thomas Edison or others who reached their full potential. They had all of their basic needs met and therefore happiness could be achieved. While Freud studied negative motivations, Maslow studied positive incentives for humans to reach full potential.

---

12. Barber, *Comfortably Numb*, 141.
13. Deacon, "The Biomedical Model of Mental Disorder," 846–61.
14. Karl Menninger shows the logical outcome of this thinking as it applies to responsibility and criminal behavior. "If one can be treated effectively by medical science for a propensity toward certain behavior, it would be absurd to punish him for this same manifestation.... Diseases are not crimes. Hence, no matter how reprehensible or offensive a piece of behavior may be, it cannot be called a crime if it is a symptom of a disease. A man may murder his best friend or his worst enemy during a delirium and yet commit no crime.... The demonstrated presence in the offender at the time of his criminal act of a condition called 'mental disease' which impairs discretion and control cancels the legal guiltiness of the offender." Menninger, *Whatever Became of Sin?*, 74–75.
15. Maslow, *Toward a Psychology of Being*, 3.

Many today have essentially the same view of what the illness is and its solution. For example,

> One of the deepest concerns of psychologists and some other social scientists has been the identification of the spring of human action. What moves us to action and/or determines the direction of our strivings? Our motives, described by concepts like needs, desires, aims, goals, and aspirations, not only shape our actions, but their fulfillment or frustration also deeply affect our inner life, our experience of ourselves and the world. Basic needs are conceptualized here as the most fundamental motives. Their satisfaction is essential for growth, development and well-being of human beings…. Basic needs have an imperative quality: they press for satisfaction.[16]

Biblical Eyeglasses

While all of these approaches provide interesting and helpful insights into humanity, I do not believe they get at the root of the problem that is influencing everything else. As Christians, we want to know what the all-knowing Creator said about humanity. In light of this, problems arise when we take a discerning look at these theories.

Think with me about Cognitive Behavioral Therapy. Of course we are rational beings according to Scripture, but it is also true that strong desires often override the rational part of our being. Practitioners might say in response that we must reorient thinking about desires. But change is more complex than reprogramming our mental processing of desires. Titus 3:3 says that humans are "slaves to various passions and pleasures." Many people intellectually know the right thing to do but their desires override thinking. According to Scripture we are worshiping beings (Matt 12:34–35), desiring beings (Rom 13:14), and much more.[17] Something deeper is going on than just thinking.

---

16. Staub, *The Psychology of Good and Evil*, 52. It is not the purpose of this chapter to fully analyze secular views. I am only trying to demonstrate how essential a biblical view of humanity is for the social sciences. If the reader would like another perspective on "needs" theory read Ed Welch's article, "Who Are We: Needs, Longings, and the Image of God in Man." In this article he is answering the following questions: Where are needs in the Bible? How should we think biblically about needs? If we are image-bearers and have needs, are we saying that God too has needs?
17. There are many worship words that describe what is going on inside of humans. For ex-

It is also true that we are bio/psycho/social beings, but consider what secular culture means by these terms. Your biology is evolved and has not been impacted by a sinful nature.[18] Your "psyche" is your mental state, with no emphasis on an immaterial part of your being. Yes, we are social beings but the ultimate relationship is missing in that you were created to be in relationship with God.

Thus, from a biblical standpoint, we can already begin to see that these theories are inadequate. You see, Karen's problems did not begin when she said, "I do." They began thousands of years ago in the Garden.

Genesis 1–3 Provide a Biblical Diagnostic Framework

Genesis 1 Defines Normal

Before we get to the diagnosis of the problem, we must understand what God intended normal existence to be pre-Fall. For things to be abnormal or disordered implies there is a norm and order. But, who determines "normal"? God made the answer clear right from the beginning.

Genesis 1:26–28 portrays humans made to be in relationship with their Creator. This was normal and healthy. The relationship was to be so close that we reflect His image. Much has been written on this, and a crucial aspect of being made in God's image is that we were made to live for His glory (Isa 6:3; Ezek 43:1–2; Hab 2:14; Rom 11:36; 1 Cor 10:31). His glory is all that He is in the sum total of His attributes and we were made to reflect those on the planet. We were made to live "godly" (God-like) lives. Imagine the whole world being filled with worshipers like this. That is exactly what His original intention was (Gen 1:28).

---

ample, we are devoted, hope in, serve, bow down to, love, fear, and treasure many things above the Lord.

18. In fact, the secular psychologies would not agree on a common human nature. As we have seen from just three examples, there are multiple views of what is wrong with humans and why evil exists. A biblical anthropology would tell us there is a common human nature. Consider Jonathan Edwards' argument: "If it be observed, that those trees, and all other trees of the kind, wherever planted, and in all soils, countries, climates and seasons, and however cultivated and managed, still bear ill fruit, from year to year, and in all ages, it is good evidence of the evil nature of the tree…. And if we argue in like manner from what appears among men, 'tis easy to determine, whether the universal sinfulness of mankind, and their all sinning immediately, as soon as capable of it, and all sinning continually…, in all ages, and all places, and under all possible circumstances, against means and motives inexpressibly manifold and great, and in the utmost conceivable variety, be from a permanent internal great cause." Piper, *A God-Entranced Vision of All Things: The Legacy of Jonathan Edwards*, 180–81.

Since Scripture says this is true, ask yourself if true mental health is possible outside this fundamental relationship. Could anyone be "self-actualized" outside of relationship with their Creator? It should also be clear that humanity has a big problem since most live alienated from Him. What led to this alienation and what is the solution? Genesis 3 gives the answer.

The Cause of Problems Is a Worship Disorder

Chapter 3 is incredibly ugly against the "very good" backdrop of chapter 1 (1:31). God told Adam and Eve that they had a high purpose for being on the planet. Now comes the test of obedience and fidelity to their Sovereign. Will they be godly or not? Will they live for His glory or their own?

To answer these questions we need to take a deeper look at a paradigm shifting verse of the Bible (Gen 3:6). Where did this act of rebellion originate? We are told that they ate because "the woman saw that the tree was good for food, and that it was a delight to the eyes, and that the tree was to be desired to make one wise." Their whole being was involved in this decision to go against what the Lord had commanded. The inner person was actively engaged in how each responded to the external pressure of the temptation. The serpent puts pressure on Eve, she influences Adam, and even though he knew better, he rebels.

They were not victims of circumstances unwittingly shaped by their environment. Instead, they were active agents who made a decision based upon being both rational and emotional. They were thinking about "being wise" and wanted (i.e. desired) to be like God "knowing good and evil" (v. 5). The emotions were stimulated by the fruit being a "delight." Their loyalty and devotion were tested, the inner person stirred, and the couple failed. According to Scripture, the term that is used for our inner being—consisting of "minds, will, and emotions"—is the heart.[19] It "became the richest biblical term for the totality of man's inner or immaterial nature."[20]

Adam and Eve could have said no, but chose not to. Ever since, the heart has been tainted. You are dealing with a Genesis 3 hangover, and so am I![21]

---

19. Heart is defined as "one's inner self, seat of feeling and emotions; inclination, disposition, will, reason, mind in general." Koehler and Baumgartner, *The Hebrew and Aramaic Lexicon of the Old Testament*, 1:514–15.
20. Bowling, "לב," vol. 1:466.
21. I first heard the term "Genesis 3 hangover" from Dr. George Zemek teaching on apologetics at The Master's Seminary.

They rebelled against God's commands, and a multitude of human problems have been unleashed as a result.

G. K. Beale, in his book *We Become What We Worship*, makes an important observation about what happened in the Garden. The chapter on the origin of idolatry explains, "When Adam stopped being committed to God and reflecting his image, he revered something else in place of God and resembled his new object of worship. Thus at the heart of Adam's sin was turning from God and replacing reverence for God with a new object of reverence to which Adam became conformed."[22]

Genesis 3 then in part reveals what Adam and Eve would put their hope in and choose to be devoted to. Would they believe the Lord, trust Him, and let Him be God and them the creation? Or would they believe the serpent, trust it and desire to be like God and rule their own lives? We all know the answer and are feeling the results. Like Adam and Eve, every morning we awake and make the same decisions. What will I love? What will I hope in? What will I serve? But now, because of Adam and Eve, I am bent the wrong way. I have a tendency to worship (i.e., trust in, hope in, rejoice in, and love)[23] the wrong things. I am guilty of idolatry.

The Rest of Scripture and False Worship/ Wrong Desire in the Heart

We see Adam's heart idolatry in the Garden paralleled in how Scripture describes sin. Scripture clearly states that life is lived out of the heart. We must guard it with all vigilance, since it is the springhead of life (Prov 4:23).[24] Our Lord reinforces this by telling us that from the heart the mouth speaks (Matt 12:34). He then adds a crucial piece to help us understand the puzzle of

---

22. In another place Beale writes, "There is no explicit vocabulary describing Adam's sin as idol worship, but the idea appears inextricably bound up with his transgression. But how is this discernible? Recall that idol worship is revering anything other than God. At the least Adam's allegiance shifted from God to himself and probably also to Satan, since he comes to resemble the serpent's character in some ways" (133). It is intriguing to think about the implications of resembling the serpent. Was it part of Satan's strategy to make Adam and Eve his own "image-bearers," instead of fulfilling their original design of being image-bearers of the true and living God? Beale, *We Become What We Worship*, 127, 133.
23. A long list could be compiled of phrases from Scripture that tell us what we are to do in relationship with God. Each one of these has counseling implications. For example, what do you devote yourself to? what do you "sing the praises of?" where do you bow?
24. There are hundreds of other references to the heart (e.g., Gen 6:5; Isa 29:13; Mark 7:21–23; Heb 4:12).

our hearts. He replaces the word "heart" with "treasure" in verse 35. In other words, our hearts are our treasures, revealing what we value. How can you tell a person's value system? What they love, hope for, trust, rejoice in, and fear, reveals "treasures."

The Bible directs us where to place our love, hope, and faith, and warns us about false loves and hoping in empty things (Ps 33:13–22; Matt 22:37–40; 1 Tim 6:17; 2 Tim 3:1–4). It is guaranteed that thought, decision-making, and emotions are wrapped around these things. But, according to Jeremiah 17:9, all of this has been tainted by the deceitful and desperately sick nature of the heart.[25]

Do you see that the problem is deeper than chemical imbalances? Brace yourself, we have another key component to add: In the heart dwell desires and passions.[26] We are desire-filled beings, and these appetites and passions are permeated with sin (Matt 5:28; Rom 1:24; Jas 3:14).

John's classic passage warns about loving the world and in particular not to love the "desires of the flesh," the "desires of the eyes," and the "pride in possessions" (1 John 2:15–17). There is a clear connection to the Garden. But here John adds that this is about the futility of false loves. Ruling desires reveal "heart themes" that are directly connected to counseling issues. Here are a few examples.

- Desires of the flesh (in Genesis 3, "good for food"): sexual pleasure, food, comfort-loving, enslavement to alcohol or other enslavements.

- Desires of the eyes (in Genesis 3, "delight to the eyes"): appearances, pornography.

- Pride in possessions (in Genesis 3, "desired"): materialism, cars, technology, degrees.

To really help people grow and change, we must help them get to the deepest disorders. Humans do not just have personality disorders, they have worship disorders. The testimony of Scripture is that the desires resulting from Genesis 3 become strong, entrenched, ruling desires (see Titus 3:3).

---

25. For one understanding of how this verse precisely relates to the believer, see my article "Jeremiah 17:9—Is It True of the Believer?" at http://biblicalcounselingcoalition.org/blogs/2013/07/11/jeremiah-179-is-it-true-of-the-believer.
26. Behm, "Heart," 3:612.

Genesis 4 makes clear that "sin is crouching at the door. Its desire is for you" (v.7). It is pictured as having a life of its own (cf. Heb 4:12 where the heart is described as being active with "thoughts and intentions"). David Powlison makes it clear why we must understand this as an interpretation of human nature: "If we would help people have eyes and ears for God we must know well which alternative gods clamor for their attention. These forces and shaping influences neither determine nor excuse our sins. But they do nurture, channel, and exacerbate our sinfulness in particular directions."[27]

The Result of Misplaced Worship Is Counseling Issues

I agree with Berkouwer who wrote, "In Genesis we observe a sin whose essential traits return in *every* [emphasis his] sin. Thus in the history of Israel[,] the fall was apostasy from the fellowship of God and the assumption of man's own way."[28] In other words, the seed of every distortion and disorder is in this seminal section of Scripture. The basis of what we view as the problem with humanity starts here.[29]

Humans Have Desire Problems

We have already noted the central place of desires within the heart but let us make clear where it started. The tree was "desired to make one wise" (Gen 3:6). Adam and Eve ate, and consequently we all have a bad case of the "I wants."[30] Their desires, not stopped by the dam of relationship with the Creator, overflowed into ruling desires. Lust takes on a life of its own. This topic is discussed frequently in Scripture showing how common the problem is (e.g., Rom 7:15–25; 13:14; 1 Pet 1:14; Eph 4:22). In counseling you can almost always ask, "What do you want that you are not getting?" And, "what are you getting that you do not want?" Unruly appetites and passions have launched thousands of counseling issues like the vast array of "addictions" humanity experiences. Sinful desires permeate the rest of the list and lead to sins not delineated.

---

27. Powlison, "Revisiting Idols of the Heart and Vanity Fair," 57. This seminal article has shaped the thinking of much of the biblical counseling world.
28. Berkhouwer, *Sin: Studies in Dogmatics*, 274.
29. We are about to see a literal list of the consequences of sin. If the consequences are literal, why would the cause be metaphorical? In other words, if the effects of sin are literal (which is self-evident from daily experience) it makes sense that a literal Adam and Eve were the cause.
30. Please note that the word in Hebrew for "desire" (Gen 3:6) is translated "covet" in the tenth commandment (Exod 20:17). Can we conclude that Moses (the author of both) saw the connection?

Humans Experience Pain/Suffering

The earth is now going to produce "thorns" (Gen 3:18) and cause Adam pain in his labor (Gen 3:17). Romans 8:21–22 reinforces this, saying that all creation groans and is subject to decay.

Other things change as well. Death was warned about (Gen 2:17) and death, with its suffering and diseases, was delivered. It should not surprise us if there are mental diseases, since the brain, like the rest of the body, has been impacted by the Fall.

We also see humans hurting each other. The first thing that Adam does when confronted with his sin is blame Eve. This is the man who seems to have been delighted when God presented his wife to him. He said, "This *at last* [my emphasis] is bone of my bones and flesh of my flesh" (Gen 2:23). What a change! I sin and I am sinned against. Much that is dealt with in counseling relates to hurt caused by others.

Humans Struggle with Food Issues

The object of desire was food, and as we saw, all desires went awry (Gen 3:6). We all have eating issues as a result. When the pressure is on, some over-eat and some undereat. You should not be surprised. It is intrinsic to the Fall.

Humans Struggle with Giving into Social Pressure

Psychology has long noted the shaping influence of others in our lives. We see it in the Garden. Eve gave the fruit to Adam, he listened to the voice of his wife, and we suffer (Gen 3:6, 17). Could this be the common human malady called "fear of man" (Prov 29:25)? Have you suffered because you listened to the voice of others?

Humans Struggle with Relationship Issues

As mentioned before, in Genesis 4 we see the word "sin" mentioned for the first time and what is the context? It is interpersonal conflict of the worst type—murder. How bad was the Fall? It was so bad that just twenty-six verses after the dreadful decision, brother murders brother. Also, instead of taking personal responsibility, Adam shifts the blame to his wife (Gen 3:12). "It was not me" has been the default of humans ever since, and it causes much pain in relationships.

Humans Struggle with Hiding and Deception

The first thing Adam and Eve did was cover and hide because of their shame and fear (Gen 3:7–10). Not only that, but the satanic character of deception (Gen 3:13) now influences humanity (John 8:44). Humans hide and deceive in many ways, like not allowing others to see the real self. Other ways deception has influenced us are too numerous to mention.

Humans Struggle with Sexual Temptation

Why were Adam and Eve ashamed of their nakedness? I understand that the primary message here is the shame from sin and what their newly informed conscience was doing to their souls. But they are the only two on the planet! Could there also be implications of sexual deviance? Are they looking at each other in a different way now? The end of chapter two tells us, "The man and his wife were both naked and not ashamed." At that point they were one flesh and happily united. But now, what was supposed to be a blessing is impacted by sin and they cover themselves.

Humans Struggle with Ungodly Communication

One of the first things that happened is Adam sinned against his wife with words. Imagine what she was thinking when she heard, "The woman whom you gave to be with me, she gave me fruit of the tree" (Gen 3:12).

Humans Struggle with Materialism

Think about it. Is not materialism the desire for more? It is the attitude that stuff will bring us security and happiness. Adam and Eve were not content with what God gave them. They wanted more, and human nature became like Gollum in *Lord of the Rings*, frantically grasping for "rings" that then grip the heart. David Powlison states, "The tenth commandment is also a command that internalizes the problem of sin, making sin 'psychodynamic.'[31] It lays bare the grasping and demanding nature of the human heart, as Paul powerfully describes in Romans 7."[32]

Humans Struggle with Disordered Emotions

For the first time we see fear and shame in human history (Gen 3:8–10). It is easy to imagine the disordered emotions that grew out of this. For example, there was probably anxiety as Adam and Eve heard God approaching (v. 10).

---

31. "Psychodynamic" would refer to processes going on internally that are impacting the external.
32. Powlison, "Revisiting Idols of the Heart and Vanity Fair," 44.

I find it interesting that every picture I have seen depicting them being driven from the Garden shows them downcast, depressed, and ashamed. How have you felt these emotions?

Humans Struggle with Self-Centeredness

This is the culminating fact that launched it all. Their sin was about wanting to be like God. Their focus turned to what they thought was best instead of what God said was best. They thought they deserved more. Pride is written all over the decision to operate independently of God.

What happens if we keep living for false hopes, shallow loves, and distorted desires? I will tell you—counseling issues. These become disordered relationships, emotions, and behavior.[33] When you begin to see people's problems this way you say to yourself, "It would take a miracle for people to change." And you would be right.

THE SOLUTION TO THE PROBLEM

The Gospel Radically Reorients Life

Miracles happen as the cross sets us free from enslaving lusts and desires (Titus 3:3; Rom 6) and reorders the worship (love, trust, and hope) of our heart. The cross is not just a message to believe to get us to heaven someday. It is a message of hope and deliverance from the tyrant of sin and the lordship of engrained lusts and desires. This amazing grace is even promised for the first time right after Adam and Eve's rebellion (Gen 3:15). Christ came to destroy the works of the devil (1 John 3:8). As we repent, our Sovereign continues to, liberate us from Satan's and sin's tyrannical rule (Col 1:13). Worship is being restored to the King.

Such a salvation can happen because the most God-glorifying person who ever lived was our Savior. He was a perfect worshiper and through the power of the gospel we can become like Him. The New Testament is clear that this is the goal of our progressive sanctification (Rom 8:29; 2 Cor 3:18). We are being made into the image of our Savior and restored to a place of obeying out of love. The purpose of the cross is to "put on the new self, which is being renewed in knowledge after the image of its creator" (Col 3:10). We

---

33. The term "disorder" is the current terminology of the DSM-5. I like this terminology, since the Lord can bring order out of disorder.

are enabled and motivated by the Holy Spirit to trust His character, putting our hope in Him (Rom 15: 4–5, 13). We are called to rejoice in and sing the praises of the Creator of the universe, instead of the empty things this planet tells us are worthy of devotion. The image of God in man is being restored— which means that the mind, will, and emotions can change because of the power of the gospel.

It seems like this is what the Lord was after with the woman of Samaria in John 4. This story is a wonderful example of the Lord going after themes of the heart.[34] Have you ever wondered why the Lord abruptly changes the subject and asks her to call her husband? He had already offered to be living water if she would believe (John 4:10). Could it be that he goes right for her heart? His request clearly demonstrated her loves and hopes. Can you imagine the counseling issues of her lifestyle? Instead of putting her hope in relationships, she needed to repent and put her trust in the Lord for her salvation. Doing so would begin to reorder the disorder of her soul (John 4:14). Significantly, the Lord then tells her that God is seeking worshipers (John 4:23). He was calling her to be one of them—and the gospel reorders another life.

The problem that was launched in the Garden is clear, and so is the solution. We have a wonderful message of hope not only for eternity but also for daily struggles. Think of your own testimony. How has the gospel changed what you serve? What you are devoted to? What you love? What you are willing to sacrifice for? What you put hope in? These questions have many practical applications.

How Does This Work Out Practically?

I tell my classes, if false worship is the problem, then true worship is the solution. Worship reorders the heart. My growth is dependent on living as a worshiper, which is made possible by the Spirit (2 Cor 3:18). The disorder of life is being reordered as my inner person is influenced by the power of the gospel and the living Word of God (Heb 4:12). I obey out of love for and trust in my Creator and Savior (John 15:10).

Practically, this means we have to help counselees understand what is being served in the inner person. Meaning, we ask heart questions. These questions are worded to faithfully represent what Scripture says about the thoughts and intentions of the heart (Gen 6:5; Heb 4:12). For example, what do you find

---

34. The rich young ruler is another example of the Lord going after a heart theme—wealth and materialism (Luke 18:18–25).

your mind dwelling on? What situations do you seek to avoid (decision-making)? When do you tend to experience fear, worry, and anxiety? As mentioned earlier, these questions usually reveal values like living for the approval of other people, materialism, comfort, pleasure, or strong desires to control life.

The natural question then is, what do you do with the answers? Biblical counselors disciple individuals to see the biblical alternative to these false themes of the soul and give practical homework so they can carry out the alternatives in real life (Matt 7:24). This would involve their thinking, emotions, and decision-making. We also show the behavior changes that should result from being a follower of Christ (Matt 28:20).

The Expulsive Power of a New Affection[35]

Let us take one worship word and demonstrate how this reorients false worship to true worship. "Love one another" is the most often repeated command of the New Testament, so love seems like a great example (e.g., John 13:34; Rom 13:8–10). Is this just because God is love and wants us to be nice to each other? No, there is a strategy to His commands. Love leads to holiness (Rom 13:8). Why? Because superior loves push out inferior loves. We pursue the objects of our desire, so grow in love for God and others. It makes perfect sense why the two great commandments *are* the two great commandments (Matt 22:34–40). We grow in holiness when we love God, because we will pursue Him. Thus, part of our job in counseling is to disciple others how to grow in love for God and each other. This actually reorients the desires of the inner person.

The medicine, then, for a sick heart is to submit to the King, and then continue to grow practically in love for God and others. I agree with John Piper, that once you understand our original purpose on the planet but then do not point people to the ultimate solution, it is "like treating fever with cold packs when you have penicillin."[36]

---

35. This is the title of an insightful sermon by a Scottish pastor named Thomas Chalmers (1780–1847). I would also remind the reader that you can take any worship word (e.g., "faith," "hope," "obey") and think how it can be useful for reorienting the heart and thus deal with counseling issues.

36. The full quote is in a context discussing the theology of Jonathan Edwards: "In other words, if God's glory is the only all-satisfying reality in the universe, then to try to do good for people, without aiming to show them the glory of God and ignite in them a delight in God, would be 'like treating fever with cold packs when you have penicillin.'" Piper, *God's Passion for His Glory*, 36.

Because of the gospel, we will grow to be like our Lord, the godliest person who ever lived, and thus we will reflect more and more glory back to the Creator instead of worshipping idols (1 Thess 1:9). This then helps people deal with their worries, fears, and depression. The impact of the Fall is being reversed in people like Karen. That is a great reason to rejoice instead of being worried, fearful, or depressed (Rom 15:13).

How to Think Biblically about the Term "Mental Illness"

Now that we have seen how the doctrines of sin and salvation impact the psychologies, and have viewed how to deal with counseling issues biblically, we are in a better position to think theologically about the term "mental illness." As we do, keep in mind that the various psychologies do not agree on the source of problems. They just know there are problems.

Before diving into this controversial subject, allow me to make a clarification lest I am accused of being anti-scientific. I enjoy studying neuropsychology and have friends who are neuropsychologists. Studying the brain is crucial and I am thankful for those gifted to do so. There are many mysteries yet to be discovered. But my assumption is that something deeper is going on in humans that must be kept in mind when doing research. I am not naïve enough to believe that the secular psychologies would operate from the presupposition that something did happen in the Garden.[37] My concern here is for the church to not be gullible and buy into the talk of mental illness without taking into consideration Genesis 3.

I began to think seriously about this topic at the church where I was pastor in Virginia. We purposefully tried to reach struggling families for the sake of ministry in general and the gospel in particular. Part of our strategy was an active children's ministry to our community. We loved the children and it was a great outreach to underprivileged children. This brought an interesting dynamic to our church, most of it positive. One of the negative things though

---

37. I find it interesting to read the speculations of secular researchers on the source of evil. They do not believe in a sinful nature but still have to explain the obvious—evil behavior. An example is, "Perhaps our dark side [evil] comes from our evolutionary heritage, in which aggression ensured our survival. Maybe it is the result of faulty wiring in our brains. The depletion of certain brain neurotransmitters, such as serotonin, has been found to parallel aggressive behavior." Simon, *Bad Men Do What Good Men Dream*, 3.

was the highly undisciplined nature of the children. It was not uncommon for a child to say to us when we were trying to address his or her behavior, "I cannot help myself. I did not have my medicine." I desire to be teachable on this, and maybe there really is a brain disease that has yet to be discovered, but even many in the secular world would not call the cluster of symptoms of these children a disease or even a disorder.[38] Do you find it sad that children at such a young age seem to think they have an illness that must be controlled by medicine?

On the other hand, I have a friend who is a neuropsychologist who studies frontal lobe injury and its impact on emotion. I am very thankful for people like him who are studying the brain and doing cutting-edge research. There are people whose physiology is definitely impacting their behavior.

Because of what I believe about the Fall and how it has impacted our bodies, and because brain research is a relatively new and developing field of science, I am confident there are yet to be discovered diseases that are influencing behavior and the inner person. To say that they are *influencing* is not to say they are *causing* behavior, though. As we have seen, humans are more complex than just a body. Among other things, we are social, emotional, rational, self-aware, worshipping/false-worshiping beings as well. We must keep in mind that a secular worldview often misses these factors or puts a different emphasis on them. As believers, we respect science but do not bow down to science. Bowing down is "scientism."[39]

William Schweitzer states this well: "Our gratitude for technological achievement does not entail a servile deference to whatever the scientific au-

---

38. A syndrome is defined by Lilienfeld, Smith, and Watts as "typically constellations of signs and symptoms that co-occur across individuals. In syndromes neither pathology nor etiology is well understood.... A disorder is the next rung on the ladder and is understood as ...[s]yndromes that cannot be readily explained by other conditions [a specific cause cannot be determined]." Compare these to how a disease is defined. Diseases are "disorders in which pathology and etiology are reasonably well understood." Then the authors make this startling statement: "With the possible exception of Alzheimer's disease and a handful of other organic conditions the diagnoses in the present system of psychiatric classifications are almost exclusively syndromes or, in rare cases disorders.... This fact is a sobering reminder that the pathology in most cases of psychopathology is largely unknown, and their etiology is poorly understood." Lilienfeld, Smith, and Watts, "Issues in Diagnosis," 2–3.
39. Scientism is a term being used to describe the tendency to give science an inappropriate amount of authority. It is defined as "an exaggerated trust in the efficacy of the methods of natural science applied to all areas of investigation (as in philosophy, the social sciences, and the humanities)." http://www.merriam-webster.com/dictionary/scientism (accessed January 31, 2014).

thorities tell us especially when a theory extends beyond any contemporary ability to test conclusively."[40] This does not mean, though, that we ignore the valid observations of science that do not contradict our worldview.[41]

My colleague in the Biblical Counseling Coalition, Dr. Jeremy Pierre, has written an article to give the church guidance:

> We should be skeptical because the paradigm of mental illness is built without the basic building materials of a biblical view of people. Absent is any consideration of moral agency as Scripture defines it: an active heart responding dynamically to God and His creation with every thought, feeling, and choice. Such an absence of the spiritual aspect of the person results in a critical misunderstanding of the person as a whole. And the care offered is inadequate for the ultimate troubles of the soul.
>
> But we should also appreciate that these diagnoses at times accurately describe physical symptom clusters ["syndromes" as defined earlier in the chapter, *my addition*] and could lead to medical interventions that offer some level of helpful influence over them. In other words, because we recognize humans as corrupted in body as well as in soul, we can appreciate medical ingenuity that helpfully addresses the potential neurobiological aspects of people's trouble. . . .
>
> Extreme mental, emotional, or behavioral problems are not *either* spiritual *or* physical. They are both, though we recognize a sliding scale of influence. Some troubles may be more neurologically engrained, thus requiring closer medical attention. Others may be less so. But, whether it's more or less, a spiritual heart is always actively in need of the grace of the Lord Jesus.[42]

---

40. Schweitzer, *Engaging with Keller*, 200–201.
41. I have tried to nuance my understanding of this in my book "Caution: Counseling Systems Are Belief Systems," 159–76.
42. Pierre, "Mental Illness and the Church," I am including an extended portion here to demonstrate the theological nuance that is needed:
   "Various folks have been pointing out the need for the church to pull its head out of the sand on the issue of mental health care. By this, we can be saying something very good or something not-so-good. Let's start with the not-so-good. We should not mean

A Story Demonstrating
a Biblical-Counseling Approach to Problems

To help us think through what we have just seen, let us go back to the story of Karen.[43] If this heartbreaking story does not demonstrate the reality of the Garden, then I am not sure what will. Just as in the Garden, it is full of shame, fear, blame-shifting, sins of the tongue, and false worship. But change happened, not only as thinking changed but also as desires and worship changed.

As the mediation unfolded, a story kept bleeding out into the process. From the time Karen was a young girl, her brothers sexually molested her, and unfortunately it lasted until her late teens. To try to shame her into silence, they regularly told her that no one would love her when they found out who she re-

---

that the church should just accept that extreme emotional, mental, or behavioral troubles are merely physical problems with physical solutions. Of all people, Christians must insist that we were created spiritual beings with the dignity of moral agency. Our thoughts and actions are not merely the product of our biology. We have freedom to act out of our nature as the image of God. And so, wisdom for living from the Word of God is always necessary in the ongoing care of a person, which includes addressing mental, emotional, and behavioral troubles.

"Now let's get to the good. What we should mean by the church pulling its head out of the sand is that Christians should acknowledge that the corruption of the fall warps not just our souls, but our bodies as well. The influence of bodily corruption on the soul is powerful, and the church needs to recognize those suffering under it in a way that points them to help—both body and soul.

"Extreme mental, emotional, or behavioral problems are not *either* spiritual *or* physical. They are both, though we recognize a sliding scale of influence. Some troubles may be more neurologically engrained, thus requiring closer medical attention. Others may be less so. But, whether it's more or less, a spiritual heart is always actively in need of the grace of the Lord Jesus....

"On one hand, medical intervention, including psychotropic medication, does not heal the ultimate problem of a person's disordered desires, beliefs, or choices. Medical intervention does not reverse the results of sin and corruption. Only the power of the gospel of Jesus does this. Visiting a doctor apart from considering how your spiritual responses are involved in your condition will not lead to an ultimate solution.

"On the other hand, medical intervention often allays the effects of sin's corruption of the body, including the brain. And so we should affirm the value of medical treatment and should encourage our people to seek medical attention when necessary. The need for medical intervention is not in itself anti-spiritual. Visiting a doctor does not necessarily mean you are failing to trust the Lord."

43. This story is used with the permission of the counselee. If there is any similarity between this story and others, it is coincidental. It should not surprise us, though, that it sounds familiar, because of common sins and common responses to being sinned against by others. We are all cut from the same cloth.

ally was and what she had done. After many years of silence she finally told her mother, who did nothing. Can you imagine the pain, anger, and bitterness? Can you imagine the distorted thinking this would cause about romantic relationships? Can you imagine the fear of being hurt by others? It became obvious that she had a lot of unresolved issues related to her abuse from decades earlier. This woman was full of hurt and self-protection.

During the mediation, both Karen and her husband humbly submitted to the process and, more importantly, to the Lord. They were convicted of their wrong responses, and asked forgiveness for how they had sinned against each other. A plan was developed to address the concerns of each. But more importantly, Karen recognized the need for help with truly dealing with the issue of abuse and the controlling tendencies she had developed as a way to protect herself. It became painfully clear to her that her mouth was directly related to her heart, as the Lord so poignantly states in Matthew 12:34–35. So, even though the marriage was now more stable, there was a lot of personal growth that needed to take place.

I arranged for a godly woman of her church to be Karen's discipler, and they developed a loving and trusting relationship. Here is how the issues were patiently approached.

> The first thing that we focused on was learning that God is sovereign and to trust Him. We went chapter by chapter each week through *Trusting God* by Jerry Bridges. Weekly she would share when she was angry, frustrated, fearful, or anxious and we would talk about it. I explained to her how these feelings and attitudes pointed to what we are serving in our hearts (idolatry). We discussed that we are called to worship Christ above all else. That he should be on the throne of our heart. It is He we serve and not ourselves and idols. No excuses. As we did this, week by week she was able to recognize her sinfulness in the situations and recognize that she was not trusting God and wanted to control people and situations. Little by little she improved greatly in this area by trusting God more and seeing her sin sooner and more easily. . . .
>
> We talked a lot about loving and respecting her husband and how to do that practically. Their relationship and her

attitude and behavior toward him was the most consistent pressure that revealed her sinful desires and in turn an area we have seen tremendous growth. She is constantly thinking and would sometimes refer to it as "stinking thinking." We talked about Phil 4:8–9 and how it related to her thinking. She worked on putting off bad behavior/thinking and putting on righteous behavior/thinking. We discussed anger a lot and how to control it by recognizing her desires, pleasing and worshipping God above all else, and trusting in God's sovereign grace and love. I gave her questions to ask herself when she felt anger, irritated, anxious, frustrated, fearful, etc. to help her identify what she was demanding instead of trusting God in the situation.

Also, to work on a proper self-image, we talked a lot about who she is in Christ now (Col 2:10). We talked about working on the areas where she needed to change and grow and accepting who God had made her in the areas that she couldn't change.

She was very fearful of being physically harmed. Again, it was believing and trusting in the sovereignty of God that has really helped her not to be as fearful (1 John 4:18–19; 2 Tim 1:7). We also talked about healthy fear and sinful fear.

We went through *Rid of My Disgrace*.[44] It addressed denial, distorted self-image, shame, guilt, and anger. The truths from God's Word taught in this book of how Christ's life, death and resurrection transform us were a life changer for her. She learned and accepted that Christ not only died for her sins, but for the guilt of sin, and shame. We saw how Christ took her shame and clothed her in righteousness. He rose from the dead to bring her healing and hope. God allowed the abuse to happen and He loves her and it can be used for

---

44. *Rid of My Disgrace,* by Justin S. Holcomb and Lindsey A. Holcomb, has been used in the lives of many who have been sexually abused.

her good and His glory. She has learned to practice the truth
that we forgive others out of the amazing forgiveness we have
received in Christ. She knows that it is only Christ that can
help her deal with her pain.[45]

I have heard Karen talk publicly about how much she has grown in Christ.
She is not as controlling [her dominant heart worship theme] or angry, and
reports that she is much more relaxed and is processing life much differently
than just a couple of years ago. Her relationship with her husband is stable
and loving and she is sleeping better. She regularly reminds herself that Christ
took her shame and guilt, and she does not struggle with the same degree of
fear. She is much more content (Phil 4:11–13). This chapter has been about
worship, so it seems very appropriate to add concerning Karen, "Praise God
from Whom all blessings flow!" The effects of the Fall are being reversed in
her life. The image of God is being restored as she grows to be more like her
Savior. If she had gone to secular counseling, these certainly would not have
been the diagnoses and prescriptions for change.

CONCLUSION

From a biblical perspective we live in a naïve age concerning human nature.
In spite of all our advances in understanding how the brain functions, we are
missing a key lens for interpreting the data we see—the doctrine of sin. Humans will never be able to be understood properly, no matter how advanced
our neuroscience or psychologies become, if Genesis 3 is not understood as
a defining moment in human history. It impacts every second of existence
and makes the best sense of what we observe. I share the same concern as Dr.
Menninger: there are serious consequences to a culture that denies the reality of sin. He said, "Notions of guilt and sin which formerly served as some
restraint on aggression have become eroded by the presumption that the individual has less to do with his actions than we had assumed, and hence any
sense of personal responsibility (or guilt) is inappropriate."[46]

I marvel at the profundity of Genesis 3 in regard to its relevance for anthropology in general and the counseling psychologies in particular. While

---

45. Brief summary sent to me via e-mail.
46. Menninger, *Whatever Became of Sin?*, 177.

it is compassionate to try to help people with their problems, I also fear that we are not accurately diagnosing the deepest issues of the soul. Therefore, our treatment plans are not getting to the root issues. As I hope you have seen, it is crucial that we keep a literal understanding of what happened at the beginning. A worship model has the best explanatory power to bring into focus the multitude of counseling issues humans face. May our gracious Lord help the church see the significance of what happened in the Garden as we endeavor to help others with personal problems.

BIBLIOGRAPHY

Baker, Ernie. "Caution: Counseling Systems Are Belief Systems." In *Scripture and Counseling: God's Word for Life in a Broken World*, edited by Bob Kellermen and Jeffrey Forrey. Grand Rapids: Zondervan, 2015.

Barber, Charles. *Comfortably Numb: How Psychiatry is Medicating a Nation*. New York: Vintage Random House, 2008.

Beale, G. K. *We Become What We Worship*. Downers Grove, IL: InterVarsity Press, 2008.

Behm, Johannes, "Heart." In *Theological Dictionary of the New Testament*, edited by Gerhard Kittel, translated by Geoffrey Bromiley, 3:611–614. Grand Rapids: Eerdmans Publishing, 1964–1976.

Berkhof, Louis. *Systematic Theology*. Grand Rapids: Eerdmans Publishing, 1996.

Berkouwer G. C. *Sin: Studies in Dogmatics*. Grand Rapids: Eerdmans Publishing, 1977.

Bowling, Andrew. "לֵב." In *Theological Wordbook of the Old Testament*, edited by R. Laird Harris, J. Gleason L. Archer, and Bruce K. Waltke, 1:466. Chicago: Moody Press, 1980.

Campbell, Ian. *Engaging with Keller: Thinking through the Theology of an Influential Evangelical*. Darlington, England: EP Books, 2013. Kindle version

Charnock, Stephen. *The Existence and Attributes of God.* Grand Rapids: Baker, 2000.

Diagnostic and Statistical Manual of Mental Disorders: DSM-5. 5th ed. Washington, DC: American Psychiatric Association, 2013.

Enns, Peter. *The Evolution of Adam.* Grand Rapids: Brazos Press, 2012.

Feldman, Robert S. *Understanding Psychology, 8th Edition.* New York: McGraw-Hill, 2008.

Frame, John. *The Doctrine of the Word of God.* Phillipsburg, NJ: P&R, 2010.

Holcomb, Justin and Lindsey A. Holcomb. *Rid of My Disgrace.* Wheaton, IL: Crossway, 2011.

Koehler, Ludwig and Walter Baumgartner. *The Hebrew and Aramaic Lexicon of the Old Testament Vol. 1.* Boston: Brill, 2001.

Lilienfeld, Scott O., Sarah Francis Smith, and Ashley L. Watts. "Issues in Diagnosis: Conceptual Issues and Controversies." In *Psychopathology: History, Diagnosis, and Empirical Foundations.* 2nd ed., edited by W. Edward Craighead, David Jay Miklowitz, and Linda W. Craighead, 1–35. Hoboken, NJ: John Wiley & Sons, 2013.

MacArthur, John. *The Vanishing Conscience.* Dallas: Word Publishing, 1994.

Machen, J. Gresham. *Christianity & Liberalism.* Grand Rapids: Eerdmans Publishing, 2009.

Maslow, Abraham H. *Toward a Psychology of Being.* 2nd ed. New York: Van Nostrand, 1968.

Menninger, Karl. *Whatever Became of Sin?* New York: Hawthorne Books, 1973.

Pierre, Jeremy, "Mental Illness and the Church," http://biblicalcounseling-

coalition.org/blogs/2013/04/19/mental-illness-and-the-church
(accessed January 31, 2014).

Piper, John. *A God Entranced Vision of All Things: The Legacy of Jonathan Edwards*. Wheaton, IL: Crossway, 2004.

Piper, John. *God's Passion for His Glory*. Wheaton, IL: Crossway, 1998.

Powlison, David. "Revisiting Idols of the Heart and Vanity Fair." *The Journal of Biblical Counseling* 27 (2013): 37–68.

Schweitzer, William. *Engaging with Keller: Thinking through the Theology of an Influential Evangelical*. Edited by Iain Campbell. Grand Rapids: EP Books, 2013.

Staub, Ervin. *The Psychology of Good and Evil: Why Children, Adults, and Groups Help and Harm Others*. New York: Cambridge University Press, 2003.

Welch, Edward. *Blame It on the Brain? Distinguishing Chemical Imbalances, Brain Disorders and Disobedience*. Phillipsburg, NJ: P&R, 1998.

_____. "Who Are We: Needs, Longings, and the Image of God in Man." *The Journal of Biblical Counseling*, Vol. 13, Number 1 (Fall 1994).

CHAPTER 11

"HE MADE THEM MALE AND FEMALE"— THE IMAGE OF GOD, ESSENTIALISM, AND THE EVANGELICAL GENDER DEBATE

Jo Suzuki

"that you may learn…not to go beyond what is written" (1 Cor. 4:6).

S ome time ago, a grader for the college entrance exam told me that he encountered a curious essay. The prompt for the essay was, "Discuss the
Women's Movement in the United States." He had been reading papers that began by explaining the civil rights movement of the 1960s or the issue of inequal-
ity in pay between equally qualified men and women, but this paper's opening
sentence was this: "American women tend to swing their hips when they walk."

The issue of gender has been a hot topic for quite some time. What is the
nature of masculinity and femininity? What are the masculine and the feminine roles at home or in the society? Do the male brain and the female brain
operate differently? Does academic writing privilege males and exclude the
distinctly female style of writing? The gender-related issues seem endless. In
evangelical Christianity, the situation is the same.

As evangelicals, we distinguish ourselves by our belief in the inerrancy
and the authority of the Scriptures. One thing the contemporary evangeli-

cal debate on the gender issue has taught us is that this belief itself does not guarantee that we can agree on how we read the Bible. It must first be interpreted. Unfortunately, this act of interpretation involves us, the interpreters, who necessarily bring in our own personal, cultural, and historical biases into the reading of the passages. The conflict in interpretation unwittingly touches these sensitive nerves and elicits strong emotional reactions.

It is, therefore, no surprise that the gender issue is one of the most volatile and polarizing issues in contemporary evangelical Christianity. For the last two decades, the two major camps, complementarians and egalitarians,[1] have engaged in heated exchanges, arguing for or against their respective positions in a civil and not so civil way. All the passages that pertain to this issue in the Bible have been exegeted and re-exegeted *ad nauseam*. Organizations and counter-organizations have been formed to promote the respective positions. So why does yet another article need to be written about it, particularly, in a book that deals with the historicity of Adam and Eve and their Fall? It is because the interpretation of Genesis 1–3 (1:27 in particular) is the key to the gender debate: only by taking the Genesis account of the Creation and the Fall of Adam and Eve in the most simple, literal, and historical way,[2] I contend, can we have the view of gender that God desires New Testament believers to have.

Cultural Beliefs and the Genesis Narrative

It is not difficult to realize that the interpretation of Genesis 1–3 is central to the biblical discussion of gender. Raymond C. Ortlund Jr. thus writes, "One way or the other, all the additional Biblical texts on manhood and womanhood must be interpreted consistently with these chapters. They lay the very foundation of Biblical manhood and womanhood."[3] The problem is that the

---

1. Wayne Grudem describes the complementarian position as follows: "men and women are equal and different—equal in value and personhood, but different in roles in marriage and the church." See Grudem, *Evangelical Feminism & Biblical Truth*, 17, n. 1. In contrast, the evangelical egalitarian position stresses the equality and denies the role distinctions.
2. I am well aware that each of the three adjectives used in this sentence can be highly contested. It is far beyond the scope of this short article to cover the critical, hermeneutic, and linguistic issues involved in the reading of the Biblical narratives. For the hermeneutic issues involved in the evangelical gender debate, see Paul Felix, "The Hermeneutics of Evangelical Feminism," 159–84. It suffices here to say that Jesus' use of a simple reading of Genesis 2:4 to correct the rabbinical teachings on divorce in Matthew 19:1–12 serves as the model of my reading of Genesis 1–3.
3. Ortlund, "Male-Female Equality and Male Headship," 95.

interpretation of these passages (or any other passages of the Scriptures) does not happen in a vacuum: we all have the tendency to read the Scriptures from the prevailing ideologies of the day and reread our meta-narratives into the simple biblical narratives to make them say what *we* want them to say. Kevin Giles, in his forward to a collection of essays written mostly from the egalitarian perspective, thus writes, "Profound changes in how people see the world always force believers to rethink their theology. When a cultural worldview changes Christians have to distinguish between what they believe as those seeking to be guided by the Bible and what they tacitly believe as those living in a given culture."[4]

Giles goes on to give three examples that illustrate how our tacit beliefs have influenced our reading of the Bible. The first is the belief in the flat earth: "When everyone thought the world was flat, theologians read the Bible to teach this"; the second, the geocentric cosmology: "When everyone thought sun revolved around the earth, the Bible was read to teach this." The third and the last example he gives, however, is a problematic one: "When everyone thought the world was created in seven literal days about 6000 years ago, Christians read the Bible to teach this."[5]

Let us look closely at these three examples. The first two illustrate how the prevailing scientific beliefs of the day were read into the simple, phenomenal language of the Biblical narratives to make them conform to their worldview. The last one is the reverse: The "literal" reading came first. Then the evolutionary hypothesis became the prevailing belief system. Now the literal reading of the Scriptures appears ridiculous to people today, because the "cultural worldview" that we tacitly embrace has conditioned us to think that the world is billions of years old.[6] Giles ironically reveals his own tacit belief, which he effectively reads into the biblical text.

It is interesting to note here that the background of the above example is the conflict between the literal reading of the Genesis Creation narrative and the cultural (or scientific) belief regarding the age of the earth. The issue discussed in this chapter also revolves around the reading of Genesis and cultural beliefs. When it comes to the view on gender relationship, no detailed argument

---

4. Giles, "Foreward," *Reconsidering Gender*, x.
5. Ibid.
6. As the inclusion of this chapter in this collection indicates, I am writing from the young-earth-creationist perspective. For this position, see Barrick, "A Historical Adam: Young-Earth Creation View," 197–227.

is necessary to show that the dominant cultural belief of our time is that of egalitarianism. The question then is this: how has this belief affected our reading of the Bible? Did it have a positive effect in helping us break away from the problematic views on gender that the past generations held (as Giles suggests), or did it have a negative effect in causing us to twist the Bible to reflect it? My answer is "yes." This chapter argues that both the current egalitarian belief and the traditional patriarchal one have caused us to misread the gender relationship depicted in the Bible, because they both share the same underlying philosophical position known as "essentialism." Once we accept the essentialized notion of gender, we project it to the biblical text and override the simple narrative account with its meta-narrative. Only by reading the Genesis Creation narrative literally and historically can we escape cultural and philosophical biases to see what the Bible truly teaches about gender relationship.

In the discussion below, I will first examine the conflict between essentialism and its polar opposite position, constructionism, in the general academic (i.e., nontheological) gender debate and discuss its implications for the gender debate among the evangelicals. I will then list and discuss the general reasons I believe that the Bible does teach the role of male headship within marriage and church, but not on the basis of the essentialized notion of gender. Finally, I will closely examine the "image of God" statement in Genesis 1:27 to argue that its literal reading reveals this relationship to be a reflection of the voluntary roles that the Persons within the triune Godhead assumed and not based on the intrinsic nature of the sexes.

Essentialism Versus Constructionism in the Academic Gender Debate

Gender versus Sex

It is often said that when it comes to discussing the general cultural hot-topics, evangelicals are always about ten to twenty years behind. Such is the case with the gender debate. Although the term "gender" has long existed in the English language, its use as a construct distinct from biological "sex" is a relatively recent development.[7] According to the gender theorist Stevi Jack-

---

7. *Oxford English Dictionary* lists 1474 as the date of the first occurrence of this term used in the sense of "males or females viewed as a group." However, it lists 1945 as the first occurrence of this term designating the sociocultural (not biological) male/female distinction.

son, "[t]he term gender has been used since the early 1970s to denote culturally constructed femininity and masculinity as opposed to biological sex
differences."[8] Jackson traces the origin of this distinction in the works of the
psychologist Robert Stoller, which the sociologist Ann Oakley borrowed and
popularized in her 1972 work *Sex, Gender and Society*. Jackson writes:

> Oakley suggested that gender is not a direct product of bio-
> logical sex. She defined sex as the anatomical and physio-
> logical characteristics which signify biological maleness and
> femaleness and gender as socially constructed masculinity
> and femininity. Masculinity and femininity are defined not
> by biology but by social, cultural and psychological attributes
> which are acquired through becoming a man or a woman in
> a particular society at a particular time.[9]

Here, Jackson is echoing Simone de Beauvoir's famous statement originally
made in French in 1949: "One is not born, but rather becomes, a woman."[10]

Why then does this distinction need to be made? If masculinity and femininity are biological, then they are universal and cannot be altered. If they are
cultural, then we can alter them by changing our culture. Seeing the problems
of inequalities between men and women, De Beauvoir, Oakley, and other academic and social activists made us aware that this problem is not natural but
cultural. Thus, it can and should be remedied.

Essentialism versus Constructionism

A positive development of becoming aware of the sex/gender distinction is
that we are now able to break away from the deterministic view of masculinity
and femininity known as "essentialism." Diana Fuss defines it as follows: "Essentialism is most commonly understood as a belief in the real, true essence of
things, the invariable and fixed properties which define the 'whatness' of a given
entity."[11] When it comes to the gender issue, essentialists do not really see the

---

8. Jackson, "Theorising Gender and Sexuality," 131.
9. Ibid., 133.
10. De Beauvoir, *The Second Sex*, 301.
11. Fuss, *Essentially Speaking*, xi. It is tempting here to diverge into philosophical discussions
    of essentialisms. See Fuss, 1–21, for John Locke's differentiation between the "real" and
    the "nominal" essence, Edmund Husserl's phenomenological essentialism, Jacques Lacan's
    psychoanalytic essentialism, etc.

distinction between sex and gender. For them, masculinity and femininity (i.e., how men and women think and behave) are not cultural but the universal and invariable property of men and women. Their essential nature determines the way they act and think. One of the most notable (or infamous) examples of the essentialist view of gender in recent years is Camille Paglia's *Sexual Personae*. In the preface, Paglia affirms her biologically deterministic view of sex difference: "My stress on the truth in sexual stereotypes and on the biologic basis of sex differences is sure to cause controversy."[12] She thus attributes the history of male dominance in the Western world on male physiology:

> My explanation for the male domination of art, science, and politics, an indisputable fact of history, is based on an analogy between sexual physiology and aesthetics. I will argue that all cultural achievement is a projection, a swerve into Apollonian transcendence, and that men are anatomically destined to be projectors.[13]

If this is indeed the case, then there is no possibility of gender equality.

There is, however, a position to the polar opposite of essentialism called "constructionism." Fuss writes:

> Constructionism, articulated in opposition to essentialism and concerned with its philosophical refutation, insists that essence is itself a historical construction. Constructionists take the refusal of essence as the inaugural moment of their own projects and proceed to demonstrate the way previously assumed self-evident kinds (like "man" or "woman") are in fact the effects of complicated discursive practices.[14]

Naturally, most feminists take this position. One of the most extreme constructionist positions is Donna Haraway's "cyborg feminism." In her highly influential "A Cyborg Manifesto," Haraway sees that, because of technological advances, we are no longer bound by the natural category of sexes but are able to modify and

12. Paglia, *Sexual Personae*, xiii.
13. Ibid., 17.
14. Fuss, *Essentially Speaking*, 2.

augment our bodies to seek new possible ways of existence.[15] She thus concludes her manifesto: "[I] would rather be a cyborg than a goddess."[16]

To those that have studied the intellectual history of the West, this opposition between essentialism and constructionism in the gender theory should look familiar. It is just another form of the ancient Sophistic discussion of *physis* (nature) and *nomos* (culture/convention), which has developed into the long-standing conflict between philosophy and rhetoric.[17] William Barrett presents another name for the same conflict, this time, the opposition between essentialism and existentialism. Barrett notes that the essentialism is deeply rooted in Western science and philosophy. In fact, it originates from the thinking of ancient Greeks that culminated in the works of Plato. Moreover, he states that in this conflict essentialism usually is the victor:

> The history of Western philosophy has been one long conflict, sometimes explicit but more often hidden and veiled, between essentialism and existentialism. And it would seem also to be the case that, to the degree to which this history takes its beginnings from Plato, essentialism has always come out on top.[18]

Why does Barrett say that the essentialism "has always come out on top"? At least, when we examine the field of contemporary feminist theory, is it not apparent that most theorists are anti-essentialists/social-constructionists? Fuss, however, makes an interesting statement: "My point here, and throughout this book, is that social constructionisms do not definitively escape the pull of essentialism, that indeed essentialism subtends the very idea of constructionism."[19] In other words, even though the contemporary feminist theorists appear on the surface as constructionists, when we examine their theories closely, we will discover that there are hidden essentialisms in them. Therefore, Barrett is correct in that essentialism eventually wins out.

What then exactly is this "pull" Fuss refers to, and what makes it so difficult for us to escape from it? There are at least three possible answers:

---

15. Haraway, *Simians, Cyborgs, and Women*, 149–81.
16. Ibid., 181.
17. See Guthrie, *The Sophists*, 55–134 and Kerferd, *The Sophistic Movement*, 111–30 for the *physis-nomos* controversy. See also Ijsseling, *Rhetoric and Philosophy in Conflict* for comprehensive discussions of the conflict between philosophy and rhetoric.
18. Barrett, *Irrational Man*, 104.
19. Fuss, *Essentially Speaking*, 5.

(1) our innate tendency, (2) our desire for political power, and (3) the nature of constructionism itself.

The "Pull" of Essentialism

Our innate human tendency favors essentialism. According to the cognitive psychologist Paul Bloom, our basic understanding of the world itself comes from the essentialist perspective. In fact, Bloom suspects that essentialism could be built into us: "We are natural-born essentialists."[20] Children in general have a strong tendency for essentialization, ascribing common hidden properties to similar objects. For example, Bloom writes, "If nine-month-olds find that a box makes a sound when you touch it, they expect other boxes that look the same to make the same sound."[21] We thus continue to maintain this childhood essentialist tendency into our quest for knowledge.

Our desire for political power also favors essentialism. Essentialism often serves those who are in the dominant political position to enforce and maintain the power structure. It is, therefore, too tempting even for social constructionists not to embrace an essentialist position. Bloom writes, "In the domains of race and sex and caste, essentialism is a myth invented by the powerful to convince people that these social categories are natural and immutable."[22] One example of this is the eighteenth- and nineteenth-century complementarians.

The term "complementarian" is now best known for Wayne Grudem and John Piper's use in the contemporary evangelical gender debate. However, the same term appears long before this in the gender debate among French Enlightenment thinkers around the time of the French Revolution. Londa Schiebinger notes that the debate first began when they faced the question of the women's position in society. Schiebinger quotes the Huguenot physician Louis de Jaucourt: "[I]t appears at first difficult to demonstrate that the authority of the husband comes from nature because that authority is contrary to the natural equality of all people."[23] Jaucourt eventually resorts to the argument denying the "natural equality."

Subsequent thinkers, however, could not ignore the inconsistency between their egalitarian belief and the women's limited place in society. Ideologically, they should have affirmed the equality of the sexes and allowed

---

20. Ibid., xii.
21. Bloom, *How Pleasure Works*, 15. See 14–18 for more examples on children's essentialism.
22. Ibid., 15.
23. Schiebinger, *The Mind Has No Sex? Women in the Origins of Modern Science*, 215.

the women to participate in democracy. Their desire to preserve the social hierarchy, however, won out; and they sought to resolve the dilemma in the form of the theory of sexual complementarity. According to this theory, "man and woman are not physical and moral equals but complementary opposites…. Henceforth, women were not to be viewed merely as *inferior to* men but as fundamentally *different from* and thus *incomparable to*, men."[24] They explained the complementary nature of the sexes by essentializing their nature: Men are rational and belong to the public sphere, whereas women are nurturers and belong to the private sphere of home. This is how essentialism is used to legitimate the traditional division of labor and preserve the social hierarchy.

Finally, the nature of constructionism itself forces it to revert back into essentialism. The point that Fuss makes throughout her book is that, no matter what kind of constructionist position one employs, there always is a hidden essentialism in it.[25] When constructionists attempt to show how gender is constructed, for example, by its cultural environment, they must essentialize the cultural environment itself in order to describe how it is done. Thus they slip right back into essentialism from which they attempt to escape. Stanley Fish puts this as follows: "Indeed, any claim in which the notion of situatedness is said to be a lever that allows us to get a purchase on situations is finally a claim to have escaped situatedness, and is therefore nothing more or less than a reinvention of foundationalism [i.e., essentialism] by the very form of thought that has supposedly reduced it to ruins."[26]

Essentialism in the Evangelical Gender Debate

When we look at the contemporary evangelical gender debate, we can easily recognize the influence of essentialism. Grudem and Piper's complementarian position restricts the male headship strictly within marriage and church. However, not everyone who affirms the male headship places this restriction but extends it beyond these two spheres. Willard Swartley thus describes one of the tenets of what he calls the hierarchical position as follows: "Women are expected to be subordinate to men—in the home, church,

---

24. Ibid., 217.
25. In particular, Fuss examines Lacanian psychoanalysis and Derridian deconstruction. She sees the "vestige of essentialism" in Lacan's notion of "The Woman" and Derrida's use of the phrase "always already." See Fuss, *Essentially Speaking*, 6–18.
26. Fish, *Doing What Comes Naturally*, 348–49.

and society" [my emphasis].[27] By extending the male headship role and the female subordination role to society in general, this position universalizes the masculine and the feminine role. Thus it takes the essentialist position regarding gender.

What about the evangelical egalitarians? In her statement about the goal of the organization Christians for Biblical Equality, Rebecca Merrill Groothuis writes,

> The goal of evangelical feminism is that men and women be allowed to serve God as individuals, according to their own unique gifts rather than according to a culturally predetermined personality slot called "Christian manhood" or "Christian womanhood."[28]

On the first glance, Groothuis's statement looks like a constructionist statement, since she characterizes Christian manhood/womanhood as "culturally predetermined." However, in denying the male headship anywhere, she essentializes the egalitarian nature of the sexes and makes it the universal standard for every Christian. Her case is a classic example of what Fuss and Fish describe as the anti-essentialists falling back into essentialism.

In sum, we first looked at how the concept of "gender" came to be understood apart from the biological "sex." Then we examined the two philosophical positions regarding the nature of gender: essentialism, which views masculinity/femininity as a universal and invariant characteristic of every male/female, and constructionism, which views masculinity/femininity as a local and cultural construct. We then saw that in the essentialist-constructionist conflict, essentialism usually comes out on top. Finally, we saw the influence of essentialism in the evangelical gender debate, especially how the "hierarchal" position essentializes the male headship and the egalitarian position essentializes the notion of equality.

We must now turn to the Bible and examine what it says about the nature of gender and the gender role in the light of the above discussions. Specifically, let us deal with the question: Does the scriptural evidence call for the essentialized view of gender?

---

27. Swartley, *Slavery, Sabbath, War, and Women*, 151.
28. Groothuis, *Women Caught in the Conflict*, 110.

The Biblical View of Gender and Essentialism

Regarding gender roles, I believe that the Bible clearly teaches male headship, but not from the essentialist position. In the discussion below , I will discuss four reasons in support of this position.

First, *the biblical command for the male headship is not universal, but local and specific.* In 1 Timothy 2:12–13, the Apostle Paul writes, "I do not permit a woman to teach or to exercise authority over a man; rather, she is to remain quiet. For Adam was formed first, then Eve." The context of this passage makes it clear that this command is restricted to the context of the New Testament local church and not society in general. Also, in Ephesians 5:22–24, Paul commands, "Wives, submit to your own husbands, as to the Lord. For the husband is the head of the wife even as Christ is the head of the church, his body, and is himself its Savior. Now as the church submits to Christ, so also wives should submit in everything to their husbands." Thus he limits the scope of the wife's submission only to her own husband, not men in general. Male headship only applies within church and within marriage.

Second, *the biblical command for male headship is not permanent.* This is easy to see in the marital relationship, because death annuls marriage. In Romans 7:2, Paul uses this principle to illustrate our death to the Law: "For a married woman is bound by law to her husband while he lives, but if her husband dies she is released from the law of marriage." Does the marital relationship continue after the resurrection? Our Lord clearly answers this question in his reply to the Sadducees in Matthew 22:23–33. In this passage, the Sadducees attempt to entrap Him by pointing out the possible complications in the levirate marriage custom after the resurrection: When seven brothers had the same woman for a wife consecutively, whose wife would she be? "But Jesus answered them, 'You are wrong, because you know neither the Scriptures nor the power of God. For in the resurrection they neither marry nor are given in marriage, but are like angels in heaven'" (Matt 22:29–30). So then, the wife's submission to her husband ends at the death of either one and will not continue after this. The question regarding the male headship within church, however, is less clear. The phrase "neither marry nor are given in marriage" in the above passage indicates that the reproductive function of our physical body is no longer needed in the glorified, resurrected state: we will no longer be differentiated on the basis of the (biological) sex differences.[29] Therefore, it is most natural to assume that the male headship within the local church should no longer exist after the resurrection. Further, if the headship within marriage is not permanent, there is no reason to assume that the one within church is permanent either.

Third, *the biblical command for the male headship is not based on the nature of sex differences.* What does the Bible teach us about the (biological) sex and (cultural) gender distinction? Genesis 1:27 clearly tells us that God created two separate sexes: male and female. What about the gender? If the gender is socially constructed, it was still being formed in the Garden. (Tragically, however, the Fall took place to mar the formation of what could have been the perfect and harmonious gender relationship.) Nevertheless, the Bible does specify one aspect of the gender relationship at the time when man and woman were created: male headship. As was discussed above, 1 Timothy 2:13 states that the command for the male headship in church is based on the order of creation: *that* man was created first, and not on *how* they were created. In other words, the Bible does not ground the male headship on the essentialized nature of masculinity and femininity. It is therefore wrong to assume that men are biologically programmed to be leaders and women, followers.

Unfortunately, many commentators of old have succumbed to the essentialist trap. John Calvin, for instance, makes the following statement in his commentary on 1 Timothy 2:12:

> [W]oman *by nature* (that is, by the ordinary law of God) is formed to obey; for *gunaikokratia* (the government of women) has always been regarded by all wise persons as a monstrous thing; and, therefore, so to speak, it will be a mingling of heaven and earth, if women usurp the right to teach [my emphasis].[30]

---

29. John Frame, although weakly (by his own admission), argues that we still maintain our sexual differences after the resurrection. His reasoning is largely based on the physical appearance of post-resurrection Jesus and of the angels, which, in my mind, does not prove it one way or the other. See his "Men and Women in the Image of God," in *Recovering Biblical Manhood and Womanhood*, 232. Daniel Heimbach also argues that sexual identity is eternal. His argument, however, consists almost completely of references from Augustine. I see little exegetical argument in it. Regarding Matthew 22:30, he believes that Jesus does not deny the possibility but the practice of marriage. See Heimbach, "The Unchangeable Difference," 281–87. It is inconceivable for me that we continue to retain the biological function no longer needed throughout eternity. Nevertheless, since the Bible is not specific about this, it is best to restrain from making any dogmatic conclusions.
30. Calvin, *Commentaries on the First Epistle to Timothy*, 68.

Again, he comments on 2:13:

> Now Moses shews that the woman was created afterwards, in
> order that she might be a kind of appendage to the man; and
> that she was joined to the man on the express condition that
> she should be at hand to render obedience to him. (Gen. ii. 21.)
> Since, therefore, God did not create two chiefs of equal power,
> but added to the man *an inferior aid*, the Apostle justly reminds
> us of that order of creation in which the eternal and inviolable
> appointment of God is strikingly displayed [my emphasis].[31]

Calvin's comments are a great reminder for all of us that, no matter how great
a theologian one is, we are still very much a victim to the cultural values of
our day and cannot escape from our tendency to read them into the interpretations of the Scriptures.

Another approach that can fall into the essentialist trap is a biological approach, which takes the scientific findings about the nature of sex differences
and reads them into the Scriptures. Having examined physiological and neural
differences between the sexes, Gregg Johnson gives the following conclusion:

> We should not conclude automatically that because men and
> women may have different gifts, traditional roles are the only
> way they may be expressed. Yet it seems very significant that
> these different gifts correspond very well to the different roles
> given to men and women in Scripture.... These unique abili-
> ties, coupled with the traditional roles, have served mankind
> well and enabled us to fulfill the commission to multiply and
> fill the earth very efficiently.[32]

Johnson, however, is careful in presenting his view. At the beginning of his study,
he offers two cautions. First, many of the findings are based on animal studies
and cannot be conclusively applied to humans. Second, the findings are "aver-
ages and patterns that cannot be completely universalized."[33] Here, it is impor-

---

31. Ibid., 69.
32. Johnson, "Biological Basis for Gender-Specific Behavior," 293.
33. Ibid., 285.

tant to make the distinction between sex and gender. It is one thing to present the evidences about sex differences, but translating them directly into gender role distinctions is highly problematic. The gender theorist Judith Butler explains the mind-boggling complexity involved in the gender formation as follows:

> Gender is not exactly what one "is" nor is it precisely what one "has." Gender is the apparatus by which the production and normalization of masculine and feminine take place along with the interstitial forms of hormonal, chromosomal, psychic, and performative that gender assumes. To assume that gender always and exclusively means the matrix of the "masculine" and "feminine" is precisely to miss the critical point that the production of that coherent binary is contingent, that it comes at a cost, and that those permutations of gender which do not fit the binary are as much a part of gender as its most normative instance.[34]

To reiterate, the male headship in family and in church is a specific biblical command and not a universal biological necessity or inclination.

Lastly, *the biblical command for the male headship reflects the inter-Trinitarian (in particular, the Father and the Son) relationship*. If indeed the male headship mirrors the role relationship within the Godhead, then it certainly is not based on the essence of the Persons within Trinity, because, as one being, the three persons' essence is the same. (Regarding the nature of the Second Person of the Godhead, the Nicene Creed states that He is one substance [*homoousion*] with the Father.)[35] To elaborate this point, I must now turn to the key text that explains the biblical gender relationship: "So God created man in his own image … male and female he created them" (Gen. 1:27).

INTERPRETIVE HISTORY OF GENESIS 1:27

The key passage in understanding the Biblical view of sex/gender is Genesis 1:27: "So God created man in his own image, in the image of God he created him; *male and female he created them*" [my emphasis]. Why did God specifi-

---

34. Butler, *Undoing Gender*, 42.
35. http://www.creeds.net/ancient/niceneg.htm.

cally state here that His image involved both male and female? If we understand what the "image of God" is, then we can also have a much better idea about the biblical view of the nature of masculinity and femininity.

Not surprisingly, the history of the interpretation of the "image of God" shows that it too was affected by the essentialisms of the day. When we examine the history of the interpretation of Genesis 1:27, we can see that what was considered to be the essence of the human is often read backwards into the understanding of the image of God. In his article "Male and Female Complementarity and the Image of God," Bruce Ware divides the historical understandings of the phrase "the image of God" into three groups:[36]

1. The structural views, which include:

    a. Irenaeus's view that it is our *reason* and volition (as opposed to our holiness and spirituality)

    b. Augustine's view that it is our memory, *intellect*, and will, mirroring the triune nature of God

    c. Aquinas' view that it is our *rationality*

    d. Calvin's view that it is our soul with its capacities (however diminished after the Fall) of *reason* and will.

2. The relational views, which include:

    a. Karl Barth's view that it is the social/relational nature of human life

    b. Emil Brunner's view that it is both our "formal" capacity to know and to love God and their "material" manifestation in our actual knowing and loving God

3. The functional views, which include Leonard Verduin's and D. J. A. Clines' view that the image of God refers to our function as rulers over the creation.

---

36. Ware, "Male and Female Complementarity," 73–75.

Ware goes on to point out the problems of these approaches:

> One of the main problems with much of the traditional un-
> derstandings (particularly with the variations of the structur-
> al view) is that these proposals were led more by speculation
> regarding how men are like God and unlike animals than by
> careful attention to indications in the text of Scripture itself
> as to what may constitute this likeness.[37]

It is interesting to note that all the structural views involve some reference to human rationality, as I have emphasized in the above. In addition,
they all do not deal with the fact that God's image in Genesis 1:27 includes
both male and female. Also, the structural views have a significantly older history: Iranaeus is the oldest, dating to the second century AD, and Calvin, the
youngest, dating to the sixteenth century. We can very well suspect here that
they were all under the obvious influence of the essentialist thinking inherited
from the ancient Greeks, which equated masculinity with human rationality.

Not being satisfied with any of the "traditional understandings," Ware
himself, following Anthony Hoekema and Clines, takes the view he calls
"functional holism," which attempts to combine all three views: "[A]ll three
are needed, the *structural* serves the purpose of the *functional* being carried
out in *relationship*" [his emphasis].[38] Yet the long definition he gives is rather
ambiguous:

> The image of God in man as functional holism means that
> God made human beings, both male and female, to be cre-
> ated and finite *representations* (images of God) of God's own
> nature, that in *relationship* with Him and each other they
> might be His *representatives* (imaging God) in carrying out
> the *responsibilities* He has given to them. In this sense, we are
> *images of God* in order *to image God* and His purposes in the
> ordering of our lives and the carrying out of our God-given
> responsibilities. [his emphases][39]

37. Ibid., 75.
38. Ibid., 79.
39. Ibid.

If we are to come up with the all-inclusive definition of the image of God, we may have to tolerate this definition. But if we want to understand Genesis 1:27, then we must answer two questions: first, what specifically is "God's own nature"? Second, what exactly are the "responsibilities" we are to carry out? The answer to the latter question is easy: as Ware himself points out in his discussion of Clines's position, it is to rule the creation.[40] God repeats His command to rule the creation twice in the immediate context: the first time in 1:26b, "And let them have dominion over the fish of the sea and over the birds of the heavens and over the livestock and over all the earth and over every creeping thing that creeps on the earth"; and the second time in 1:28b, "Be fruitful and multiply and fill the earth and subdue it, and have dominion over the fish of the sea and over the birds of the heavens and over every living thing that moves on the earth."

The first question about the nature of God, however, brings us back to the same problem that confronted the structural views—that is, we are tempted again to essentialize human nature and read it back to the nature of God. Is there any way to understand the nature of the image of God without falling into the essentialist trap and reading non-biblical understandings of human nature into Genesis 1:27? I believe there is, and to do this we must revisit the relational view.

Non-Essentialist Reading of Genesis 1:27

There is a lot to like about the relational view. First and foremost, it seeks to understand the phrase "image of God" strictly from the context of the passage. Ware writes, "Clearly we should affirm with Karl Barth that our understanding of the image of God should be directed as fully as possible by the text of Scripture."[41] Both Ware and Frame nevertheless object to the relational view because other references to the image of God (such as in Genesis 9:6) only refer to one man and not to male and female as a unit.[42] If indeed the image of God refers to the social and relational nature of the humans as represented in the phrase "male and female," we see it only in Genesis 1:27 and nowhere else.

I believe, however, that this is not a sufficient enough reason to dismiss the relational view. The image of God reference in Genesis 1:27 is uniquely different from other references. Here, it refers to the pre-Fall humanity. The

---

40. Ibid., 75. Clines convincingly argues that the image of God in the Old Testament is an image of the king as a ruler. See Clines, "The Image of God in Man," 92–99.
41. Ibid., 77.
42. Ibid., 76. Also, Frame, 228.

image of God in Genesis 9:6, in contrast, refers to the post-Fall (post-Flood) humanity. It is exegetically conceivable that the reason the "male and female" aspect of the image of God does not appear after 1:27 is related to this change in the human condition (as we will see below). As Clines points out (as does Ware), the aspect of "rulership" is at the core of the notion of the image of God.[43] Yet how the "rulership" manifested before sin tainted humanity must have been different from after the Fall. The notion of the image of God is broad enough to emphasize different aspects of God's character within the common core reference about His "rulership." In the following section, I will examine the context of Genesis 1:27 to modify the relational view and argue that in this narrative Moses emphasizes one aspect of the image of God by using the phrase "male and female": the unity and role differences within the Godhead as reflected in the male-female relationship.

So what does the immediate context of Genesis 1:27 say? Genesis 1:26 begins with this: "Then God said, 'Let *us* make man in *our* image, after *our* likeness'" [my emphasis]. The New Testament believers can readily identify these repeated plural references that God uses about himself as a reference to His triune nature. Moreover, there is one other passage in Genesis where we encounter God yet again using "us" to refer to Himself. Genesis 11:6–7 reads, "And the Lord said, 'Behold, they are one people, and they have all one language, and this is only the beginning of what they will do. And nothing that they propose to do will now be impossible for them. Come, let *us* go down and there confuse their language, so that they may not understand one another's speech'" [my emphasis].

What do these two passages have in common? They both have something to do with the unity within the interpersonal relationships. Genesis 1 deals with male and female reflecting the triune nature of the godhead, and Genesis 11 deals with the people uniting themselves under one language to build the tower, obviously against God's will. If these textual implications are indeed correct, the image of God is more than just the social nature of humans as Barth suggests.[44] It refers to the *unity* of the interpersonal relationship that a husband and a wife ought to have had in marriage before the Fall.

The emphasis on the marital unity is abundant in the immediate context. The entire creation of Adam and Eve account emphasizes the unity of the first couple. Genesis 1:27 sets the stage: humans are created as a male/female

---

43. Clines, ibid.
44. Barth, *Church Dogmatics* 3.1.185.

pair. Then the more detailed account that follows in Genesis 2 specifically emphasizes the close union of the husband and the wife, first, by the manner in which Eve was created, second, by Adam's exclamation upon seeing Eve, and finally, by the institution of marriage. In 2:21, God takes a part of Adam to form Eve, rather than using more dust and breathing into it like He did with Adam, emphasizing the unified nature of the two. Adam's response to seeing Eve also emphasizes the unity between them: "This at last is bone of my bones and flesh of my flesh" (2:23b). And the institution of marriage indicates that the married couple forms a closer unit than the parent-child relationship: "Therefore a man shall leave his father and his mother and hold fast to his wife, and they shall become one flesh" (Gen 2:24).

Not only the Creation account, but also the account of the Fall in Genesis 3 (in particular, the curse proclaimed against the wife in 3:16b) emphasizes the unity of the married couple, albeit in a negative way. In her classic study of the "woman's desire" in 3:16b, Susan T. Foh concludes:

> God's words in Genesis 3:16b destroy the harmony of marriage, for the rule of the husband, part of God's original intent for marriage, is not made more tolerable by the wife's desire for husband, but less tolerable, because she rebels against his leadership and tries to usurp it.[45]

This explains why the image of God in the sense of the unity between husband and wife is not repeated again after Genesis 1:27 in the Scriptures: it is forever broken because of the Fall.

If the image of God in Genesis 1:27 refers to inter-Trinitarian unity and the pre-Fall marriage relationship, this carries enormous implications for the issue of biblical gender. As we saw above, the command for the male headship predates the Fall and is based on the order of Creation (1 Tim 2:13). If the marriage relationship mirrors the inter-Trinitarian relationship, then the difference of roles in the marriage relationship also mirrors the roles within the Godhead. Wayne Grudem thus writes:

> In fact, the idea of headship and submission did not even begin with the creation of Adam and Eve in Genesis 1 and 2....It be-

---

45. Foh, "What Is the Woman's Desire?," 383.

gan in the relationship between the Father and Son in the Trinity. ... It has *always existed* in the eternal nature of God Himself. And in this most basic of all authority relationships, authority is not based on gifts or ability (for the Father, Son and Holy Spirit are equal in attributes and perfections). It is just there. [Grudem's emphasis][46]

Both the gender-role difference, just like the role difference within the Trinity, is *not* based on the essence: every male is not born to lead and female to follow. We know very well, both from history and from personal experience, that some women are much more gifted in leadership than some men. Yet the Scriptures explicitly command these gifted women *voluntarily* to restrict their gifts and assume the submissive role within marriage and within church. Why does God give us such a seemingly unfair command? Is not our God the god of justice and equity? We see the answer in how the Son of God dealt with His role. Philippians 2:6–8 says:

[The Son], though he was in the form of God, did not count equality with God a thing to be grasped, but emptied himself, by taking the form of a [servant], being born in the likeness of men. And being found in human form, he humbled himself by becoming obedient to the point of death, even death on a cross.

Jesus Christ was equal in essence with God the Father, but He *voluntarily* restricted His equality and *voluntarily* took on the lowly form of a servant to accomplish our redemption by dying on the cross! When Christian women (no matter how gifted they are) *voluntarily* restrict their freedom and assume the submissive role in marriage and in church, they reflect the humility of our Lord. This act is far more precious in God's eyes than any exercise of their leadership gifts.

Yet there still remains the issue of fairness and equity. Regarding the women's role, Grudem writes, "[S]ubmission to a rightful authority is a noble virtue. It is a privilege."[47] Regarding the nature of men's roles, Ortlund makes a

46. Grudem, *Evangelical Feminism & Biblical Truth*, 47.
47. Ibid.

useful distinction between male headship and male domination. He describes the former, "In the partnership of two spiritually equal human beings, man and woman, the man bears the primary responsibility to lead the partnership in a God-glorifying direction," and the latter, "[T]he assertion of the man's will over the woman's will, heedless of her spiritual equality, her rights, and her value."[48] These statements do mitigate the implications of unfairness in the biblical gender roles, but do not eliminate them. Still then we must ask: Is not our God the god of impartiality?

The answer, again, is found in the role that Jesus assumed in the Trinity. The role of Sonship involved not only His voluntary submission and humiliation but also a reward. The Philippians passage quoted above continues:

> Therefore God has highly exalted him and bestowed on him the name that is above every name, so that at the name of Jesus every knee should bow, in heaven and on earth and under the earth, and every tongue confess that Jesus Christ is Lord, to the glory of God the Father (2:9–11).

His exaltation is the reward for His voluntary submission to fulfill His role. What about the Christian women who voluntarily submit to their roles in marriage and in church? There is no question that their act of obedience will be richly rewarded, if not in this life, it will surely be in the kingdom to come. In Colossians 3:23–25, after giving instructions to wives, husbands, children, and fathers regarding their role, the Apostle Paul gives the following instruction to the bondservants:

> Whatever you do, work heartily, as for the Lord and not for men, knowing that from the Lord you will receive the inheritance as your reward. You are serving the Lord Christ. For the wrongdoer will be paid back for the wrong he has done, and there is no partiality.

Here, the bondservants receive a promise of future inheritance for their faithful service to their earthly masters, because they are really serving their heavenly Master in doing this. This promise is the evidence that God shows no

---

48. Ortlund, "Male-Female Equality and Male Headship," 3.

partiality: the faithful acts of service, be it by the bondservants to their masters or by women under the headship of men in marriage and in church, will receive compensation, if not in this life, then in the life to come.

Once we realize that the male-female role relationship reflects the relationship among the Godhead (especially, between the Father and the Son), we can also realize that, just as the subordinate role of the Son in the Trinity came with great reward, the subordinate role of women in marriage and in church also will involve a future exaltation. God is indeed a god of impartiality.

Conclusion: Biblical Suspension of the Ethical

We began this study with the discussion of how we have the tendency to read the prevailing ideology of the day into our interpretation of the Scriptures. In the study of gender, this tendency appears in the form of essentializing masculinity/femininity: when the prevailing ideology was patriarchy, as in the days of Calvin (and even in eighteenth- and nineteenth-century France), the concept of male superiority was essentialized and then read into the Bible. Today, we do the same thing with egalitarianism: we essentialize the notion of gender equality, make it into a universal principle, and then read it into our interpretations of the Bible. The simple, literal, and historical reading of the Genesis account, however, gives us a different view of gender: masculinity and femininity in the Bible are never essentialized, that is, they are never made into a universal and invariant principle that applies to every male and female. The Bible does command the male headship not as a universal principle but as a local, specific instruction limited to only within the sphere of marriage and church. If this command sounds unethical to our ears, it is because we have essentialized the notion of gender equality and accepted it as our universal ethical principle. So, then, the evangelical gender debate really is a conflict between the simple reading of the Scriptures and our universalized ethical sense derived from the essentialization of gender equality.

The conflict between what God says in His Word and what our ethical sense informs us is not unique to this debate. Soren Kierkegaard's exposition of Abraham sacrificing Isaac (Gen 22) in his *Fear and Trembling* is one of the best known expressions of this conflict. What God commanded Abraham to do can be considered "unethical" in more than one way: it was an act of murder, not only of an innocent, but also of his own child, of his only child, of his only child of old age, and of his only child of promise that God specifically gave Abraham. Yet Abraham suspended his "ethical" sense in favor of obedience to God's specific command. Kierkegaard calls this act the "teleological suspension of the ethical."[49]

Of course, what Abraham had to do was extraordinary and incomparable. Yet the principle stays the same. In his commentary on Kierkegaard, the philosopher Calvin O. Schrag points out that the "ethical" here stands for "a universal moral requirement."[50] When this universalized ethical code contradicts with what the Bible says, we must make a choice. We must biblically suspend the ethical in order to obey the Word of God.

As we see in Genesis 3, the gender problem is one of the oldest problems that has confronted humankind. And it still continues on to this day. Throughout history, the essentialized notion of male superiority has been used to dominate women; and now the essentialized notion of gender equality is making it difficult for Christian women to accept their role in marriage and in church. As long as the curse is in effect, there is no end to the conflict between the sexes. The only remedy we have is in the hands of the redeemed with the help from the Holy Spirit to obey the Word of God in love, humility, and simplicity of faith. Thus we will truly become the image of God by reflecting the unity and unbroken fellowship of the Trinity. Our Lord prays this on our behalf: "Holy Father, keep them in your name, which you have given me, *that they may be one, even as we are one*" (John 17:11b [my emphasis]).

BIBLIOGRAPHY

Barrett, Matthew, and Ardel B. Caneday, eds. *Four Views on The Historical Adam*. Grand Rapids: Zondervan, 2013.

Barrett, William. *Irrational Man: A Study in Existential Philosophy*. New York: Anchor Books, 1958.

Barrick, William D. "A Historical Adam: Young-Earth Creation View." In *Four Views on The Historical Adam*. 197–227.

Barth, Karl. *Church Dogmatics*. 4 vols. Trans. J. W. Edwards, et al. Edinburgh: T. and T. Clark, 1958.

---

49. Kierkegaard, *Fear and Trembling/Repetition*, 54–67.
50. Schrag, "Note on Kierkegaard's Teleological Suspension of the Ethical," 66.

Bloom, Paul. *How Pleasure Works: The New Science of Why We Like What We Like*. New York: W. W. Norton & Co., 2010.

Butler, Judith. *Undoing Gender*, New York: Routledge, 2004.

Calvin, John. *Commentaries on the First Epistle to Timothy*, Grand Rapids: Baker, 2005.

Clines, D. J. A. "The Image of God in Man." *Tyndale Bulletin* (1968): 92–99.

De Beauvoir, Simone. *The Second Sex*. New York: Vintage Books, 1973.

Felix, Paul. "The Hermeneutics of Evangelical Feminism," *The Master's Seminary Journal* 5/2 (Fall 1994): 159–84.

Foh, Susan T. "What Is the Woman's Desire?" *The Westminster Theological Journal* 37 (1974/75): 376–83.

Frame, John. "Men and Women in the Image of God." In *Recovering Biblical Manhood and Womanhood*. 228–36.

Fuss, Diana. *Essentially Speaking: Feminism, Nature & Difference*, New York: Routledge, 1989.

Groothuis, Rebecca Merrill. *Women Caught in the Conflict*. Grand Rapids: Baker, 1994.

Grudem, Wayne. *Evangelical Feminism & Biblical Truth: An Analysis of More Than One Hundred Disputed Questions*. Wheaton, IL: Crossway, 2012.

Guthrie, W. K. G. *The Sophists*. Cambridge: Cambridge University Press, 1971.

Habets, Myk and Beulah Wood. *Reconsidering Gender: Evangelical Perspectives*. Foreword by Kevin Giles. Eugene, OR: Pickwick Publications, 2011.

Haraway, Donna. *Simians, Cyborgs, and Women: The Reinvention of Nature.* New York: Routledge, 1991.

Heimbach, Daniel R. "The Unchangeable Difference." In *Biblical Foundations for Manhood and Womanhood.* 281–287. Ed. Wayne Grudem. Wheaton, IL: Crossway, 2002.

Ijsseling, Samuel. *Rhetoric and Philosophy in Conflict.* Trans. Paul Dunphy. The Hague: Martinus Nijhoff, 1976.

Jackson, Stevi and Jackie Jones, eds. *Contemporary Feminist Theories.* Edinburgh: University of Edinburgh Press, 1998.

Jackson, Stevi. "Theorising Gender and Sexuality." In *Contemporary Feminist Theories.* 131–46.

Johnson, Gregg. "Biological Basis for Gender-Specific Behavior." In *Recovering Biblical Manhood and Womanhood*, edited by John Piper and Wayne Grudem, 285–98. Wheaton, IL: Crossway, 2012.

Kerferd, G. B. *The Sophistic Movement.* Cambridge: Cambridge University Press, 1981.

Kierkegaard, Soren. *Fear and Trembling/Repetition.* Edited and translated by Howard V. Hong and Edna H. Hong. Princeton, NJ: Princeton University Press, 1983.

Oakley, Ann. *Sex, Gender and Society.* London: Temple Smith, 1972.

Ortlund, Raymond C., Jr., "Male-Female Equality and Male Headship: Genesis 1–3." In *Recovering Biblical Manhood and Womanhood*, edited by John Piper and Wayne Grudem, 228–36. Wheaton, IL: Crossway, 2012.

Paglia, Camille. *Sexual Personae: Art and Decadence from Nefertiti to Emily Dickinson*, New Haven: Yale University Press, 1990.

Piper, John and Wayne Grudem, eds. *Recovering Biblical Manhood and Womanhood (Redesign): A Response to Evangelical Feminism.* Wheaton, IL: Crossway, 2012.

Schiebinger, Londa. *The Mind Has No Sex? Women in the Origins of Modern Science.* Cambridge, MA: Harvard University Press, 1989.

Schrag, Calvin O. "Note on Kierkegaard's Teleological Suspension of the Ethical," *Ethics* 70.1 (October, 1959): 66–68.

Swartley, Willard. *Slavery, Sabbath, War, and Women: Case Issues in Biblical Interpretation.* Scottdale, PA: Herald Press, 1983.

Ware, Bruce. "Male and Female Complementarity and the Image of God." In *Recovering Biblical Manhood and Womanhood,* edited by John Piper and Wayne Grudem, 228–36. Wheaton, IL: Crossway, 2012.

CHAPTER 12

THE HISTORICAL ADAM IN EDUCATION—WHY KEEPING HIM REAL IN OUR CURRICULUM MATTERS

Alexander Granados

In the flaring parks, in the taverns, in the hushed academies,
your murmur will applaud the wisdom of a thousand quacks.
For theirs is the kingdom.[1]

EDUCATION AND THE LIE OF THE GARDEN

We may wonder about the value of Christian higher education. After all, it appears that research universities, comprehensive universities, four-year colleges, community colleges, and for-profit institutions can give Christian students the skills and information for vocation. However, according to the Bible, knowledge apart from God actually produces a fallen understanding of the world and perpetuates the disaster of Genesis 3. The fear of the Lord is the beginning of wisdom (Prov. 1:7). Hence, while educational institutions can provide certain pieces of information, from a biblical worldview,

---

1. Fearing, "Conclusion," v.

they will ultimately fail in that they cannot produce wisdom. The nature of education in today's society has in essence adopted the lie of the Garden. The serpent tempted the woman by undermining what God really said for an unsanctioned way to obtaining knowledge (Gen 3:1–7). However, true wisdom is not ultimately based upon reason but divine revelation, which alone counteracts our fallen condition. As such, our job in education is to exalt divine revelation above our reason. The issue of the historical Adam thus is pivotal in the matter of education, for the reality of the lie in the Garden continues to this day in education, and our stance on Adam impacts how we deal with revelation and reason.

My erudite colleagues have written from different disciplines, addressing why they believe that the issues of a historical Adam and Fall are too great to compromise on. They have labored exegetically, historically, scientifically, and hermeneutically to remove objections surrounding the historicity of Genesis 1–3. They have explained the implications of Genesis 1–3 as it relates to systematic and biblical theology, pastoral ministry, the nature of the Christian life, science, sexuality, politics, and business. Because they have comprehensively addressed the issues, my contribution will be concise. Why does it matter that we keep Adam real in our Christian higher education curriculum? I propose that accepting an ahistorical Adam may have ramifications that would reshape our entire Christian higher education curriculum. There is good reason for this. As we will see, the Christian higher education curriculum was historically reshaped by the shift in higher education in the late nineteenth century, and the modern struggle in Christian higher education threatens to reshape it once more. My goal is to succinctly discuss these historical issues and ultimately provide a vision for a true Christian higher education.

THE SHIFT IN HIGHER EDUCATION

The words of the Preacher, "the writing of many books is endless" (Eccl 12:12, NASB), are affirmed by the copious books written on the topic of higher education. In 1994, George M. Marsden published *The Soul of the American University: From Protestant Establishment to Established Nonbelief*. The book provides a historical narrative on the influence of Protestantism in shaping higher education in America during the late nineteenth century. In the same year, Douglas Sloan, published *Faith and Knowledge: Mainline Protestantism and American Higher Education*. Sloan addresses the central role Protestantism played in the founding, administering, and teaching tasks of colonial American higher education. I will not attempt to regurgitate all the issues presented in these books and numerous other books that chronicle the history of higher education in America. For centuries, Christian colleges and universities played a major role in both Western intellectual history and the history of the church. Christian colleges and universities affirmed the usefulness of a liberal arts curriculum as preparation for service to both church and society. Christian scholars emphasized an empirical approach both to science and to the study of language and literature. The basis for higher education in America was the belief that in the academy, moral and spiritual formation, and the usefulness of liberal learning, are joined to the unity of truth in an all-encompassing doxology to the God of Creation. Christian colleges and universities prepared students with a liberal arts education focusing on theology or law, and for the active life of pastors and administrators in church or civil society.

But, arguably, the purpose of higher education shifted in the last half of the nineteenth century. The singular aim of higher education—to discipline the mind and build the character of wealthy elite students with a rigorous liberal arts curriculum and strict adherence to religious dogma—came under scrutiny. The appetite for freedom and autonomous spirit of the Enlightenment gave rise to those who labored to transform higher education. Their desire to create a religiously neutral civilization took aim at dismantling what they perceived to be the intellectual stronghold of narrow-minded and elitist Christians in the church, academy, and civil society. James Axtell describes how, "under the weight of the western land-grant universities (representing Utility), German scholarship and higher criticism (representing Research), and Darwinism (representing Science),"[2] the prolonged death of the liberal arts college came. I will briefly examine this triad of issues that radically transformed the landscape of higher education in the late nineteenth century.

Utility

The development of land-grant colleges and universities began when Congress passed the Morrill Act of 1862; higher education was intended to be democratized by opening access to the industrial classes. The land grants given by Congress or state legislatures were to be used for the endowment and

---

2. Axtell, "The Death of the Liberal Arts College," 340.

maintenance of colleges and universities teaching agriculture, military tactics, and the mechanical arts as well as classical studies, so members of the working classes could obtain a liberal, practical education. These colleges and universities revised the higher education curriculum to fulfill their democratic mandate for accessibility, openness, and service to the toiling peoples. Today, there is one land-grant institution in every state and territory of the United States. Several land-grant institutions are among the nation's most prestigious public research universities.[3]

This was a significant shift in higher education because land-grant colleges and universities were no longer tied to a religious denomination or charter. Land-grant colleges and universities ultimately became secular state institutions for the humanistic education of the masses. Every year, millions of Christian students enroll at public and land-grant institutions because of their academic reputation, affordability, and promise of a good job. But the education they receive teaches evolution as fact and biblical creation as myth. The average Christian sitting on the pew at church has, for years, been indoctrinated in the secular K-12 and university classroom to not interpret the Bible literally.

Sadly, this is why most Christians easily accept an ahistorical Adam. In addition, faculty at Christian colleges and universities who have been educated at secular institutions can often struggle to integrate faith and learning. They readily find in theistic evolution a reconciliation of their faith and secular learning. This of course begins to be what is taught in the classroom at our Christian colleges and universities. Students graduate not believing in biblical Creation, and our churches are filled with more congregants who do not interpret the Bible literally. It is a vicious circle.

Research

German biblical scholarship in the late eighteenth and early nineteenth centuries gave rise to the speculative principles of higher criticism that are based on reason rather than revelation. Higher critics like Friedrich Schleiermacher (1768–1834), Ludwig Feuerbach (1804–1872) and David Friedrich Strauss (1808–1874) popularized the application of literary historical-critical methods in analyzing and studying the Bible and its textual content. Originally, higher criticism was simply a scholarly approach to studying, evaluating, and critically assessing the Bible as literature in order to understand it better.

---

3. Behle, "Educating the Toiling Peoples," 73–75.

Regrettably, the critical methods employed to evaluate the Bible and its text soon began to denigrate the Bible into fable and myth. Rationalism, naturalism, higher criticism, and contemporary philosophical trends launched an assault to de-historicize Scripture.

American universities imported the German higher criticism model in the 1870s and 1880s. Christian colleges and universities began to question and deny the inspiration (1 Cor 2:7–14; 2 Tim 3:16; 2 Pet 1:20–21), authority (1 Cor 2:13; 1 Thess 2:13), inerrancy, and infallibility (Matt 5:18; 24:35; John 10:35; 16:12–13; 17:17; 1 Cor 2:13; 2 Tim 3:15–17; Heb 4:12; 2 Pet 1:20–21) of Scripture. The belief that Jesus Christ represents humanity and deity in indivisible oneness (Mic 5:2; John 5:23; 14:9–10; Col 2:9) was disavowed. The teaching that our Lord Jesus Christ was virgin-born (Isa 7:14; Matt 1:23, 25; Luke 1:26–35) and that He was God incarnate (John 1:1, 14) was rejected. Naturally, the literal-grammatical-historical interpretation of Genesis 1–3 was jettisoned. The embracing of the new critical views of Scripture by Christian colleges and universities had a disastrous impact on the Christian higher-education curriculum. Higher education in America was tragically transformed.

Science

Higher education experienced another radical transformation when universities explicitly began promoting research and the pursuit of scientific inquiry. The scientific community engaged in a fierce epistemological battle between scientists who promoted natural theology and the glory of the Creator and scientists who philosophically or methodologically excluded God completely. Darwin's publication of *On the Origin of Species* in 1859 forever changed the relationship between science and Christianity. Science and its evolutionary theory challenged the literalness of Genesis 1–2 and God's personal and purposeful involvement in the original creative act.[4]

The incessant external pressure to conform to this world's philosophies and ideologies and relentless internal attacks against divine revelation in colleges and universities, left many in shambles. The educational curriculum was relegated to an assortment of secular and religious courses. Theology, which previously was considered the "queen of the sciences," and the Bible, if offered, became courses like any other. Higher education increasingly be-

---

4. Hutchison, "Darwin's Evolutionary Theory," 61.

came hostile toward its religious roots and divine revelation was no longer the foundation of a comprehensive educational curriculum. A Christian world-view was segregated from all academic disciplines. Without divine revelation as an anchor, colleges and universities promoted scientific research, elevating man's intellect and reason. Research devoid of God's glory as its goal became nothing more than the worldly creation, dissemination, preservation, and ap-plication of human knowledge for the betterment of a global society. Higher education's ultimate purpose became career training for self-promotion.

Thus a shift in higher education took place and changed how Americans look at education. Instead of seeing education as being about the mind and character, it became about a job. An intellectual examination of the Bible was supposed to deny the Bible rather than understand it. Even more, the Bible was completely sectioned off from the whole of education. As a result, we as Ameri-cans often struggle to see how education, the Bible, and our intellectual pursuits really come together, for our culture essentially teaches that they do not.

THE MODERN STRUGGLE IN CHRISTIAN EDUCATION

When institutions like Harvard, Yale, and Princeton succumbed to the shift-ing pressures on higher education, divine revelation lost its place of promi-nence in their curriculum. The fortresses of a once-stalwart Christian educa-tion became hostile to God and His Word. The classical Christian liberal arts approach to unify all truth for the glory of God was discarded. Many historic colleges and universities surrendered to a vocational, research, and scientific method of education. The curriculum became specialized, fragmented, and focused on practical education for a materialistic career devoid of God.

In the late nineteenth and early twentieth centuries, new Christian colleg-es and universities were founded in response to the secularization of higher education. In 1910 and 1915, *The Fundamentals*, a multi-volume work, was originally published to raise a defense and standard for biblical Christianity.[5] It is in an analogous spirit that we endeavor, one hundred years later, to voice our concern. In the twenty-first century, the secularization or death of many Christian colleges and universities is prophesied. History is repeating itself. The triad of issues that transformed higher education in the nineteenth centu-ry continues to make inroads in our churches, seminaries, colleges, and uni-

---

5. Torrey, Feinberg, and Wiersbe, *The Fundamentals*.

versities. Our institutions are yielding under the weight of financial burdens,[6] research, and science that continue to pressure them to compromise their biblical convictions, and they are losing their identity. This accentuates all the more why the issue of a historical Adam is important. It is the tip of the iceberg for Christian colleges and universities to go the way of the institutions of the past.

After all, the discussion regarding the role of research and science in Christian higher education is not new. Christian scholars have for centuries attempted to establish a harmony between faith, revelation, reason, and science. Such efforts have produced rigorous debate and various views. The historicity of Adam is one of the issues in this ongoing debate. It has been thrust into prominence and public discourse as the publication of *Four Views on the Historical Adam*[7] demonstrates. The evolutionary creation view (no historical Adam) and the different views of a historical Adam (archetypal, old-earth, and young-earth) reveal the diversity of the authors' interpretive traditions and why the divergent perspectives exist. I believe that the key issue has and always will be an epistemological one: what is our theory of knowledge and how do we gain knowledge? Our interpretive traditions are bound and guided by our epistemology. Do we believe divine revelation to be the source of all truth, and reason the instrument to study, recognize, and apply it? Or do we fall prey to the lie in the Garden and, armed with a proud and rebellious reason, stand in judgment of and question the veracity of divine revelation?

As we observed, these types of issues are not new—Christian higher education has been in crisis for over two centuries. If we do not learn from history, we are doomed to repeat it. This is why keeping Adam real in our Christian higher education curriculum does matter. We lament how Harvard, Yale, Princeton, and other institutions that were once the citadels of Christian

---

6. The challenges of affordability and sustainability have made attractive, incentives that promote efficiency at the expense of historic biblical affirmations. Changes effected to secure faculty, staff, students, and funding over time are effectively altering the identity of Christian higher education. Openly hiring faculty and staff and admitting students who deny the biblical values and convictions of the institution have proven to be devastating compromises. Students' and parents' inability to afford a Christian college or university education has forced many into secular institutions or settling for a hybrid education that is primarily secular and at best partially biblical. Boards of trustees, presidents and administrators, faculty, staff, students, alumni, donors, and churches are all the stewards of Christian colleges and universities. We must labor to address the pressing issues of affordability, sustainability, and decreasing enrollment, and hold firm to our biblical convictions.

7. Barrett and Caneday, *Four Views on the Historical Adam.*

higher education are no longer the lighthouses of our faith. When the history of Christian higher education in the twenty-first century is written by future generations, which additional colleges and universities will we grieve for and remember as former bastions of truth?

HAVING A VISION FOR TRUE
CHRISTIAN HIGHER EDUCATION

We discussed above that the shift in higher education brought a change in how we think about how education should work. There is confusion about how the Bible, education, and our intellectual pursuits all fit together. What we need is a clearer vision of Christian higher education. Based upon this, we can further see why keeping Adam real is so necessary.

Every year undergraduate students throughout the United States and around the world apply, are accepted, and attend Christian colleges and universities in America. These students are seeking an education that will instill in them the knowledge, skills, and attitudes necessary for their chosen professions, cultivate their spiritual growth, strengthen their moral character, and develop their abilities as global citizens and leaders (Phil 1:27). Christian students desire more than just training for a career and a life of self-promotion. They seek an education that will impart invaluable transformative qualities of character and mind suitable for their Christian calling along with useful technical skills and knowledge. They want to be equipped for a life of enduring commitment to Christ and instructed to think like Christ, value like Christ, and serve as Christ has called them to serve in the home, church, academy, community, and marketplace.[8]

Creator, Creation, and Learning

The distinctiveness of Christian higher education begins with an understanding that there is an infinite, personal God. God has created all things "both in the heavens and on earth, visible and invisible" (Col 1:16, NASB) for His glory. Our Christian worldview affirms God's existence and His activity in the world. Christian scholarship begins with the recognition of God's existence and His sovereignty over creation, including man and his intellectual pursuits (Ps 24:1). The knowledge of God is the beginning of all learn-

---

8.   Schwehn, "A Christian University," 30.

ing (Prov 9:10). A Christian, more than any other person, can appreciate the process and the product of learning. Because of spiritual growth and biblical knowledge, we can appreciate such inexplicable issues as man's finiteness and God's omniscience. The Lord has revealed to us His nature in Scripture and in the general revelation of creation. In light of that, every classroom experience can be a worship experience. A lesson in science or history, math or literature, is a window to the Creator. This stands in stark contrast to the world's contention that absolutely no truth is absolute truth, that reality is relative, and that life is self-sustained. In essence, man becomes God. This is the lie in the Garden (Gen 3:1–7).

Learning under Christ's Lordship

Christian higher education is Christ-centered education. It recognizes the lordship of Christ over all of life, including every academic discipline. It affirms that all Christian scholars must bow the knee to Him and that every thought must be brought captive to Christ (2 Cor 10:5; Col 2:8). The lordship of Christ affirms that all scholars will one day give an account for their activities, including those of an intellectual nature (Phil 1:9–11; Jas 3:1). Recognizing that all scholarship begins from a theoretical base, namely the scholars' worldview, Christian higher education affirms the metaphysical, epistemological, and axiological distinctives of a uniquely Christian worldview perspective. This perspective must permeate teaching and scholarship.[9]

The lordship of Christ demands that the foundation of Christian knowledge be grounded in the Scriptures. Few people today will boldly claim God's Word as sufficient, inerrant, and authoritative, providing the basis from which to craft a truth-based worldview. Carl F. H. Henry correctly states, "The revelation of God in his Word is for Christianity the primary epistemological principle from which all its other truths are deduced."[10] The Bible is truth (John 17:17) and as such provides the Christian scholar with confidence that truth is knowable. The pursuit of truth has particular meaning for the Christian scholar who has the authority of the Word of God as a foundation and basis for knowledge.

The Christian scholar understands that there are two basic classifications of revelation. General revelation is the disclosure of God's eternal power

---

9. Carson, "Can There Be a Christian University?," 26–27.
10. Henry, God, Revelation, and Authority, 1:219.

and glory through nature and history. Special revelation is the disclosure of God's redemptive purpose and work through Jesus Christ and the Scriptures. Henry's additional observation regarding revelation is insightful: "Scriptural revelation takes epistemological priority over general revelation, not because general revelation is obscure or because man as sinner cannot know it, but because Scripture as an inspired literary document republishes the content of general revelation objectively, over against sinful man's reductive dilutions and misconstructions of it."[11] Scripture is the ultimate authority in the universe. The Scriptures alone provide epistemological certainty against the relativistic flux, nonrationality, and theoretical changes within the frameworks of our academic disciplines.

Purposes of Christian Higher Education

People often think that education is the solution to the world's problems. But we know better, and that is why Genesis 3 is important because the idea of "education as solution" is based upon the lie in the Garden. On one hand, Christian higher education affirms the dignity and greatness of humanity as created in the image and likeness of God (Gen. 1:27) and that creativity and rationality, which are essential to higher education pursuits, are both bound to the *imago dei*. However, mankind has fallen in revolt against God. The story of Adam in Genesis 3:1–7 reveals that the basic problem of man is his desire to be like God. Man's desire to be like God was manifested by his wish to possess a knowledge that is both infinite and wholly autonomous. Man not only wanted to have knowledge like God's, but also wanted to be like God and not die. This desire to be as God is what led man to sin. The notion of education as salvation repeats exactly what happened in the garden.

Instead, Christian higher education understands that the Fall has affected the totality of humanity and all aspects of personhood, including the intellect. As a result of man's transgression, his relation to God, his nature, his body, and his environment changed. Thus humanity, both corporately and individually, is in need of regeneration, restoration, and reconciliation with God. Christian higher education affirms that redemption occurs through the finished work of Christ alone, not educational betterment. Keeping Adam real aids in making sure Christian higher education points to the true solution of mankind's problems.

---

11. Ibid., 1:223.

In addition, the Christian scholastic community bears a special responsibility to model excellence in our teaching, research, and service to the broader academic community as ambassadors for Christ (2 Cor 5:20). If our motivation for scholarship and teaching is doxological, then excellence must follow. Christian scholars bear the responsibility to demonstrate this excellence in their academic vocation (Matt 5:16). Our scholastic activities must bring glory to God through both the pedagogical articulation of our Christian worldview and by demonstration of professional quality and excellence in our work. The Apostle Paul's engagement in Athens at Mars Hill is especially illustrative of this principle (Acts 17:16–34).

The foundational trilogy of American higher education—teaching, research, and service—has special bearing on Christian higher education. The pursuit of truth and quest for knowledge (research), the dissemination and acquisition of scholarship and research by the individual, both theoretical and practical (teaching and learning), and compassionate application of truth (service and ministry), all have special meaning to the Christian scholar. The Christian academic community shares particular responsibility in light of these realities.

Concluding Thoughts

We can often be confused about Christian higher education. Society has accepted that we can split intellectual pursuits and education from the Scripture. We have seen that if we are to be consistent with what the Bible teaches, we should pursue learning. Christians should desire to be educated because of what they believe about their Creator. There is no sacred or secular (1 Cor 10:31; Rom 11:36). We treat the pursuit of education as an act of worship that honors and glorifies God (Rom 12:1–2). Christian higher education affirms the education of the total person: the intellectual, physical, affective, social, moral, aesthetic, and spiritual.

At the same time, true Christian higher education is grounded upon Scripture first. It is the ultimate source of knowledge, which pervades every area of life. That is why keeping Adam real is important in our curriculum. This is not only because it affirms Scripture's authority. It is also because mythologizing those "lies in the Garden" is exactly what secular education wants us to do. Secular education argues that man can obtain knowledge apart from divine revelation. Man can replace God. This thereby repeats the serpent's lie.

As a result, society believes that education can solve all the problems to its own demise. Affirming the historicity of Adam becomes important for shaping the way we understand education and its purposes. It provides the true solution to the world's problems in the gospel. It is what makes our education distinctively Christian.

Therefore, true Christian higher education can never segregate the authority of Scripture and wisdom from the rest of education and intellectual pursuits. Its role will never be limited simply to offering Bible courses. Christian higher education seeks to provide for students a Christ-centered educational experience. The primary and overarching purpose of Christian higher education is to expand students' awareness of the glory of God. This goal gives Christian educators a different starting point and framework for their teaching, namely, a Christian worldview. An idea that follows from this worldview is the extreme importance of providing for students an educational environment that will build up their faith and their ability to engage serious scholarship. Christian higher education imparts specialized training and education for promoting the Christian message and nurturing Christian communities. It provides the tools to think and act as Christian disciples and servants in our increasingly complex world.[12]

BIBLIOGRAPHY

Axtell, James. "The Death of the Liberal Arts College." *History of Education Quarterly* 11, no. 4 (Winter, 1971): 339–52.

Barrett, Matthew, and Ardel B. Caneday, eds. *Four Views on The Historical Adam*. Grand Rapids: Zondervan, 2013.

Behle, J. Gregory. "Educating the Toiling Peoples: Students at the Illinois Industrial University, Spring 1868." In *The Land-Grant Colleges and the Reshaping of American Higher Education,* edited by Roger L. Geiger and Nathan M. Sorber, 73–94. New Brunswick, NJ: Transaction Publishers, 2013.

Cairns, Earle Edwin. "A Blueprint for Christian Higher Education." *Faculty Bulletin of Wheaton College* 16, no. 3 (1953): 1–107.

---

12.   Cairns, "A Blueprint for Christian Higher Education," 41–63.

Carson, D. A. "Can There Be a Christian University?" *Southern Baptist Journal of Theology* 1, no. 3 (Fall 1997): 20–38.

Fearing, Kenneth. "Conclusion." In *Vision of the Anointed: Self-Congratulations as a Basis for Social Policy*, ed. Thomas Sowell. New York: Basic Books, 1995.

Henry, Carl F. H. *God, Revelation, and Authority*. 6 vols. Wheaton, IL: Crossway, 1999.

Hutchison, John C. "Darwin's Evolutionary Theory and 19th-Century Natural Theology." In *Vital Apologetic Issues: Examining Reason and Revelation in Biblical Perspective*, ed. R. B. Zuck, 61–81. Grand Rapids: Kregel, 1995.

Marsden, George M. *The Soul of the American University: From Protestant Establishment to Established Nonbelief*. New York: Oxford University Press, 1994.

Schwehn, Mark R. "A Christian University: Defining the Difference." *First Things* 93 (May 1999): 25–31.

Sloan, Douglas. *Faith and Knowledge: Mainline Protestantism and American Higher Education*. Louisville: Westminster John Knox Press, 1994.

Torrey, R.A., Charles Lee Feinberg, and Warren W. Wiersbe. *The Fundamentals: The Famous Sourcebook of Foundational Biblical Truths*. Grand Rapids: Kregel, 1990.

CHAPTER 13

A SIN OF HISTORIC PROPORTIONS

John MacArthur

The doctrine of original sin is one vital biblical tenet that mainstream Protestants, Catholics, Eastern Orthodox believers, and the early church fathers alike have generally affirmed in unison. Scripture teaches this doctrine plainly: When Adam tasted the forbidden fruit, he forfeited his innocence forever, and fell hard. He fell into permanent bondage to sin. He fell under the wrath of God. He fell into condemnation.

And the entire human race fell with him. That first act of disobedience brought sin and death, corruption and condemnation, upon all Adam's natural offspring. As father of our race, head and progenitor of all humanity, Adam plunged us into sin. So says Scripture.

An important corollary, of course, is that we were born sinners; sin is part of our very nature. We were not pure and innocent until some point in childhood or adolescence when a voluntary, sinful act of our own brought us down. We were fallen from the start. We entered this world with a bent toward evil. In our natural, fleshly, unregenerate state, all our appetites, thoughts, and actions showed that we were in full agreement with Adam's disobedience. Like David, we were born in iniquity—guilty sinners from the moment of conception (Ps 51:5)—and desperately in need of divine grace.

Scripture is very explicit about this. The key text on the subject of original sin is Romans 5:12–19. It includes these emphatic statements: All the sin and death in this world is traceable back to one man. "Through one man sin entered into the world, and death through sin" (Rom 5:12, NASB). We inherit from Adam both *guilt* ("Through one transgression there resulted condemnation to all men," v. 18) and *corruption* ("Through the one man's disobedience the many were made sinners," v. 19 NASB). So that first sin of Adam's—humanity's original sin—was singularly significant. Romans 5 says so again and again: "Adam's offense…the transgression of the one…one transgression… one man's disobedience" (NASB) resulted in condemnation to all the rest of us.

Furthermore, there are many meaningful, God-ordained parallels between Adam and Jesus Christ. "For as in Adam all die, so also in Christ all shall be made alive" (1 Cor 15:22, NASB). Christ is head of all who are "in Christ"; Adam is head over all those "in Adam." Through Adam we received human life; in Christ we receive eternal life: "So also it is written, 'The first man, Adam, became a living soul.' The last Adam became a life-giving spirit" (v. 45, NASB).

In other words, "Adam . . . is a type of Him who was to come" (Rom 5:14, NASB). Paul uses a Greek expression, *tupos,* which speaks of a stamp or a tool for making coins. As the contrasting heads of their respective races, Adam and Christ are like coins struck from the same die. Christ (fully human, yet without sin), and Adam (in the purity of innocence prior to his fall) both embody the human ideal. Yet the results they obtained could not be more different. That is the whole theme of this vital section in Romans 5. The apostle is drawing comparisons and noting contrasts between how Adam's *disobedience* doomed all those in Adam versus how Christ's *obedience* redeems those who are in Christ.

Adam is therefore repeatedly set alongside Christ in verse after verse. Those in Adam are fallen with him because of his sin. Those in Christ are redeemed by Him through His obedience. The way sinners are redeemed thus mirrors and reverses the way they fell. The point is made again and again that Christ's headship over the redeemed race exactly parallels Adam's headship over the fallen human race.

Therefore to deny the historicity of Adam is to undermine what Scripture says about Christ's role and function as our Redeemer.

Let us acknowledge that the doctrine of original sin is not easy to receive. It goes against every human wish and intuition. It is hostile to the fundamental dogmas of secular humanism, natural philosophy, and every man-made religion. It punctures the human ego, subverts carnal pride, and flatly contradicts the way most people like to think about themselves—especially in this age of self-esteem. It reminds us that we are *not* fundamentally good; we are fallen creatures.

The natural mind hates that idea, so the doctrine of original sin has been a fierce battleground in religious circles ever since Jesus told the Pharisees, the strictest sect of Jewish Old Testament scholars, "You are of your father the devil, and your will is to do your father's desires" (John 8:44). Pelagians, cultists, and various other peddlers of heresy have generally repudiated the doctrine of original sin. Christians committed to the authority of Scripture and sound, biblical doctrine have always defended it.

That is fitting, because there is no more vital truth in all of theology than the doctrine of original sin. Going back to apostolic times, this has been deemed a cardinal, nonnegotiable, indispensable tenet of biblical Christianity. No wonder. Deny this doctrine and you undermine the very foundation of gospel truth. Eliminate the Fall or the headship of Adam and you compromise everything the Bible ever says about sin, redemption, human nature—even the work of Christ.

Meanwhile, no doctrine in all of Christian theology can be more easily and thoroughly substantiated by empirical evidence. It is quite obvious that the whole human race is fallen. "All have sinned and fall short of the glory of God" (Rom 3:23). That truth is evident no matter where you look in the world. G. K. Chesterton famously called the doctrine of original sin "a fact as practical as potatoes. . . . the only part of Christian theology which can really be proved."[1] In short, the fallenness of the human race is an undeniable reality, and those who wish to deny or discard it condemn their thoughts, their scruples, and their spiritual perception to utter moral and theological confusion. Whatever worldview they adopt will be wrong. To deny original sin is to stumble right out of the gate.

ADAM: HISTORY, NOT ALLEGORY

This significant fact ought to be immediately obvious to anyone who considers the problem of sin properly as a theological issue: Any *biblical* understanding of human fallenness hinges necessarily on the historical person of Adam. To waver or back-pedal on the historicity of Genesis 3 is no trivial

---

1.   Chesterton, *Orthodoxy*, 24.

misstep. Apart from a real, singular, specific individual from whom all of us descended (someone who in his capacity as head of the race fell into sin at the very start), the origin and universality of human sin are insurmountable mysteries. Without Adam, the tenacity of sin's grip on our hearts is just a hopeless theological conundrum. Without the first Adam, there is no way to make sense of the atonement offered by the last Adam (1 Cor 15:45). To put it as simply as possible: *Doubt the historicity of Adam, and you have no good reason to believe any of the rest of the Bible.*

On the other hand, it is utterly impossible to explain the problem of sin by any merely "scientific" method—much less by dogmatic appeals to constantly changing secular theories about human origins. Consider the reality and universality of shame, our innate sense of guilt, and the workings of the human conscience. The moral dilemma we find ourselves in simply cannot be adequately explained by the notion that human life evolved from lower life forms.

Therefore, we must let Scripture frame our understanding of Creation and the Fall—as well as the underlying question of how to interpret Genesis. On all these matters, Scripture speaks with simple, straightforward clarity, and it makes perfect sense of why humanity is in such a desperate state morally and spiritually.

Jesus clearly believed in the historicity of Adam. When some Pharisees attempted to put him to the test with a question about divorce, He replied by pointing them to the example of Adam and Eve: "Have you not read, that He who created them from the beginning made them male and female, and said, 'for this cause a man shall leave his father and mother, and shall cleave to his wife, and the two shall become one flesh'?" (Matt 19:4–5; cf. Mark 10:7, NASB). Nothing in the words of Jesus about Genesis ever indicated that the record of events documented in that book should be read as anything other than authentic history. Even the genealogy of Christ given in Luke 3:23–38 traces His earthly parents' lineage all the way back to Adam.

The Apostle Paul had even more to say about Adam, and it adds up to a definitive affirmation of Adam's historicity. In 1 Timothy 2, where Paul gave the rationale for why men, not women, should stand in the place of leadership when the whole church comes together, he refers to the order of Creation and the events that led to the Fall: "For it was Adam who was first created, and then Eve. And it was not Adam who was deceived, but the woman being quite deceived, fell into transgression" (1 Tim 2:13–14, NASB). Dealing with a similar topic in Corinth, he makes a slightly different argument from Genesis, but again, the argument hinges on the historicity of Adam and Eve: "Man does not originate from woman, but woman from man; for indeed man was not created for the woman's sake, but woman for the man's sake" (1 Cor 11:8–9, NASB).

As I have written elsewhere:

> A clear pattern for interpreting Genesis is given to us in the New Testament. If the language of early Genesis were meant to be interpreted figuratively, we could expect to see Genesis interpreted in the New Testament in a figurative sense. After all, the New Testament is itself inspired Scripture, so it is the Creator's own commentary on the Genesis record.

> What do we find in the New Testament? In every New Testament reference to Genesis, the events recorded by Moses are treated as historical events. And in particular, the first three chapters of Genesis are consistently treated as a literal record of historical events. The New Testament affirms, for example, the creation of Adam in the image of God (James 3:9). . . . To question the historicity of these events is to undermine the very essence of Christian doctrine.[2]

THE FALL: ACTUAL, NOT MYTHOLOGICAL

The definitive New Testament text dealing with Adam as a historical figure is Romans 5. There, in the context of his inspired exposition on original sin, Paul teaches without qualification that Adam was a true, historical individual. Our first parent was not a species of higher primates marking a majestic turn in the epic of evolution. He was a unique creature, made by God in His own image, formed individually from the dust of the ground. Everything the Bible has to say about sin and redemption hinges on that fact.

Here is the full text of Romans 5:12–19 (NASB):

> Just as through one man sin entered into the world, and death through sin, and so death spread to all men, because all sinned—

---

2.   MacArthur, *Battle for the Beginning*, 23.

for until the Law sin was in the world; but sin is not imputed when there is no law. Nevertheless death reigned from Adam until Moses, even over those who had not sinned in the likeness of Adam's offense, who is a type of Him who was to come.

But the free gift is not like the transgression. For if by the transgression of the one the many died, much more did the grace of God and the gift by the grace of the one Man, Jesus Christ, abound to the many. And the gift is not like that which came through the one who sinned; for on the one hand the judgment arose from one transgression resulting in condemnation, but on the other hand the free gift arose from many transgressions resulting in justification. For if by the transgression of the one, death reigned through the one, much more those who receive the abundance of grace and of the gift of righteousness will reign in life through the One, Jesus Christ.

So then as through one transgression there resulted condemnation to all men, even so through one act of righteousness there resulted justification of life to all men. For as through the one man's disobedience the many were made sinners, even so through the obedience of the One the many will be made righteous.

That passage lays bare the roots of human history. For those who wonder why the world is like it is, there is the answer. Adam's original sin is the key to human history. It reveals why humanity cannot avoid evil, much less conquer it. It reveals why death reigns. It reveals why human society is morally and spiritually caught in a downward spiral, and why human history is so full of tragedies, conflicts, and evil events.

Paul's entire line of argument in this passage starts and ends with the historicity of the Genesis account of Adam.

ORIGINAL SIN: THE ACT OF ONE MAN, NOT MANY

Paul begins by saying as plainly as possible that sin entered the world through one man (v. 12). In verse 12, Paul begins a thought that he never completes, because he interrupts himself with several parenthetical asides. But the context makes clear what he was about to say. The idea that would have completed the original sentence is then clearly stated in verse 15. Here is Paul's central point in his own words, without the parenthetical ideas: "Just as *through one man* sin entered into the world . . . much more did the grace of God and the gift *by the grace of the one Man,* Jesus Christ, abound to the many." More simply still: Just as the Fall resulted from the misdeed of one disobedient man (Adam), redemption is provided through the obedience of one truly righteous Man (Jesus Christ).

If Adam was not a historic person, the whole point is meaningless.

When we speak of "original sin," and when Scripture says "sin entered into the world" through Adam, the point, of course, is not that sin *per se* originated with Adam. It did not. Sin originated with Satan. "The one who practices sin is of the devil; for the devil has sinned from the beginning" (1 John 3:8, NASB). Satan's sin clearly predated Adam's, and Satan came to Eve as the evil tempter, already having fallen himself.

Moreover, strictly speaking, Adam's sin was not even the first human sin. Eve tasted the forbidden fruit before he did (Gen 3:6). She knew full well that God had forbidden her to eat the fruit, but she ate anyway. Although she was deceived by the serpent, what she did was still an act of deliberate disobedience for which she was culpable. She clearly felt the guilt of it (v. 8).

What, then, makes Adam's sin so significant? Why does Scripture identify him as the "one man" through whom "sin entered into the world, and death through sin, and so death spread to all men" (Rom 5:12)? Why was *Adam's* disobedience the "one transgression resulting in condemnation" (v. 16)—especially coming as it did *after* Eve's sin?

The answer lies in Adam's position as father of the human race. He stood in a unique position as head and representative of the whole species. He alone was made from the dust of the ground. Eve was fashioned from a rib removed from his side. The rest of the human race would issue by procreation from the union of Adam and Eve. So the entire human race descended from Adam and bears the stamp of his likeness, just as he bore the likeness of God.

That means there was a brief time between Eve's creation and the conception of the first child when just two individuals, Adam and Eve, constituted the whole human race. Adam was head; not only because he was Eve's source, and first in the creative order (1 Tim 2:13), but also because as God designed marriage, "the husband is the head of the wife, as Christ also is the head of the church" (Eph 5:23, NASB). Morally, intellectually, and spiritually, Adam and Eve were fully equal—and both were perfectly innocent. But positionally and functionally their roles were different by God's design. Adam was head. Eve was his beloved companion and helper (Gen 2:18).

People sometimes tend to think of headship as if it were all about privileges, power, and perks. Indeed, abusive men have sometimes behaved as if that is what headship in a marriage entails. But the biblical concept of headship is more about responsibilities than rights. It is about provision, protection, strength, service, and self-sacrifice, not tyranny or intimidation. The model of godly headship, of course is Christ, who "loved the church and gave Himself up for her" (Eph 5:25, NASB).

So Adam had an enormous responsibility. As head of the race, he was uniquely and directly accountable to God for his leadership. When he and Eve sinned and tried to hide from the presence of God, Scripture says, "The Lord God called to *the man,* and said to him, "Where are you?" (Gen 3:9, NASB, emphasis added).

Because he was the singular head and representative of the entire race, Adam's sin had disastrous consequences for all of humanity. Thus in Romans 5, the Apostle Paul deals with Adam's sin as the pivotal issue. Adam—not the serpent and not Eve, but Adam—is the "one man" through whom "sin entered into the world, and death through sin, and so death spread to all men" (Rom 5:12).

Before the creation of Eve, while the first man was still alone in the Garden, God had given Adam total freedom with just one small restriction: "From any tree of the garden you may eat freely; but from the tree of the knowledge of good and evil you shall not eat, for in the day that you eat from it you shall surely die" (Gen 2:16–17, NASB). It ought to have been an easy command to follow.

In fact, it was a very simple test. We are told there were actually two significant trees in the Garden: "the tree of life…and the tree of the knowledge of good and evil" (Gen. 2:9). There is every reason to suppose that if Adam had simply tasted the tree of life before eating from the tree of the knowledge of good and evil, he and his offspring would "live forever" (3:22) with his innocence intact.

But the tempter came, beguiled Eve, and she enticed Adam to disobey. *His* sin (not Eve's) brought a disastrous change to the human soul and constitution. That which had been perfectly pure, unstained by sin, undefiled by any disobedience, and totally free from guilt was now thoroughly corrupted instantly. And not for Adam only, but for all his offspring as well.

Notice carefully the language of Romans 5:12: "Through one man *sin* entered into the world." The noun is singular, referring to sin as a corrupting principle, not "sins"—speaking of discrete, individual sins. Paul is describing how the very character of human nature became depraved. When Adam sinned, he and his posterity together came under the bondage of the corrupt and decaying principle of sin.

Why was Adam's sin—this one sin, not any of his subsequent transgressions or failures, but the tasting of the forbidden fruit—why was *that* the cause of our downfall? Why did Adam's failure to obey that one simple commandment have such far-reaching ramifications for all of us?

Because in his position as our head and representative, Adam was a delegate for the whole human race. Indeed, at that point in human history, he and his wife *were* the whole race. We were in a sense "still in his loins" (cf. Heb 7:10)—not literally present in Eden, but nevertheless represented by Adam in his dealings with God. So Adam was acting on behalf of all mankind. (That is, by the way, what his name means: "mankind.") He not only was our first parent, but as head of the whole race, he also acted on our behalf like an agent or a proxy. Therefore when he sinned, all humanity incurred God's condemnation along with him. In the words of Romans 5:12 again: "Death spread to all men, because all sinned." That is not saying we share Adam's guilt because we subsequently sinned sins of our own. Paul uses a simple aorist verb, "all sinned." The idea is that we sinned *in Adam*.

How is that equitable? you might wonder. *It does not seem reasonable. Why should we be condemned for Adam's disobedience? We were not literally there. We did not consent beforehand to Adam's wrong choice.*

Yet in the realm of human relationships, that kind of representative headship is common. The head of a corporation signs contracts that incur binding commitments and duties for others in the company. The head of a nation might make strategic or political choices that plunge the whole kingdom into war and subject his countrymen to serious danger or death. Decisions made by fathers can result in either shame or blessing for whole families. Indeed, that is precisely what the doctrine of original sin teaches: the sin of our first father had a catastrophic effect on all his offspring.

In real life we are *often* affected in significant ways by decisions made by the heads of whatever entities we belong to. That is a common (and necessary) aspect of how relationships and responsibilities work in human society. We do not generally give this principle much thought, and we do not resent its implications—until we disagree with an executive order raising our taxes or something of that sort.

But in the case of Adam's sin, we cannot claim injustice. We demonstrate our complicity with his choice all the time. We sin willfully and often all by ourselves. No doubt by the time we reach adulthood, each of us is personally guilty of far worse sins than Adam's initial act of disobedience. So when Scripture says we share Adam's guilt, we cannot protest our own innocence or complain that we ourselves might have been a better representative for the race. We really are just as guilty as Adam.

Furthermore—and this is the central point Paul is making in Romans 5—in the same way Adam stands as our head and representative in the Fall, Christ stands as our proxy and heavenly mediator in the work of redemption. Jesus bore the wrath of God and the full penalty of sin on the cross as the perfect substitute and representative of all who would ever believe. All the merit of His perfect obedience is imputed to those who are united with Him by faith (2 Cor 5:21). And even now, he is their head and high priest, representing them before the very throne of God.

So if the arrangement by which we fell seems unfair because Adam was essentially acting in our stead, bear in mind that it is the only means by which we could ever be saved. Christ in all His glorious perfection likewise stood in our place and acted in our stead. Just as Adam was our head and representative at the Fall, Christ is the head and representative of all who are redeemed by faith. That is Paul's central point in Romans 5: "As through the one man's disobedience the many were made sinners, even so through the obedience of the One the many will be made righteous" (v. 19, NASB).

The parallelism Paul uses depends on the literal historicity of Adam. Indeed, the whole principle of redemption hinges on what Genesis says about the fall of humanity. If Adam was not a real person who as head of the human race led us all into sin through one act of disobedience, the truth that one Man's *obedience* has purchased redemption is likewise called into question; the central message of Christianity is discredited; and we have no sure and steadfast anchor for our souls (Heb 6:19).

Once we truly embrace the central truth of Romans 5, the implications are obvious and immediate. It strikes a fierce blow to the evolutionary hypothesis—and to the notion that Adam is a figurative or mythical character. The biblical account of Creation is not some kind of prehistoric drama made up to accommodate primitive minds. If Adam is not a real man whose one act of disobedience corrupted the whole race, then Christ is not a real Savior whose obedience supplies righteousness for those who believe. If, on the other hand, we truly believe in "the last Adam" (1 Cor 15:45), we are forced by simple logic to acknowledge that the first Adam must be a literal historical person as well.

THE SIN PRINCIPLE: A FACT, NOT A THEORY

The facts are clearly on the side of Scripture. The whole chronicle of human history proves the doctrine of original sin to be true. The account Paul gives in Romans 5 is a simple but precise summary of the entire human dilemma: Sin entered the world. Death followed and spread to all men. Everyone sins. Everyone is guilty (and every sentient person knows it). Everyone dies. Those are indisputable, inescapable facts whose ground and meaning are totally unintelligible apart from Scripture.

Paul makes an intriguing argument from those facts: "Until the Law sin was in the world, but sin is not imputed when there is no law. Nevertheless death reigned from Adam until Moses, even over those who had not sinned in the likeness of the offense of Adam" (Rom 5:13–14, NASB).

Here is the chain of thought the apostle is laying out: Death is the wages of sin (Rom 6:23). Sin is the transgression of God's law (1 John 3:4). Why, then, did people die prior to the giving of the law at Sinai? Without any direct and explicit code of law or behavior inscribed on stone from God, they had no commandment to break. They therefore could not have sinned in the same manner as Adam.

And yet "death reigned from Adam until Moses" (Rom 5:14, NASB). Every individual born after Adam has died—including those who lived before any written law was handed down.

Paul's point is this: the fact that they died is ample proof that they were in fact sinners. Moreover, they were sinners by nature, not merely in deed. Like us, they were fallen, guilty, deserving of condemnation—no different in that sense from those who died under the law. That is because sin is a fatal cancer that has infected all humanity. Individual sins are not mere blemishes that can be daubed over or removed if we simply do something to atone for our own faults. The sins we commit are expressions of the fatal flaw in our very nature. Our sin is not occasional. The wrongs we do are not merely "mistakes" or accidental indiscretions that are inconsistent with who we really are. Sin has infected every faculty and every aspect of our person—and it is eating away at us until death occurs.

That is why the gospel speaks about passing from death into life (John 5:24). The work of Christ is the remedy—the *only* remedy—for the failure of Adam. Adam *cannot* be merely a myth or an illustration. He is the living, breathing reason we are in this mess. And Christ is the only way out of it.

BIBLIOGRAPHY

Chesterton, G. K. *Orthodoxy*. New York: John Lane, 1908.

MacArthur, John. *The Battle for the Beginning*. Nashville: Thomas Nelson, 2001.

CONCLUSION

The discussion of this book has revolved around the reality and ramifications of Genesis 2–3. Based upon current thinking, we might be tempted to believe that the historicity of Genesis 2–3 only deals with science and the interpretation of Scripture. However, upon closer examination, our interpretation of Genesis 2–3 impacts a variety of other disciplines. The reach of the Fall extends to not only theology and science but also business, law, literary studies, gender roles, and the social sciences. All of these disciplines testify that Genesis 2–3 is no small matter. It is not merely a self-contained academic debate. Rather, it intersects all areas of life and thereby shapes our worldview.

Thinking through these ramifications demonstrates an important truth: details matter. Those who read Genesis 2–3 ahistorically contend that the text is not an account of material origins but one that merely describes the theology of who we are. Put differently, the story of Genesis 3 does not tell us *how* we came to be but *what* we are.[1] The details do not address *how* things happened, but rather are a means to an end of communicating broader theological realities.

However, the various essays in this book reveal a problem with that idea. Namely, they show how the details in Genesis 2–3 shape certain disciplines and our worldview. The advent of thorns and thistles implies a change in the nature of entropy, which generates scarcity and grounds the need for legal regulation. The specific order of Creation is the starting

---

1.   John Walton, "A Historical Adam: Archetypal Creation View." In *Four Views on the Historical Adam*, edited by Matthew Barrett and Ardel B. Caneday, 116–18. Grand Rapids: Zondervan, 2013.

point for gender roles. The interactions that happen after the Fall show a connection between sin and the counseling problems people have even today. Tensions in the judicial system are based upon factors surrounding the Fall. The reality of Adam and his headship of humanity is the foundation of original sin. The promise of Genesis 3:15 demands some tie with history, otherwise the Messiah would be merely a nice idea, as opposed to a real person who made a real difference in this world.

The contributors to this volume have observed that the details of Genesis 3 work themselves out in Scripture and in the world we inhabit. They are not just mechanics of a fictional story for showing general theological ideas. Rather, those details are real, and the evidence for them is everywhere in our fallen world. Those details comport with what we observe in our meager existence. They are the grounds for a Christian to understand the entire spectrum of life.

At this point, we reach a crossroads. Our interpretation of Genesis 3 is not merely an academic decision about a passage or even a decision about how science and faith work together. This is a decision about the way we think about Christianity as a whole.

I can use the analogy of throwing a pebble into the water. When you throw a pebble in a pond, a ripple ensues. The nature of the ripple will depend upon a variety of factors including how fast you throw the rock, the size of the stone, and the angle it hits the water. Change a factor and you end up changing the ripple.

Quite a few chapters in this book have illustrated that the details of Genesis 3 determine a lot of what we see in this world: laws, scarcity, communicative problems, counseling issues, sin, managerial complications, entropy, and gender conflict. However, if those details are not real, then they are not the cause for what we observe. If they only deal with the "what" and not the "how," then a new story must come into play to introduce us to "how" things really came to be. What happens if the new story that tells "how" things happen contradicts the story of "what" is supposedly true?

If we replace the historical account of Genesis 3 with an alternative (say, evolution), then our viewpoints on all of those issues must be adjusted. We would need to re-think how we handle scarcity and communication in business, think through the nature of law and government, view the sexes, and read literature. After all, evolution tells a very different story of how scarcity, gender roles, and our own "nature" came to be.

However, relegating Genesis 3 to merely a story of "what" we are as op-posed to "how" things came to be, would change something far deeper. How did sin come into the world without Adam? Does evolution provide an expla-nation for the origination of evil and sin? If not, should we believe that sin is real? What justification do we have if that is not how the world came to be? If we cannot truly account for the reality of sin, then what makes us confident that it is the source of people's problems? Why should we not accept a purely biological cause for people's problems? If everything is only evolutionary and biological in nature, why do we need the gospel? More to the point, how do we even know if the gospel is real? If Genesis 3 is just a story that deals with the realm of ideas (as opposed to history), then is the Messiah, originally prom-ised in Genesis 3, just a nice concept? Is He as mythical as the first Adam?

With these alterations, the "ripple effect" becomes a deluge of conse-quences. If Genesis 2–3 does not explain "how" things came to be, something else will and that will define what reality is. It will become our new starting point and with that, everything will change. Such an alteration will not be a slight modification of our theology. If we are to be consistent, it will be an entire paradigm shift of worldview. It will strike the very foundation of our faith. We indeed are at an important crossroads.

The irony is that we do not need to even go down this road of dramatic change. As other chapters in this book argue, Genesis 2–3 is historical. It is hermeneutically and linguistically justifiable to read it as history. It is a story that makes bold claims not only on "what" is but also on "how" everything came to be. The fossil record and genetics do not determinatively or conclu-sively contradict those assertions, contrary to popular opinion. Having done the hard work (and still having much more to do), we have seen that the Bible can withstand the toughest challenges.

This too brings another important point. Those who are faithful to the Lord need not fear and shy away from the disputes of our day. The goal of this book is not to blindly and blithely wait around, but rather to think critically through these difficult matters. Part of believing God is having the confidence that the truth of His Word will never fail. Such conviction makes us bold to examine these issues thoroughly and from a variety of angles. As we grapple with the text and take every thought captive, we can more clearly see that the claims of Scripture are not only true, but also are the only full explanation for reality. As we engage in careful research and contemplation, we have all the more reason to trust God and His Word.

Thus, this book serves as a reminder that the issues of Scripture never exist in a vacuum. For us, the historicity of the Fall fuels profound meditation on the terrible consequences of Paradise lost and also the triumphant hope of the Seed (Gen 3:15, NASB) who will crush sin, Satan, and death once and for all. Paradise lost will be paradise regained. Christ will restore the edenic state. May we wrestle with those realities as we contemplate Adam's sin of historic proportions.